IN MY BOOTS

A Memoir of Five Million Steps
Along the Appalachian Trail

Amanda K. Jaros

Black Rose Writing | Texas

First printing

Some names and identifying details may have been changed to protect the privacy of individuals.

ISBN: 978-1-68513-565-2
LIBRARY OF CONGRESS CONTROL NUMBER: 2024945983
PUBLISHED BY BLACK ROSE WRITING
www.blackrosewriting.com

Printed in the United States of America
Suggested Retail Price (SRP) $22.95

In My Boots is printed in Minion Pro

*As a planet-friendly publisher, Black Rose Writing does its best to eliminate unnecessary waste to reduce paper usage and energy costs, while never compromising the reading experience. As a result, the final word count vs. page count may not meet common expectations.

For Great-Aunt Jeannette

PRAISE FOR
IN MY BOOTS

"Amanda K. Jaros's *In My Boots* does what some of the best works of nonfiction do: it takes the reader on a journey—in this case, a journey that is as much mental and emotion as it is physical. In this book, as Jaros writes, wilderness consumes, but equally at the forefront is Jaros's own psychological and emotional environment, which makes for a startling brave debut."
–Amy Butcher, author of *Visiting Hours: A Memoir of Friendship and Murder* and *Mothertrucker: Finding Joy on the Loneliest Road in America*

"In My Boots treks in the literary footsteps of Bryson, as well as Strayed and Muir. Step by step, Jaros takes us through all the blisters and bliss that is the Appalachian Trail, offering hard won lessons on how to outdistance the fears and limitations of one's past and "hike your own hike." An intimate and invigorating inside passage. A triumphant debut."
–Marc Nieson, author of *Schoolhouse: Lessons on Love & Landscape*

"Amanda K. Jaros takes readers on a thrilling journey of self-discovery and healing as she treks over the 2,000-plus miles of the Appalachian Trail. Throughout the book, Jaros portrays both the struggles and triumphs of hiking and her childhood experiences of emotional abuse with unflinching honesty. I was hooked by her engaging prose and carried along with her joy and determination as she grew over the miles from a frightened child and timid young woman into a powerful force of nature. *In My Boots* is certain to take a place of honor alongside classic hiking memoirs."
–Andrea Lani, author of *Uphill Both Ways: Hiking Toward Happiness on the Colorado Trail*

"In her memoir *In My Boots*, Amanda K. Jaros takes us on her 2,000-mile hike from Georgia to Maine. It's a story of transformation, and in this strong debut memoir, Jaros shows us that the journey is much more than putting one foot in front of the other."
–Rachel Dickinson, author of *The Loneliest Places: Loss, Grief, and the Long Journey Home*

"*In My Boots* brings to life thru-hiking the Appalachian Trail--from the joy of cresting mountains, the awe of coming face to face with elegant moose, to the pain of blisters and misery of walking in rainstorms. Through a close-up lens readers experience the author's individual courage and determination as she confronts her own spiritual angels and demons. I felt as though I knew each member of the constantly shifting, colorful rainbow of individuals that made up the trail community moving along the over 2000 mile path. I felt every step. *In My Boots* is an epic heroine's journey."
-**Joan Griffin, author of** *Force of Nature: Three Women Tackle the John Muir Trail*

"Don't miss Amanda K. Jaros's (Trail Name: Tamarack) amazing story of personal struggle, trauma, resilience, and perseverance during her epic Appalachian Trail journey. Jaros answers the question: How can a woman backpack solo for more than two thousand miles with the crushing weight of her past slowing her every step?"
-**Cam Torrens, Appalachian Trail thru-hiker and award-winning author of the** *Tyler Zahn* **suspense series**

IN MY BOOTS

APPROACH

I can't do this.

The sun traversed the sky as I hiked over rocks and tree roots worn down by thousands of footsteps. I stumbled into a flat gap, as good a place as any for my twentieth stop of the day. My breath caught in my chest. My thighs burned. Feet ached. This was pure physical suffering. Every step was a battle against the mountain, my pack, my body. I slid my pack down my back into the dirt and plopped myself on top of it. I pulled out my crisp, clean map one more time, but couldn't figure out where I was. Trees above bent to the cold winter wind, and the sun gleamed through the bare canopy onto my sweating shoulders. I was too weak. My body couldn't take the strain. My mind couldn't take the challenge. It was only day one, and I started to cry.

The day had begun with such promise, such hope. Earlier that morning, my mother and I had left behind the shiny buildings of Atlanta, drove past the strip malls and suburbs which eventually faded into farmland, and finally, slipped into the Georgia wilderness. Excitement and unease lurched in my throat when I'd spotted the sign for Amicalola Falls State Park, home of the Approach Trail which led eight miles to the top of Springer Mountain and the beginning of the Appalachian Trail. This trek seemed so improbable. And yet, there I was. When my mom parked in a space near the visitor center, I paused. I let the warm air from the car sink into my skin for one more moment before opening the door and stepping out into the cold.

"Well, you're off on your adventure." Mom sniffled and walked around to my side of the car. "Let me take your picture."

The camera clicked, and in the snap of a second, my wavering smile was caught forever on film. A young woman dressed in a purple microfleece sweater, blue shorts over purple leggings, and heavy-duty Montrail boots. Her red hair was pulled back from her face and her hands were clasped together. She leaned casually against a nondescript sedan as if there was nothing momentous about this day.

I took my camera back from my tearful mother and slipped it into the blue pouch around my waist. My posed half-smile was gone, replaced by an edge of tension. A cold wind whipped. It was time.

My mother had seen me off to college each fall for four years, including one study-abroad semester of my boarding a plane to Australia, and at every goodbye, she shed tears. I didn't think this goodbye was much different, other than she thought she'd never see me again. I wondered what parting words were best in this situation. *Thanks for the ride into the backcountry, Mom. I'll call you if I break my leg and end up in the hospital. If I don't get eaten by a bear, I'll see you in six months.*

"You've got to get going," I said instead. "You've got a plane to catch to see Nate." My brother had followed in our father's footsteps and joined the Air Force. This weekend, he would receive his pilot assignment. After depositing me at the trailhead, Mom was headed across the country to his base for the announcement.

My loaded pack weighed in at fifty-eight pounds. Almost half my weight. I grabbed the shoulder straps and heaved it up onto my leg. The weight dug into my thigh, and I didn't know if I could swing it around onto my back. More importantly, I didn't know if I wanted to. It seemed like a stupid idea to carry this giant green thing up a mountain. I'd read that you should chuck out anything you didn't use every day and vowed to keep that in mind. Mom helped me maneuver it onto my shoulders. My spine compressed as it settled onto my back. I adjusted the hip belt, fiddled with my shirt under the straps, and pretended not to notice that the thing towered above my head.

Mom reached out and pulled me to her. It was an awkward embrace because I stood nearly eight inches taller than her and was trying to balance fifty-eight pounds on my back. But also because she wanted to hug me longer than I wanted to hug her.

I pulled away.

"I'll call you when I get to a pay phone," I promised. "It's fine. I'll be fine."

She nodded. "I love you," she said.

"I love you, too," I said. "We'll talk soon." I picked up my trekking poles resting against the car and walked away.

•   •   •

A thru-hike of the Appalachian Trail had been a lofty goal. Especially considering that the previous summer's first climb of Katahdin, in Baxter State Park, Maine, had been my first climb of any mountain. Ever. If I hadn't already lost my breath on that ascent, it would have been taken from me when I arrived at the flat expanse of the tableland a mile from Baxter Peak. I gasped. Extending out beyond the edge of the mountain was blue, green, brown, of all shades and tones, blending into one boundless view. Sprinkled throughout were sparkling dots of water and the cut-through of a river. I swooned and had to sit down, unable to comprehend the vastness. I had expected to be impressed at the top of Katahdin, but I hadn't expected to fall instantly, madly in love. The Penobscot people named the mountain Katahdin, which means, "Greatest Mountain." And it was.

I dragged my tired body to the peak on that first climb and joined the many small groups of hikers sitting with their snacks. They clustered around an old, faded, rectangular wooden sign. It was exceptionally worn from years of weathering sun and storms. It read:

KATAHDIN
Baxter Peak, elevation 5269 ft.
Northern Terminus of the APPALACHIAN TRAIL. A mountain footpath extending over 2,000 miles to Springer Mountain, Georgia.

I'd gone to Baxter State Park after graduating from the University of Michigan. My friends all had plans after college: they were getting engaged, going to work for large corporations, and starting graduate school. I, on the other hand, had never had a boyfriend, wasn't prepared for grad school, and was sure that no corporation would find me a worthy investment. I'd heard of the Student Conservation Association, a sort of Peace Corps in the US, and decided to apply. I marked down my interests—nature, environmental issues, human rights, animals—and my skills—none worth mentioning. I declared to the SCA application Gods that come May, I would be available to go anywhere in the country to help save the planet.

When a call came from the chief naturalist at Baxter State Park, something stirred in me. I would be given space in a cabin, a stipend, and forty hours of work each week. It felt like a huge risk, stepping away from everything I knew, heading to the wilderness. I wondered what I would do at the end of the summer, but being an assistant naturalist and teaching environmental education was the closest thing to what I was qualified for. I accepted.

Over the summer, I climbed Katahdin many times, doing butterfly and bird surveys, talking to hikers, and studying the rare soils and lichens in the alpine zone. I met many enthusiastic campers, but as autumn closed in, I met people who had a different look about them. They were not ordinary hikers up from New York City or Boston for a week. These people appeared worn down, depleted. Many had emaciated bodies and clothing in tatters, backpacks that were brown from ground-in dirt. They gathered in groups in the campgrounds, laughing easily and loudly. Mostly, I saw that they carried a look of triumph and strength in their eyes. When I learned they had walked to Katahdin from Georgia, I was shocked. I had no idea such a thing was possible. I immediately bought the first book I could find about the Appalachian Trail.

That book was *There are Mountains to Climb*, by Jean Deeds. Jean was a middle-aged woman facing an empty nest, retirement, and questions about what to do with the second half of her life. After college, I hadn't known what was next, but as I turned the pages of Jean's book, it dawned on me—I would hike the Appalachian Trail.

When the internship ended, I moved back to my parents' house in New Jersey and spent the winter delving into the world of the Appalachian Trail. I collected what facts and figures I could find from a welcoming and informative online forum called Trailplace. The AT ran 2,160.7 miles from Springer Mountain, Georgia, to Katahdin, Maine, passing through fourteen states. It took about five million steps to thru-hike the trail, and though about 2,000 people attempted a northbound thru-hike each year, only a quarter of them succeeded. When I began my hike in 1999, a total of about 5,000 people had completed a thru-hike and were listed by the Appalachian Trail Conference as 2,000-milers, about ninety percent of them men.

Knowing I needed more than Internet advice, I'd headed to the Eastern Mountain Sports store in a nearby mall. After applying for a job, I was soon on payroll folding t-shirts and selling backpacks. It didn't seem to matter that I knew nothing about the gear I was trying to convince others to purchase. All my coworkers had significant outdoor experience and shared it with me.

I ordered a complete set of forty-six topographic maps from the ATC. I bought Dan "Wingfoot" Bruce's *Thru-hiker's Handbook*, which taught me about mileage, trail towns, and road crossings. Wingfoot's *Thru-hiker's Planning Guide* told me how to create my hike budget, plan a trail menu, plot my resupply stops, and more.

My mother had cried at the thought of her daughter alone in the wilderness for six months. My father didn't take me seriously until the day I spread out my books and planners in the living room. Wingfoot suggested resupply stops every five to seven days, and I marked the towns on my chart: Neel's Gap, Hiawassee, Nantahala Outdoor Center… I tallied the mileage in between. My father came into the room and asked what I was doing.

"I'm planning my thru-hike on the Appalachian Trail," I said.

"What?" he said. "You can't do that."

I looked at him: tall, with a runner's lithe form, and thin red hair. I sensed the tensing of his muscles, the anger rising like magma. If the lava reached the crater and erupted, I was in trouble.

My father's wrath burned through my life. Once sparked, he fumed for hours, or days. Anything, at any time, could send him into a rage: a misplaced set of keys, the wrong tone of voice, a toy left out on the carpet. Or a daughter who didn't fit his mold of what a perfect daughter should be. His was a violence of words, emotion, volume, power. His anger made him yell, often. "I have a right to be angry!" he'd scream.

The rare physical violence toward me came in the form of spanking; sometimes a grabbed arm and smack on the bottom, one time a chase up the stairs to my bedroom where he held my face to the floor and repeatedly hit my rear end, hard. He often reminded my brother and me we were lucky. "You have nothing to complain about," he'd yell. "I'm going easy on you compared to how my father dealt with me!" The story went that when he got into trouble, his mother would send him to his room, taunting him with, "Just you wait 'til your father gets home." When his father returned from a long day at the office, my dad was taken out to the garage and beaten with a belt. I was definitely grateful to avoid such punishment, but I never doubted that he was one explosion away from giving it a try.

Like so many other times, as I sat planning my hike in his living room, I knew I shouldn't challenge him. I should keep my mouth closed and eyes averted and allow the surge of his anger to pour over me. Sometimes, as his face grew more animated, melting his many freckles into redness, I wondered if that red scalp would blow off like in a cartoon. But always I'd focus on holding in my own anger, sadness, fear. *Don't respond.* That only made things worse. *Nod, tell him he's right.* He was always right.

But I was twenty-three years old this time, and he was not right.

"Actually, I am. I'm going to Georgia in March. And I'm going to walk to Katahdin."

His lips tightened together. We stared at each other for a moment. His eyes squinted in the soft, yellow lighting. Then I turned back to the papers in front of me, holding my breath, staring at the page until he stomped away.

I hadn't cared if my parents didn't want me to do it or that I had no experience backpacking. Standing on the Katahdin tableland for the first time had been a moment of awakening. It was the greatest sense of accomplishment I'd ever felt. The greatest awe. The greatest freedom. I hadn't tiptoed to the top; I had grunted and groaned and hauled myself against gravity under my own power and will to the peak of the Greatest Mountain.

I had found my calling.

•   •   •

I had known for many months that I would come to the beginning; I would come to the moment when I would start walking. Thirty yards behind the Amicalola Falls Visitor Center was a stone archway, the entrance to the Approach Trail. Katahdin, the mountain I had fantasized about all winter, waited 2,160 miles and 464,500 feet of combined elevation change north of here. Hundreds of other mountains and an unknown number of days stood between us. I took a couple of deep breaths, gripped my trekking poles tightly, then passed through the stone archway and set out.

Walking with fifty-eight pounds on my back was unlike anything I'd ever done. The first hour was the most torturous of my life. My shoulders felt like they were dislocating from their sockets. My legs wobbled with fatigue. Blisters formed on both heels, which surprised me considering that I'd worn these Montrail boots the previous summer with great success. They were two-pound tanks that protected my feet from every rock, root, or bear attack. That they were hurting me from the inside was incomprehensible.

A mile in, I took a break near the Amicalola Lodge. I unbuckled my pack and dropped it in the middle of the trail, which skirted the edge of the Lodge parking lot. Through the trees, I could see colorful cars lined up in neat rows. That was my world, one where you didn't have to exert yourself unless you felt like taking a light jog on the fitness trail. I considered walking over to the Lodge, pulling out the traveler's checks tucked into my Zip-locked wallet, and checking in. It made so much more sense than what I was actually doing. But the hiking would get easier. It had to.

I grunted as I lugged my monstrous green turtle shell onto my shoulders again. Standing up straight was a challenge, but the trekking poles helped me balance, and I resumed my tortoise-like crawl.

The Approach Trail was as uninspiring as they came. It wasn't one long uphill, like climbing Katahdin. This trail curved steeply up one side of a mountain, gaining significant elevation, then turned sharply back down the other side, losing all the elevation I'd just acquired. Then on to another.

It was endless, and I was getting nowhere. In the gaps between the mountains, I took off my pack to rest my shoulders. I nibbled on GORP—Good Old Raisins and Peanuts—at every break, hoping that perhaps my pack was just a few peanuts too heavy.

After several hours of trudging alone, voices materialized behind me. I stepped to the side of the trail and looked back to see three men moving fast, their packs significantly smaller than mine.

"Hello!" one shouted. They paused long enough to introduce themselves: Kurt, Brad, and Colin, out for a spring break hike. As they moved on, they yelled, "See you at the top."

Motivated by their energy, I hurried behind them, trying to keep pace. It was a fruitless attempt. I slipped back into my plod as their voices disappeared ahead. I was the slowest person on the Approach Trail, a fact soon proven by a single young man and later by a couple who easily passed me with a smile and nod. Every time another hiker zipped by, I sped up, only draining my energy reserves more.

I can't do this.

Several hours in and unsure of my location, I dropped my pack, plopped down, leaned my head forward into my hands, and cried. The tears came out in great, breathless bursts. I had been so sure of myself in my parent's tidy house. So sure that a summer at Baxter and a winter at EMS was enough experience to get me back to Maine on foot. Maybe everyone was right. I should have been working on my career, whatever that was. I should have been earning money. Settling down. Finding a husband. Being a productive member of society.

But what exactly was a productive member of society? If I didn't even know who I was or what I wanted out of life, how could I contribute anything?

Crying on the Approach Trail had not been referenced anywhere in Wingfoot's book. There had been no planning sheet for emotional distress. If I gave up now, I'd have to return to my parent's house, my childhood restraints. *And then what?* I'd put all my savings and six months of planning into this hike. There was nothing else on my life's agenda. *I don't want to go back there.* The least I could do was get to the first mountain.

I wiped the tears from my cheeks. With every muscle in my body protesting, I forced my arms to lift my ridiculous pack and my legs to resume the struggle against gravity. Step, breathe. Step, breathe. Step, breathe. I moved forward, tears mingling with sweat and dripping down onto my shirt.

A few high clouds blew in, dispersing the sharp sunlight into a hazy glow. Without warning, the steep mountainside leveled out and opened into a wide clearing bordered by dense trees and shrubs and rock slabs covering the ground. The edge of a cliff loomed ahead, and the sun gazed back across the world at me. It appeared still in its orangey radiance above the horizon.

My shaky legs and numb shoulders carried me to the edge of Springer Mountain where I dropped my pack. The hills and trees and forests of brown rolled inch by inch into the vague blue-green of distance. There was nothing manmade in sight: no cities corrupted the hillsides, no cars streaked past in oblivion, no buildings jutted into the sky or forced sharp angles into the softness of the wild. In that way, it was very much like being atop Katahdin, removed from everything and everyone.

I felt entirely alone.

"Want me to take your picture?"

I spun around to find a dark-haired man with glasses, about my height, sporting spotless khaki zip-off hiker pants and a green rain jacket. He'd come out of nowhere. He carried a very large backpack too, which he unclipped as I replied, "Sure. Thanks."

"Where you headed?"

"Oh, just over there to the Springer Mountain Shelter." As the words came out of my mouth, I wondered if I should tell him. There was no sign of Kurt, Brad, or Colin, or the other hikers who had passed me today. It was just Springer Mountain, me, and the khaki guy. The voices of my relations warning me about hiking alone sprang to mind, and I hoped he wouldn't pull out a knife.

When my friends and extended family learned about my hike, I heard every kind of fear and form of dissuasion possible. No one I knew had any long-distance backpacking experience, and most had never hiked farther than a few laps around the mall, but they all had advice on gear, clothing, and safety. Despite never having handled a weapon in my life, they suggested I bring a gun. There had been eleven murders on the AT over its sixty-five-year history, a minuscule number compared to any city I'd ever visited. It was possible to get attacked by a bear, have a tree fall on you, or get lost and die of exposure, but I was willing to risk it all for the chance at adventure.

I studied khaki guy as he rummaged through his gear. His water bottles and some small stuff sacks escaped his pack, tumbling onto the rocks. I noticed he was overweight, and I thought I could probably outrun him if necessary. His awkwardness and silly smile made me think he was more like a teddy than a grizzly.

"Where are you headed tonight?" I asked.

"Stover Creek Shelter. Only three miles away, if you want to join me." The man had a gravelly voice, though I could hear a bit of laughter behind every word. "I'm Mike, by the way." He held out his hand.

"I'm Amanda," I replied, shaking it. "I won't be doing any more miles today. I just came up the Approach Trail." I was still out of breath. How could he even be considering going three more miles, particularly when he didn't appear to be in very lean shape to begin with?

"Oh, man! Why'd you do that?" He chuckled. "I just came from US 42."

That explained the perfectly clean pants and lack of sweat. US 42 was a dirt forest road that crossed the AT just a mile north of Springer. I had considered, then quickly rejected this route. I'd heard the road was rugged, and I didn't want to make my mom navigate a rental car through a backcountry wilderness. It seemed like a safer route to start at Amicalola Falls and hike the Approach Trail. Clearly, I'd made the wrong choice.

"How about that picture?" Mike asked, gesturing to the camera.

We traded cameras. I stood next to the bronze plaque that marked the beginning, or the end, of the Appalachian Trail, leaned forward onto my trekking poles, and smiled into the pain.

"How far you going?" Mike asked after I took his picture.

"Maine," I replied. It seemed so strange to say, considering that earlier I'd been ready to throw the whole shebang back on the bus to the airport.

"Me too! Congratulations!" Mike grinned. "We're on our way."

He seemed so happy, no doubt because he'd only hiked one mile so far. I was probably happy, too, but after eight miles, the pain over every inch of my body dulled the joy. I sat down on the rock by the plaque as Mike packed up his gear. I noticed a white blaze painted onto the rock and reached out to it. These two-by-six-inch rectangles were painted on trees and rocks the entire length of the trail, marking the way. It had been a painful day, but as my fingers scraped the rock under the first official blaze, I promised myself that I would walk past many, many more of them.

Mike said goodbye, and I watched him disappear beyond the second blaze painted on a tree trunk. With my plodding speed, it was likely that our paths wouldn't cross again. I kind of hated to see him go.

•   •   •

I woke before light in the Springer Mountain Shelter. My thin Ridge Rest sleeping pad did nothing to prevent my hips and shoulders from throbbing against the wooden floor. I turned over, wondering why I was cold despite my zero-degree sleeping bag. I didn't want to think about what the day held, so I shut my eyes.

Something skittered across me. Then another creature scurried past my head. I sat up quickly, scattering mice into the dark corners. I shivered and pulled the drawcords tighter around my face. This could not be real. I had slept for hours with mice running all over me. I'd figured our human presence would be enough to scare the critters away, but no, not at all.

Though there was little light in the sky, I knew I would not fall back to sleep. Heath and Joe, two guys out for the weekend, stirred in the loft above, and I decided it was time to get on with it. It took more than an hour to eat breakfast, use the privy, go to the nearby spring and filter water, and figure out how to force all my gear back into my pack.

Throughout the morning preparations, I chatted with Heath and Joe about their trip and their previous hiking experiences. They said they hoped to thru-hike the AT someday and asked me numerous planning questions. I refrained from suggesting that it might not be all it was cracked up to be. I was only on day two, after all. Finally, I dragged my pack to the edge of the shelter and prepared to maneuver it onto my back.

"Hey, before you go, can we get a picture with you?" Heath asked, pausing from his oatmeal. "You're our inspirational thru-hiker," he went on when I didn't respond.

"Well, yes, sure," I hesitated. "Thank you."

I had spent twelve hours at the same campsite as these people. We'd chatted for an hour. It hardly seemed like an experience worthy of a photograph. Heath stood next to me, and Joe set the timer on the camera, then rushed to my other side as the tiny red light flashed faster. We all smiled, arms around each other as if we'd spent our whole lives together.

It was the first time in my life anyone ever called me their inspiration. And I hadn't even done anything yet. I would never see Heath and Joe again, but when I said goodbye to them, I knew that we had traded something rare. Someday in the future, they were going to look at that picture of us and make their plans to hike the AT. I had offered them the hope that they too could follow their dreams. They had given their simple friendliness, their unreserved confidence in my trek. With that kind of gift bestowed upon me, I'd better do something to earn it.

INTO THE FACE OF FEAR

My second day on the AT was similar to the first, right down to the tears, the questions, and the struggle. My pack was no lighter and gravity no less imperious. Even though the trail rambled in a long descent all morning, I stopped often for a rest, or a drink, or a snack; any excuse to take off the pack. At Long Creek Falls, I mixed up some powdered hummus for lunch and chatted with a couple from Atlanta who was amazed at my hike. Like Heath and Joe, they wanted to take a photo of me. It had been a dirty, sweaty thirty-six hours, and was possibly the least photogenic moment of my life, but I smiled as their camera clicked.

My muscles were clenched tight from the agony of the day before, making every movement harder. I kept my head down, looking solely at the dirt path, not noticing anything but each step. Every body part hurt, but my feet were complaining the most. The growing blisters on my heels demanded my complete attention.

I didn't have a sense of how long a mile actually was, but these miles were clearly longer than regular miles. That, or else someone had mismarked the trail. Each landmark that I was supposed to pass—Stover Creek Shelter, US 58, the Benton MacKaye Trail junction—took longer to get to than I expected. In my mind, eight miles was not far, so this really should not have been so difficult.

By mid-afternoon, my blisters nearing the size of quarters, I rounded each bend sure I would find the shelter and the wonderful moment when I could remove the insidious weight from my back. But with each turn, I only found another long stretch of trail bordered by brown trees and rocks. The disappointment crushed me each time and caused me to slow even further. I plodded and grumbled through eight cold, cloudy hours; one for each mile.

As I pulled myself up another incline, I decided I had to stop and pitch my tent; I could not take one more step. At the rise, I looked up from my feet, my lungs throbbing. There, a small wooden sign indicated that the Hawk Mountain Shelter was to the left. Wingfoot said in the guidebook that it was 0.2 miles off the trail, a fact which didn't thrill me. This meant 0.2 down, and tomorrow, 0.2 back up. I didn't want to do an extra almost half-mile, but that was where the flat campsites, water, and privy were. The realization that I had actually made it through the day gave me a jolt of energy as I turned down the side trail marked with blue blazes on the trees.

I heard voices and the clink of gear before I saw the shelter. When it finally came into sight through the trees, I discovered it was already overflowing. Brightly colored gear hung from every corner, and socks, boots, and packs spilled out from the open front side onto the ground nearby. I'd thought that by starting in the first week of March I would get out ahead of the major throng of would-be thru-hikers, but it looked like everyone had the same thought.

After last night's mice, I wasn't interested in sleeping in a lean-to again. I greeted everyone with a smile and wave, then went around the back to find a place to set up my tent. Blue, green, and orange domed tents stood out against the muted browns and grays of the surrounding forest like strange alien incubation pods. I settled on a spot apart from the other pods, hoping for some semblance of privacy.

I unbuckled my pack and dropped it to the ground, then waved my arms around to stretch out my shoulders. From the outside of the pack, I unstrapped my red fuel bottle, gray sleeping pad, and the empty plastic milk jug I would use for collecting water. Opening the top flap to search for my tent, my gear poured out like a waterfall of rainbows accumulating in the dirt around my feet: red stuff sack filled with cooking pot and lid, single-burner stove, and spoon; light green stuff sack bursting with food; dark green stuff sack compressing the sleeping bag; blue stuff sack holding my small allotment of clothes; and a gray bag for the water filter. I also pulled out my Teva sandals, Swiss army knife, and two Nalgene water bottles, followed by a large baggie with a journal, pens, a trail guide, and a map, a small baggie with a few first aid items, and a ball of purple cord for bear bagging. At the very bottom of the giant pack was another black and blue stuff sack that held my tent.

I'd gotten the Sierra Designs Orion CD tent while working at Eastern Mountain Sports. A customer had returned it claiming it leaked, but my co-workers advised me the leaks were because the original owner had failed to seal the seams on the rain fly. I knew it was too heavy for backpacking, but I set it up in the store and climbed inside. Lying on the floor looking up through thin mesh walls at the fluorescent store lights, I imagined looking up into a ceiling of shimmery leaves with a warm sunset peeking through. Behind me were days of peaceful wilderness walking, ahead of me, more of the same. The dreamy possibility gripped me, and I bought the discounted tent, along with some seam sealer.

That night would be the first time I would use the tent in the woods. It was a simple setup; the poles clicked into place with ease. The fly slid over the top without snagging. It was technically a two-person tent, but when I climbed in to unfurl my sleeping pad and bag, I found it a tight fit for me and all my gear. When everything was arranged, the cozy space invited me to stay. I longed to pop some ibuprofen, sink into my puffy, warm sleeping bag, close my eyes, and not get up again. But I needed to lighten my food bag.

I sat in the tent's doorway and released my feet from my tank boots. The blisters rubbed, making me cringe with a pain that rivaled what I imagined having a leg bitten off by a bear would feel like. I put on my Tevas, and my feet sighed with relief. I hobbled back to the picnic table in front of the shelter with my food bag. Mike, the teddy bear from yesterday, was there, massaging his feet off to the side. A few others were organizing gear and talking. In the middle of the shelter, amid all the movement, a woman was tucked into her sleeping bag. Was she asleep? Or dead? If she'd spent the past two days doing what I had done, I had to wonder.

Three young men and a young woman were sitting at the picnic table discussing water filters. They were using up most of the table, and I didn't know how to wedge myself in, or what I should say to these strangers. I hung back, fiddling with the strap on my stove bag acting like this was a critical strap situation that needed my attention before I could join the conversation.

"Hey," the woman said, noticing me. "You need a place to cook? Pull up a bench." She pushed her pile of granola bars aside. "I'm Margaret."

I thanked Margaret for the space, then opened my stuff sack and began to set up my stove.

A couple of guys from Ft. Lauderdale out for the weekend also introduced themselves. As did Charlie, who was skinny as a stick and seemed unfazed by the challenges of backpacking. He was eighteen and told us that the woman asleep in the shelter was his mom. Thru-hiking with my mother was not something I could even begin to imagine. Just two days ago, I had been standing with her in a parking lot trying to assure her one more time that I was not going to die in the woods. My mom loved the midwestern landscape where she'd grown up. She liked gardening, visiting the beach, and bird watching. She appreciated nature, but she was happy to appreciate it from an air-conditioned, easy-to-clean, view through a window. The edge of the State Park parking lot was as wild as she got.

"So, what about trail names?" Margaret asked. "Anyone have one yet? I don't. Obviously."

"I'm going to call my mom, Mom," Charlie said.

Everyone chuckled.

"Well, ya'll better come up with them fast, before you do something stupid that earns you infamy," said one of the Ft. Lauderdale guys.

Rarely did people go by their given names on the AT. Instead, it was a tradition to adopt a new name. Trail names were often clever and witty, maybe something profound from your home life, maybe a pun on the way you hiked the trail. I'd walked all day in fear that I'd end up with an awful name like the ones I'd come across online—Spaghetti-O, Snoreball, JetButt, Snotrocket—each backed up by a corresponding epic trail failure.

"I'm way ahead of you all," Mike chimed in from the shelter. "I'm going with I.O.W.A. Jurnee." Met with only blank stares, he clarified, "Idiot Out Walking Around on a Journey."

For a moment, I thought he was kidding. A childish, goofy grin bloomed on his face. But I thought back to my interaction with him on Springer, and I realized that this was Mike being serious. "My last name is similar to the word journey," he said. "And so far, I feel like an idiot out here. So, I figured I'd just get a jump on things."

Yesterday on Springer I'd had a sense that I liked Mike. As everyone around the table laughed at his self-deprecating attitude, the feeling came up again. I'd only known him for a day, but so far, he was always smiling.

No one else, including me, had a trail name yet. I wanted mine to be special, to mean something. On a new adventure, I didn't have to be the person I used to be. I could be anyone, if I could just figure out who that was.

My pot of water was boiling, and I poured in the pasta. As a vegetarian, all my food was low calorie, and when planning, I'd known I would need to supplement and spice up each meal. Last fall, I'd bought a food dehydrator and spent months drying fruit to add to my oatmeal and vegetables to add to the boring packages of noodles and rice. I pulled out the bag of veggies and small containers of salt, pepper, garlic, ginger, and dried tomatoes, opening them one by one.

"You're seriously carrying all those spices? In plastic containers? They must weigh a ton," Mike teased me. "Maybe we should call you Spice Girl."

"No way, Idiot Out Walking Around," I shot back. "I'll find myself a good name." And silently vowed to get rid of the spice kit at the first opportunity.

"Better hurry."

•   •   •

The next morning, staggering under the weight of my pack, I knew I had to unburden myself from some of my gear, like the spice kit. There was no way I was going to walk an extra 1.9 miles to the post office in Suches, Georgia. I had already learned that any additional mileage, however small, was not worth the suffering. The only other option was hitchhiking, which no one in my family would ever condone.

I stumbled along the trail, Dave Matthews Band's "Ants Marching" playing in a loop in my brain. The song had a good beat for keeping my feet moving, and my mind rolled back and forth over the lyrics. *Dave says I should take some chances.*

When I came out of the trees at GA Route 60, I had a choice to make. I unbuckled my pack, stowed my trekking poles on the side, and when the first vehicle came along headed in the right direction, I stuck out my thumb.

I felt terrified. What would my father say?

As a child, I tried hard to be good: stayed quiet, got good grades, never crossed a teacher, followed the rules, ate the dinner Mom served, and cleaned up after myself. In high school, I went to the movies, not out drinking. I joined wholesome clubs like the church youth group. I worked on the weekends with Safe Rides, driving my less responsible classmates home from late-night parties.

I believed if I remained vigilant, always staying ultra-focused on my father's mood or where he was in the house, I could anticipate his attacks and not incite the flame. But no matter how good I was, my father's assaults were unpredictable, coming weekly, sometimes daily.

And though I tried to be perfect, there were times I forgot to tiptoe through each day. When Nate went to college, I was fourteen, and I loved it when my parents went out and left me home alone. The house was safe. I could snack on whatever I wanted without reproach. I could turn my radio up loud. I could lay on my floor and read until my eyes went crisscross and hours flashed by in a blink. *Darnit!* Until reality crashed back in, and I realized I forgot to put a tape in the VCR to record Dad's favorite TV show.

As I waited for my parents to return, my stomach tangled in knots. I wondered if I should tell him or just wait until he discovered the mistake on his own. Either way would likely be bad. I didn't have to decide because not long after they got home, he pushed the VHS tape into the VCR and hit play. Minutes later, I was called downstairs.

I walked into the family room, lit by warm yellow light. Dad held the remote in his hand and he stared at the TV screen. Mom was in the kitchen pulling dishes out of the dishwasher and putting them back on shelves.

"What happened to my show?" Dad asked without looking at me.

I leaned casually against the dining table at the edge of the open family room. I couldn't lie about what I'd done, that would only make things worse. "I was reading, and next thing I knew, it was already starting. I don't think I missed much."

"You missed fifteen minutes! I ask you to do one thing while we're out," Dad yelled, finally turning toward me. "One thing! And you screw it up."

"I'm sorry." Tears choked the back of my throat, but I had to hold them in. "I didn't mean to."

"God dammit!" he yelled, chucking the remote control onto the couch. My body tightened. I took short breaths.

"Steve, calm down," Mom said, as always. But that was always the wrong thing to say.

"I *am* calm, Laurie!" He turned his attention to her. "She's so irresponsible!"

I edged away from the table toward the hallway, hoping he was almost done. I wanted to get out of this room and away from him. As he smacked the back of the lounge chair, I thought of the little kids I babysat for. They kicked and threw stuff when they were upset too.

My thought slipped out before I could stop it. "You're in a bad mood."

He whipped around. "What did you say?" He took several steps closer to me. His eyes were sharp, scanning me, not wanting to miss a word I said or a breath I took.

"Nothing." I paused. I knew not to say anything, but my frustration got the better of me. "It's just that you seem to be in a bad mood."

"I am not in a bad mood!" he screamed.

Stop talking now. "No, you're not," I said, looking at the ground. My vision went blurry as fear consumed my body.

"You screwed up!" He kept yelling. "And you won't take responsibility for it."

"I said I'm sorry."

"Don't give me that attitude! Don't I have a right to be angry when you mess something up?" His freckled face was sweating with rage. His voice was loud and solid, ready with a quick comeback for anything I might say.

"Steve..."

"She needs to know she's an irresponsible brat!" He stared at me, willing me to say one more thing, one more whisper so he could keep his tirade going.

Tuck in all your feelings and defer. It was the only way to get out. I kept my eyes down.

For several minutes he glowered over me as I stood frozen. "Unbelievable." He walked back to the couch and snatched up the remote control. "Get to your room."

I spun and left the room quickly. As I walked up the stairs, I let out all the breath I had been holding in. My chest shuddered. My hands unclenched. By the time I made it to my bedroom door, the tears were falling hard. I shut my door silently. If I slammed it or made any noise, he would follow me to keep fighting. I needed him to forget I existed.

I grabbed a stuffed raccoon and gripped the fluffy creature to my chest. Within minutes, its matted fur was soaked by tears. I slipped silently into my closet.

The small, dark space had become my sanctuary. I had scooched the shoes aside and pushed the newspaper mat that I'd made in Sunday school into the far corner, under the hanging clothes. I kept a flashlight, a book, and my diary there. I pilfered snacks from the kitchen: small packets of fruit gummies, Ziploc bags full of chips and peanuts, granola bars, and dry cereal. The closet was a good place to find quiet time with my books, but mostly, the whole setup was because I needed to be prepared. After being screamed at, a bag of salty chips or some candy helped take the sting away. After the intense fear of facing my angry father, I needed a safe place to hide.

Standing at the side of a Georgia road, I knew I could not hide. I felt deliriously rebellious. A rusted, blue truck, driven by an old man, pulled to the side of the road. The man leaned across the seat and rolled down the window. He was headed into town and was happy to give me a ride. I sized him up. He seemed like any other old man driving a truck, but was getting rid of the spice kit worth this risk?

I threw my pack into the truck bed and climbed in. The heater was on full blast and felt wonderful after the nonstop cold of the previous few days. The man was quiet, only asking where I wanted to be dropped off. By the time I had settled into the seat and warmed my fingers, we pulled up to the post office in Suches. I thanked him, stepped out into the cold, and hauled my pack out of the truck bed.

I did my business quickly, digging out the items to get rid of. I kept the veggies I'd worked so hard on, but stuffed the spice bottles, extra water bottle, extra spoon, some straps, a few energy bars, and one of the two books I was carrying into a box, addressed it to my parents in New Jersey and paid at the counter. My pack didn't look any smaller, but when I heaved the beast again, I told myself I could detect a slight improvement.

Wilting under its weight, I crossed the road and steeled myself for another opportunity to get kidnapped. This time I was picked up by a young man with a red winter hat pulled down over his ears. He asked lots of questions about my hike, and I mumbled vague responses. As I climbed out and thanked him, something inside me unwound. Neither this fellow nor the old man earlier had shown any signs of being a deranged killer. They were nice, normal, Georgia men living in these mountains, glad to give a thru-hiker a ride. People who lived around here, around any part of the trail, were probably used to seeing hikers with their thumbs out. Next time I might come across the local madman, but for today, I had survived.

•   •   •

Over the afternoon and evening, some low, misty clouds moved in. I finally pulled into Jarrard Gap. I had hoped to make it a few miles farther to a shelter, but cold and weary, I stopped a few miles beneath Blood Mountain, the highest peak we'd come to yet, the highest peak on the Georgia section of the AT. I sat by a campfire with some of the hikers I'd met in the past few days: Kurt, Brad, Colin, Mike the Wandering Taoist, and Chris, a guy I found extremely attractive. They smoked pot and drank the couple of beers they'd brought with them. I'd never smoked pot and wasn't interested in starting now. My awkwardness, plus the descending cold from the mountain sent me to my tent early.

All night, the wind whipped up through the gap; the empty tree branches bent low with every hard gust, then sprang back as the wind softened, scattering the detritus of broken wood, again and again. The rain fell, then turned to ice and entombed all the tents pitched in the gap.

A sound like shattering glass jerked me awake. My body felt wrecked, and I didn't want to get up. Alone in my tent, I lay listening to laughter outside as more cracking sounds rent the air. The chill stung my shoulders as I pulled an arm out of my bag and tapped gently on the tent wall. It was as hard as the ground beneath me; I was encased in ice. I began hitting the walls, splintering the ice.

"Need some help?" Came a voice I couldn't identify. The fellow hiker broke the ice from the outside, and I was soon able to unzip and emerge into a shining crystalline wonderland. It was a world utterly changed from the night before and unlike any forest I had ever seen.

Every branch and twig shone with a new coat of glistening ice. I gazed around the wide camping area, watching those who had already escaped their ice-enclosed tents and stood in various stages of breakfasting and breaking camp. Their colored tents and raincoats and backpacks burned red and orange and yellow against the icy backdrop.

The morning air in the gap filled with clouds. It was three miles to the top of Blood Mountain, then two and a half miles down the other side to the store at Neel's Gap, where I, like everyone else, was headed. I still hadn't perfected my morning packing routine and I left camp last, not long after all the guys. Trees crusted over with ice lined the trail and fog surrounded me as I pushed forward.

The ice slowed everything in the forest. The trail rose out of the gap in a gentle meander past birch and beech and maple trees. I moved along, focusing mostly on the ground beneath me, passing boulders as big as cars. The only sounds were the crunch of my boots on the frozen trail, already cracked from those who had previously passed, and the in-and-out challenged puffing of my breath. Occasionally, the heart-shaped tracks of white-tailed deer traversed my path, stringing across the glacial mountainside like highways into another lifetime. I paused often to search for a white blaze to confirm I was still on the right path.

After several hours, the steepness of the trail finally eased, and I followed a rock slab pathway toward a clearing. Between patches of pristine snow, boulders of all sizes sprinkled the area. Through the fog appeared the Blood Mountain Hut—a small, dilapidated stone building missing its front door. The hut was tucked between a few bare oaks and an impressive boulder which equaled it in size. There, I saw Chris, Brad, Kurt, and Colin sitting on the cold rocks, laughing together, trying to fill their hunger with CLIF Bars and PowerBars. Like them, I didn't unbuckle my pack, but sat on a rock and leaned back on my pack. It was too chilly to stay still for very long.

"Great climb, huh?" Chris asked. We compared notes about the ascent and talked about the ice and the lack of view. Even though the summit of Blood Mountain was partially enclosed by a high-elevation scrub forest, there were massive rock outcrops all over the area, and had it been a clear day, we would have been rewarded with stunning views.

"We'll see you down at the road," Chris said, as he and the others left the hut. I rested a bit longer, but with only two more downhill miles to go, I didn't linger. The ache for food that didn't require rehydration drove me on.

Clouds still engulfed the peak, and here, like everywhere, ice coated every branch and boulder. Small pathways led in many directions, but leaving the hut, the AT route was unclear. I headed the way the guys had gone, but after a few paces, I couldn't find any white blazes on the trees.

After searching for several minutes, I finally found one.

Beneath my feet.

The blazes had been painted on the gray granite rocks. And the rocks were covered with ice, making the blazes impossible to make out. I wanted a few words with the person whose brilliant idea that had been.

Using my trekking poles as extra legs, I picked my way over the ice. The soles of my boots couldn't grip the slick ground, and my pack made balance laughable. My feet slipped out from under me. I jabbed my poles into the ice and only just caught myself from crashing down. It was too precarious.

I couldn't do it.

If I tried to walk any farther, I would fall. So, I sat. I stuck my feet in front as if I were on a sled, thrusted my poles to the sides in hopes they would help steer me, and pushed off. The ice was smooth and glassy with bumpy and uneven patches everywhere. I slid, fast, listing to one side until I skidded onto a patch of dry rock and tumbled to a stop. Sitting awkwardly on the ground, I tried to catch my breath. The cold seeped through my rain pants, which were soaking through. The trees offered no hint that I was going in the right direction, and there were still no white blazes.

I reconsidered this hike. Maybe five days of backpacking was enough. I proved I could make it up and over mountains. I proved I could survive with everything I needed on my back. Did I need to go farther? Was the risk really worth it? The questions had been simmering under the pain all week, but now they came fully to life.

I was deeply unsure of my goal. I wanted to walk, not slide my way to Katahdin. Yet, there I was, sitting on frozen ground on a mountaintop, lost. I could go forward or I could go back. But I could not stay on Blood Mountain forever.

Mother fucker.

I took a guess where the trail might be, aimed away from where I thought the mountain's edge was, and slid. Down. Down with gravity. Down with increasing speed and decreasing control. Down as the rock slab steepened. My pack pulled me off balance as I bumped along. I couldn't manage its weight. Below, the rock slab gave way to a leaf-covered forest floor, and when I reached the line of trees, my right leg slammed into a trunk and jerked sideways.

"Shit!" I screamed, lurching to a halt.

I pressed against the ice-encrusted leaves beneath me and tried to unfold my leg. A shot of pain tore into my knee. Gulping for breath, I lay back on the crunchy ground and assessed the rest of my body, relieved to discover it was shaking, but undamaged. Then I looked back up from the direction I had come. A sloping wall of glistening ice towered over me, reminding me how truly small I was. Up there, somewhere, was the Appalachian Trail. And I didn't know how to get back to it.

I was off the trail, hidden. *I can't do this.*

Anger welled up and I beat the ground. I screamed. I swore at anything that could hear me. But I was alone. It was there, on an icy mountainside with a messed-up knee that I could give up. *How long does it take to freeze to death?* When I ran out of tears, a sort of desperation wiggled its way inside.

My father was right. *I can't do this.* I shivered, feeling the sting of cold through my wet clothes. With a chill overtaking me, a memory bubbled up. My earliest memory. Of fear.

I was three or four years old, and I awoke in the night in my bedroom. I couldn't say what woke me—a noise, a bad dream—whatever it was, I knew I needed my mommy. She would make it right. There were shadows, quiet, and a stillness so complete as I walked on the cold tile floor through the dark hallway to my parents' room.

I didn't pause at the ajar door but pushed it open to go inside and find her. The blackness grew even deeper. I stepped up to the foot of the huge bed where I could just make out two breaths softly swishing in and out. The sound stopped me. I'd forgotten, he would be there too. And if he was there, which side of the bed was he on?

Sometimes Mommy was on the side of the bed by the door, where the glowing green numbers shined from the nightstand. Sometimes she was on the other side, farther away. I needed her, but if I went to the wrong side and got Daddy, I could get in trouble. He would not make me feel better, and he might even make me feel worse.

I stood searching into the darkness, barely tall enough to see the forms on the bed, considering what to do, needing her more than ever now, wishing I knew where he was, so I could avoid him.

The memory dissolved without resolution. Maybe I picked the right side, and my father never knew I was in their room that night. Maybe I picked the wrong side, and he got angry. Or maybe he didn't and tried to comfort me on that particular night. But the blurry edge of memory whispered that maybe I turned and went back to my room, deciding that I would find some way to cope on my own with whatever had gotten me out of bed, for it was surely safer than what would happen if I woke him.

Fear had been a constant in my life. And now I was looking once more directly into the dark face of it. The steep ice slab rose high above me; it was a milky white, created in the night by an early spring mountain storm, created with no thought at all of me or my kind, created by the force that built these mountains. I couldn't wait here for someone to save me. I had to move. I had to save myself.

Cautiously guarding my knee, I pushed myself onto my feet. I looped my trekking poles over one arm and tightened my hip belt. Keeping my center of gravity low, I dug in. I clawed my way up. Every pressure on my right leg sent a ripple of agony to my knee, but it didn't seem broken, so I kept on. I examined the ground with each movement, seeking small cracks in the rock, clumps of grass, and ice-free areas to grip, using whatever I could find. I stopped frequently, looking for a white blaze, a clear path, another hiker. Nothing.

My pack had never felt so light; I barely noticed it as the adrenaline kept me moving up. I pulled myself onto a fairly level patch of rock with no ice and paused to scan the mountainside.

There! Finally, a blaze! It was faded and looked like a blotch of snow on the tree, but indeed, it was a white blaze. The trail went on past boulders, downhill through the laurel, on a worn dirt path not covered by ice.

I limped down the mountain's backside, wiping more tears from my cold face. Finally arriving at Neel's Gap, I crossed the road to enter the store, looking for someone I knew, something to steady the confusion. But there was no one. Nothing familiar.

The store was dry and warm but overcrowded with an assaulting array of backpacks, stoves, water filters, and other colorful gear. The fluorescent lights burned at my eyes. I used the pay phone to call the number for a nearby campground to see if they had any available space for the night, then wrapped my hands around a hot chocolate.

As I waited for the campground shuttle, I tried to process what I had just experienced. Sitting next to a warm building that radiated safety, with cars zooming by, it didn't seem so treacherous. Then I stood and felt the pain shoot through my knee again and knew my story could have easily turned in a different direction. One with flashing lights and rescue workers and unhappy phone calls to New Jersey. But if I could slide off an ice-coated mountain, claw my way back up, and still find my way to a warm store and a cup of hot cocoa, I had to believe I could do this. *I can make it to Maine.*

SUNBEAMS AND RAINBOWS

Men populated the Appalachian Trail. Some were on their way to Maine; many were hiking for a weekend or spring break. They'd come up quickly from behind, overtaking me as I trudged through my battle against blisters, gravity, and an injured knee. I'd step to the side of the trail, and we'd exchange a few nice words. They'd say that they'd see me at the next shelter as they pulled ahead. Then I'd never see them again. Testosterone dictated their direction, and they needed to prove how fast and far they could go. Some of them carried beer and pot and happily imbibed each evening at camp. I shared a beer a couple of times, but I usually only stayed for a short time before leaving them to their activities.

There weren't other women around. I heard Margaret left the trail due to severe migraines. And I hadn't seen Charlie and Mom for days; I didn't know whether they were ahead or behind. One or two groups included a woman, but I didn't learn their names as they passed by.

While I walked, I thought about my college friends. I'd followed both my parents and my paternal grandfather's footsteps by going to the University of Michigan. They all, along with other relatives, had participated in the Greek system. Desperate to find a place to fit in, I succumbed to the familial pressure and joined a sorority my sophomore year.

I was hardly the image of femininity that sororities demanded; I'd never learned to put on makeup properly and I always cut my legs when shaving. My mother coveted jewelry and shoes and was forever taking me to department stores to buy new clothes. While I enjoyed getting new stuff, I felt ashamed of my too-tall body and sought out oversized, frumpy items that hid any semblance of the maturing young woman underneath. And for every school event or church service, I wrestled with my ultimate nemesis: pantyhose. I frequently cursed the inventor of this most restrictive and odious female clothing item.

I wondered what my mother and sorority sisters would say if they saw me now, many days from a shower, only two sets of clothes to choose from, no makeup at all, sleeping on the hard ground or inside a dusty old shelter with a bunch of strangers, and not a pair of pantyhose within miles. I was still searching for a trail name and wondered what name they might give.

As much as I didn't fit in a sorority, I wasn't sure I fit in the wilderness either. My experience on Blood Mountain had left my knee throbbing with every step. I wrapped it tightly with an ace bandage every morning and took Advil several times a day, but the pain kept my enthusiasm for hiking in check. The winter sun set early, but the cool days seemed to last forever as I traipsed up and down the mountains, dragging myself from one shelter to the next. I arrived each night at my destination completely spent, barely enough energy to cook dinner and get into my sleeping bag.

One evening, I came close to collapsing on the trail. I thought the shelter was near, but the bends in the trail never brought me there. Finally, every muscle and bone drained, my body wouldn't go any farther. On a wide, forested ridge, I stopped walking. I was cold. I was always cold on these wet, drizzly mountains. Rocks and logs covered the ground all around, save for the flat trail itself. I pitched my tent in the middle of the trail, climbed inside, and crumpled into tears.

As I sobbed into my sleeping bag, I thought about all the tears I'd shed in my life. After an attack from my father, I would cry in my bedroom, all the fear and frustration I'd been holding in slowly oozing out. If my father heard me crying, he would pursue me to keep fighting, so I gasped into a pillow. Stifling myself.

Often, later, a soft knock would come at my door. My mother entered, a layer of sorrow underneath her always perfectly made-up face. She sat next to me on the bed and rubbed my back. After one particularly painful attack, I couldn't understand her allowance of all this. My face still wet with tears and the lump of distress still in my throat, I asked, "Why do you stay with him?"

I waited for an answer. Surely, she would explain that this was all okay, we'd be okay. Surely, there was some explanation for why she let him treat me like that. Surely, she must love him.

As forceful and aggressive as my father was, my mother was equally the peacemaker. A caregiver to her core, for most of my life she had worked as a pediatric nurse. She grew up in a time when a wife's main job was to be supportive of her husband. Though my father's rage had not been apparent during their courting, once married, my mother had no intention of not being a proper wife. She would manage her household, raise her babies, and tend to her man. Trying to keep the peace, she found justifications for his behavior. He was having trouble at work. He'd just been on a long trip. He was worried about paying the bills.

"He's a good provider," she said. Then she retreated from my room, leaving me dumbfounded at her ability to excuse him.

As night took over the mountain, the tears and memories faded as I remembered that I'd never camped alone before. I suddenly felt the sharp reality of solitude. I softened my breath and turned my attention to the sounds outside. Every noise was a mystery. Faint crinkles, gentle drips, distant creaks. I was reminded of sitting in my closet as a child, trying to pinpoint the location of the voices in the house. Here, I listened just as intently. Bears were possible nighttime marauders, but what did other animals do at night? I remained alert for hours, trying to discern exactly what made each noise. It wasn't until a long stretch of relative quiet that the fatigue of the day won out.

I woke when I could just see the blue of my tent walls. Cold stung my face, the only part of me exposed to the air. My warm bag bid me stay inside, but my tent was blocking the path, and I wanted to get going before any other hikers came by. I slipped my shorts on over my long underwear, pulled on my sports bra and a long-sleeved shirt, and wrapped my raincoat around me. I opened the tent door and saw a velvety light filtering through the trees.

I climbed out into the hazy morning forest and turned to the southeast. My eyes fell upon an astonishing sight. The fluorescent orange sun had risen and perched itself upon the distant gray-blue mountains, as if it were a basketball stopped in time on the rim of the hoop. It balanced there, precarious, held in place by the clouds above, which just touched the top of the orb. The light intensified as the perfect frame reflected pinks and oranges and reds, clouds and mountains alike rippling with color. I let the light pierce my eyes, feeling a shot of energy course through me. It was like I could see, or more accurately, sense every particle of light shimmering in the air. I had made it through the dark night. A thought whispered by that everything would be okay. *I'm alive.*

Within minutes, the sun shifted, rising into the clouds, and all color faded back to gray. The moment was gone, but the image was burned into my mind. I turned to my gear, packing up as quickly as I could. The cold pressed me forward, and my body warmed with the exertion. After about ten minutes of walking, I heard noises and soon reached the shelter I had been aiming for the previous night. Had I gone just a bit farther yesterday, I would have slept there, safe and secure among my kind.

And yet, as I watched the other hikers through the trees, I wondered if any of them had seen that sunrise. The night had challenged me, but I'd earned a beautiful reward. Maybe if there were hard times, there would equally have to be easy times too. I was glad to know that I had in fact been close to other people, but now I knew I could manage without them. Relief trickled in; I wasn't alone.

•   •   •

Many people likened the trail to a roller coaster, probably due to the lack of switchbacks and the intense steepness of each climb and descent. For me, the roller coaster also took me on a constant emotional up and down. I cried through my tenth day on the trail as I hiked six miles to my first scheduled town stop. The blisters ripped at my feet; each step was like having nails hammered into my heels. The memory of the glowing sun tucked between mountains and clouds stuck with me, but my trek thus far had been dominated by pain. I struggled all morning, ready to quit the hike for good.

When I reached Dick's Creek Gap in the early afternoon, I wiped the tears away and stuck my thumb out for a ride to the Blueberry Patch Hostel, near Hiawassee, Tennessee. I caught a ride from a woman who lived near the Blueberry Patch, and a few miles later, she dropped me off at the front door of a pale blue barn.

A man with gray-streaked black hair and a bushy black beard came outside and introduced himself as Gary. As he showed me into the old barn, now converted into sleeping quarters, he explained he was a former thru-hiker and understood the need for good accommodations. I dropped my pack and followed him around the idyllic farm nestled beneath the mountains. Gary's wife, Lennie, a mousy woman in a long flowy farm dress, appeared when we were looking over their extensive garden and the blueberry fields beyond. They were both quite short, and I felt giraffe-like towering over them. Yet, I felt dwarfed by their abundant generosity as Gary pointed out where I could refill my stove gas and Lennie offered to do my laundry. I thanked them profusely, then went back to the barn and slumped onto a bed in relief.

Mike, now IOWA Jurnee, was already there and had decided to take the next day off. One of his pack straps had broken, and he was awaiting a new one in the mail. With my aching knee, my beaten spirit, and a weather forecast showing more rain and ice, I decided I'd take the day off too. My first zero-mile day.

Normally, Lennie provided breakfast for hikers at the dining table in the barn. But since Jurnee and I were the only visitors, in the morning she invited us up to the house. Entering the petite, bright kitchen, the aroma of sweetness overtook me. The table overflowed with jams and syrups and berries and cheese biscuits and eggs and stacks of creamy blueberry pancakes. I'd been filling myself for ten days with fuel—pasta, rice, oatmeal, CLIF Bars, peanuts—survival food. Now I felt as if I'd been wandering the desert eating sand. This table spread with color and life and rising steam reawakened my sense of taste and opened the depths of my stomach.

Lennie offered me a seat, and I began to eat like never before. As soon as my plate emptied, she filled it again. Jurnee kept up the conversation with our hosts, while I focused on more blueberries, more syrup, more biscuits. It felt decadent to stuff my belly and not heave the backpack this morning. The feeling morphed into gratitude when Jurnee and I returned to the barn as the rain poured down.

"Whaddya going to do now?" I asked him.

"Nothing," Jurnee replied, relaxing on one of the well-used couches. "What are you going to do?"

"Nothing." I put another log into the fire. "I'm not walking anywhere, that's for sure."

"I talked to my brother earlier," Jurnee said, chuckling. "He was telling my nephew about my hike, and the kid goes 'Uncle Mike sure is an idiot to do that.'" Jurnee took his glasses off and rubbed his face with his hands. "We *are* idiots, aren't we?"

I agreed and placed another pillow under my knee to elevate it. Though we'd camped many of the nights since Springer in the same place, with a day of nothing but two couches and a wood stove to keep us busy, I was glad to finally get to know Jurnee better. He was different from the other young men who kept passing me by. He explained his job, but all I understood was that he was a numbers-computer guy who worked in an office. Though he didn't come right out and say it, I gathered that he was having an early mid-life crisis. He decided to take some time off, get outside, and hike the trail.

As the rain poured down outside, Jurnee started flipping through some old *Backpacker* magazines, and I turned to my mail. I'd distributed my hiking schedule and mailing list to my friends and family with an invitation to drop me a note along the way. I knew my mom would write, but when Lennie gave me my food box, she also handed me six letters from various relatives and friends. I opened each one slowly, savoring each word. They wrote about their lives: boyfriends, parties, pets, new jobs. It seemed as if nothing had changed out there. And yet, for me, everything had. I wanted to write them all back, but I didn't know how to convey everything I had been experiencing. I was only beginning to understand it myself.

I also opened a letter I'd written to myself two months before, on a good day, a day I'd been dreamy and hopeful about the whole thing. Reading it in the cozy barn made my eyes water.

Congratulations! You've made it to the first mail drop! You took that first step and left the "real world" behind. No matter where you go tomorrow, you are a success! I'm sure there are still fears swimming around in your head—health, stamina, feet, food, cold. Hopefully, you haven't lost any fingers or toes yet. Despite all these fears, I know you know you can do this. Remember that eighty-year-old woman who just kept putting one foot in front of the other? Do that. Remember that last hike up Katahdin, that glorious day, that strength—never let go of that. I have faith in you, so keep going, girl.

I closed the letter and tucked it away, planning to read it again. Then I moved on to open the food box. In my parents' living room, I had set out twenty-three toaster-sized boxes and filled each one with a week's worth of food, one or two twenty-dollar traveler's checks, batteries, the next section's trail maps and guidebook pages, rolls of film, extra plastic bags, blank writing paper, toilet paper, and anything else I thought I might need in town. Based on my estimated hiking speed, my parents would send each box so that it arrived at the next town before I did. As I sorted through the box, I realized that I'd overpacked. Again. I spent a while on the barn floor, divvying up items that would go in the backpack and those to go in the box headed back to New Jersey.

Back at Neel's Gap, I had made a brief call to my parents to tell them I was still alive, omitting any mention of Blood Mountain. Now, with a full day off, I had plenty of time to fill them in on my hike thus far. I was apprehensive to talk to my dad. What would he say? I prepared myself to downplay my knee injury and play up my happiness factor. I had to convince them I was completely confident and had zero doubts about why I was out there.

Mom answered the phone, relieved to hear my voice. She called out to Dad, somewhere else in the house, and a few minutes later he clicked onto the line. They had a lot of questions about my feet, my food, and my gear. But there were no questions about whether I should come home. They seemed happy for me. Or maybe just surprised I had made it this far. It was almost as if they were supportive.

My parents shared the news that my brother had been assigned the F-16 and would head off to another Air Force base to train to fly the fastest fighter jet there was. Nate's graduation would take place in about three weeks in Mississippi, and my parents and I discussed my plans to leave the trail to join them for a few days. I knew they were proud of him. My dad had put in many years as an F-15 pilot before leaving the military to start a career with a commercial airline, where the work was more stable and lucrative. And before him, my grandfather had served in the Army in WWII. The family history of military service was deeply honored.

Mom got weepy when it was time to say goodbye. I reminded her I had succeeded at the first leg of the journey and had learned a lot along the way.

"Everything's fine," I said. "I'll call again soon." I tried to reassure her. As I hung up the phone, I wondered if I was really trying to reassure myself.

•　　　•　　　•

By noon, I was starving. "Let's go to town," I said to Jurnee.

"We just had breakfast!" Jurnee hadn't gotten his hiker stomach yet. Though he was beginning to burn off the extra layers of city life, he still had a roundness to him. While everyone else gobbled any calories they could find, Jurnee mostly nibbled GORP and energy bars to get him through the day.

"Yeah, like three hours ago," I replied. "Come on. There's a six-dollar all-you-can-eat buffet with lots of vegetarian options."

"Fine, fine. I also want to stop at the outfitter to check out the packs." We put on our raincoats and headed to the road to get a hitch.

By the time we returned from lunch, a trip to the grocery for snacks, and a visit to the Take-A-Hike outfitter, a few other hikers had arrived at the Blueberry Patch for the night. We shared our positions on the couches and spent the afternoon playing cards and telling stories. I opened the notebook I'd brought where I'd written out a few dozen quotes, song lyrics, and bits of literature to carry me onward. I flipped through the pages, stopping at a poem I had printed out called "Ithaca," by Constantine P. Cavafy. The poem took its readers through Odysseus' travels across the seas as he voyaged back to his homeland. It struck me as similar to hiking the AT. I wasn't headed to any Phoenician markets nor Egyptian cities, and I hoped I wouldn't come across a Cyclops or Lestrygonians, whatever that was. But I read the poem repeatedly, knowing it was about travel and adventure and feeling the magic of the rhythmic language.

The rain subsided, and the sun broke through the clouds. I went outside to fill up my fuel bottle from Gary's gas can and looked up toward the mountains. A sharp rainbow arched down from the highest visible peak to the edge of the open blueberry field. The light was shining through a thinning cloud passing to the south.

I dashed back inside for my camera, despite knowing that rainbows were never captured well on film. I'd had a vague notion before I began this trek that I would see rainbows and waterfalls around every corner, glorious sunsets every night, and maybe even some magical unicorns along the way. Instead, I'd walked sixty-seven miles under a monstrous backpack. I'd scaled more than a dozen mountains, one of which almost killed me. I'd spent every day surrounded by arrogant, though friendly, young men, trying to figure out where I fit in. And I'd questioned myself perpetually as I hiked through rain, snow, ice, cold, and a few stray rays of sunshine. But I'd done it. I had the encouraging letter from myself to prove it.

The day off had given me a chance to refresh myself, to remember that my body did not have to be in pain at every moment, to replenish my strength. A reset button had been hit, and I wanted to get out there and try again.

Jurnee came out to see the rainbow, and we stood in the damp, cool air under the misty colors hovering innocently above.

"I've decided on a trail name," I said.

"Well, what is it?" Jurnee asked.

I'd seen no magical unicorns, but the rainbow reminded me that being in nature was a huge part of why I had come to the AT and a nature name was appropriate. I loved all of the natural world, but particularly trees. My favorite was one I'd learned about last summer in Maine, the only deciduous pine tree, the larch, also known as hackmatack, also known as tamarack. They were dormant and bare right now; their needles having turned to gold and dropped to the ground last fall. In the summer they were scraggly, unkempt, their branches jutting out from the trunk at odd angles, covered in little clumps of soft green needles. They were distinctly different from the rest of their pine family. As was I; I'd done something that scared most people, and no one in my family would have ever attempted. I felt a kinship with the deciduous pine, doing life my own way.

I took a deep breath, ready to say it aloud for the first time. "Tamarack," I said. "My name is Tamarack."

TRAIL MAGIC

"Why haven't you hooked up with a group yet?" asked the woman with the southern drawl. "With the Smokies acomin' up, I sure don't want to hike alone."

Melissa was a college student who had taken a semester off to hike the trail. We were sitting by a campfire at Bly Gap, 0.1 miles north of the Georgia-North Carolina border. Crossing paths with another solo woman was a rarity, so she and I began talking at once. While I was celebrating the completion of one whole state, Melissa was obsessing about being on her own in the woods.

"Have you been hiking alone?" I asked her.

"No, ma'am," she replied. "Cleo and KC are some kinda crazy, but they're the only other women I've met." She ran her hand through her short brown hair and shot a furtive look across the campfire to see if they'd heard her. The two stout, middle-aged women sat on one side of the fire ring clearing, whispering to each other, ignoring everyone else.

"Mama doesn't want me out here alone," Melissa continued, "so I'm thinking to stay with Pete and Ryan. But I'd rather hike with y'all."

Pete and Ryan, whom I'd just met, were drinking beer, stoking the fire as the smoke wisped back and forth in the wind. It did seem as if people either started with a hiking partner or joined with others quickly. I hoped to make friends, but I'd come to the trail alone and hadn't planned on hitching my pack to anyone else's. Plus, everyone except Jurnee hiked so much faster and farther than I did, and I enjoyed spending each evening laughing with him.

"I get it," I said. "I don't know how these guys do fifteen miles a day already. The next few days are going to be ten milers for me. I'm not even sure I can do that."

"We should hike together," she said.

"Sure," I replied, immediately questioning my response. Melissa was exuberant and fun, but her pack weighed half as much as mine, and she was already putting in high miles. Not to mention that after this one evening together, I knew her constant chatter wasn't my style.

I'd never been a group kind of person. As a kid, I'd rejected Girl Scouts—too structured. I played softball for a season but got hit in the forehead with a fly ball and never played again. I couldn't sing or act, so I failed to get a part in any of the many school plays I tried out for. I'd joined cheerleading in second grade, which had started out as great fun. When seventh grade hit and the social classes divided out, I sank swiftly to the bottom of the popularity pool. None of the pretty, perfect, popular girls wanted me on the cheerleading squad. So, I quit. My high school social circle included a few close girlfriends, but I never joined in with their main circles.

When I started college, the TV show *Friends* was wildly popular, and every Thursday, I joined my dorm hallmates in the room of the one girl who had a TV. I marveled at Monica and Rachel's brightly colored New York City loft and the cute boys across the hall. The jokes kept coming, and my hallmates joined the laugh track. I pretended I understood too, pretended I could have jumped into that vivid storyline and been one of the gang.

I was privileged to have my parents paying for college. I had a small, safe room with a dining hall meal plan. I attended classes of my own choosing. I should have been happy. But sitting with my hallmates, watching the beautiful twenty-somethings solve all their problems in thirty short, commercial-laden minutes, I knew something was wrong with me.

When the show ended, the other girls would start talking and laughing about a party or a boy, while I had nothing to contribute. I'd retreat to my room, shut the door behind me, and start to cry. The pain welled up from deep in my chest. I'd lower myself down onto the gray carpet square that blended in with the gray cinder block walls, weeping.

Some of my hallmates, ones who would have fit in nicely on the set of *Friends,* formed a group that I wanted to be a part of. One of them occasionally stopped by to invite me to study or out for a slice. When a knock came, I took a few deep breaths, hoping that they wouldn't notice my puffy, red eyes. When no one came to knock, I felt worse. The crying wouldn't stop until I had worn myself down to a nub of nothing. After a time, I'd pull myself up, forcing myself into bed or to the shower or the open astronomy or philosophy textbook. I wanted the pain to end. I wanted everything to end. I didn't have a specific plan for making this happen, but I prayed that some magical force would dissolve me into oblivion.

I had no energy to fight it. I'd drag myself through the week to classes, through the weekend alone in my dorm room, until another Thursday when *Friends* rolled around. No one had died and no one was hurting me. I had everything I needed, and yet, regularly I would be destroyed by intolerable, debilitating pain. It was almost as if I hadn't left my parents' home at all.

•   •   •

I walked with Melissa through the cold morning on our first day in North Carolina. As she talked, I admired the leafless forests still held tight by March's grip. Mile after mile the landscape unfolded in all shades of brown and tan. The only sign of human life was the footpath weaving through and the occasional low rumble of a plane passing overhead. The land seemed muted and static, but the afternoon sun softened the crisp snap of winter, and I heard a few birds rustling and chirping as I walked.

Melissa reiterated we should hike together, but when I decided to stop at Standing Indian Shelter for the night, she pushed on. I wished her a good climb up Standing Indian Mountain and assured her I'd see her the next day, but I had a feeling our paces wouldn't line up.

Jurnee was already staking his claim in the shelter as I dropped my pack on the opposite side. I took the register from its shelf, and in the smattering of sunshine, I opened the tattered composition notebook. I'd come to love reading the entries in these books. People wrote poems, sketched, or left notes to other hikers. It was a brilliant, organic system of communicating up and down the trail that I'd taken to straightaway.

A group of chipmunks skittered past, interrupting my reading. They were making a fine living off hikers who dropped crumbs or left their food bags unattended for too long. I turned back to the hikers' notes, wondering if the chipmunks were relieved, as I was, at the day's warmth.

By evening, two younger girls, a dark, bearded fellow, and Hercules, a white-haired man I'd met the day before, arrived at the shelter. As everyone undertook the various camp chores of getting water, cooking dinner, and unpacking gear, the conversation unfolded with the usual questions: "When did you start? How heavy is your pack? What kind of stove do you use?"

The two girls called themselves Algae and Paranoid. They were seventeen years old and just out of high school.

"Geez, what did your parents say?" I asked. "Mine never would have let me do this at seventeen. They didn't even want me to do it now."

"They were fine with it," Algae said, looking at her friend. "I guess cuz we're together."

"Yeah, I wouldn't have come alone," Paranoid added. "We've been friends forever, and we're going to different schools…"

"So, we decided to do this before college," Algae finished for her. "You're here by yourself?"

"Yeah" I replied. "I don't know anyone who would even dream of doing this."

"Well, you can hang with us. Lizzie is scared of everything," Algae said. "That's why we call her Paranoid."

"Whatever!" Paranoid gave her a shove. "You freaked out about that spider."

I laughed at them, slightly envious. My relationship with my best friend had been tenuous in our last years of high school and quickly dissolved after we'd graduated. The girls started a fire in the fire pit, and Hercules wandered over and found a seat on one of the log stumps.

"What's wrong with your feet, girl?" he asked sternly. Algae's boots were off and she was poking at the peeling skin on her feet. "They look nasty."

She grimaced as Paranoid, arranging some kindling on the fire, answered for her. "She's got some kind of fungus going on. That's why we call her Algae. See the green bits there." She pointed at Algae's feet with a stick. They did have a mossy tint to them.

"I know how Hercules got his name," Jurnee declared. He stood by the shelter and lifted Hercules' old-school, metal-frame pack. Or, tried to. It was almost larger than mine and clearly weighed much more. "You'd have to be a God to lift this thing. What do you have in there?"

"Everything I need," Hercules said in a deep voice, visibly puffing up his chest.

"Right." Jurnee chuckled. "What don't you need?"

"The kitchen sink," Hercules replied.

The air of lightness about these people contrasted starkly with last night's covert conversations and hushed tones. The only one not joining in was the dark-haired man, who sat nearby holding his pot of pasta. He was listening but hadn't said anything throughout our talk. I couldn't tell if he was brooding or just shy.

"What's your name?" Jurnee asked him, joining us by the fire with his GORP.

"Slow Buffalo," he said in a soft voice. He told us he'd started the AT four years ago but only made it to Virginia, where he was from, and now he'd come back to do the whole thing. After listening to him for a few minutes, I decided he wasn't brooding at all. He was probably an introvert who didn't know how to join in conversations, a characteristic to which I could completely relate. He had a sly smile that he hid under all that facial hair and a gentleness about him I hadn't seen in many men.

The conversation turned to food, as it usually did, and we began to list our favorite candy.

"Reese's Peanut Butter Cups," I said. "No question."

Other favorites were peanut M&M's, gummy bears, and Snickers. Then Algae chimed in, "Why limit yourself to one? Aren't they all worth the pain of carrying on your back?"

"Girl has a point," Hercules said. And there were nods of agreement.

The six of us sat around the fire, talking into the dusk. Most nights I tucked into bed by dark, which arrived around six-thirty, but the fire and company were so welcoming that I stayed up until eight o'clock when everyone else was ready to retire too. And even then, I didn't want it to end.

"No snoring, Hercules," Jurnee insisted as we situated ourselves on the hard shelter floor.

"I'll sleep on my side. Then I won't snore," Hercules grumbled. Minutes later, his loud rumble took over the shelter.

Jurnee sniggered in the darkness. "Well, that worked," he said.

•　　　•　　　•

Over the next couple of days, spring broke through winter's thick wall. I'd started wearing shorts and leaving my coat packed. I saw a few butterflies. One afternoon I spotted a handful of juncos jumping around in a copse. I paused to watch them and noticed at least a dozen more. They ignored me as they hopped under the hemlocks. Searching for seeds, chattering to each other, dancing in the warmth of spring.

Our group of six kept the same pace. Many other hikers passed us, but I was happy to be slowly adding up the miles with them. Just a few nights before, I had been feeling awkward and beaten, uncertain about this whole thing. Then over the span of one evening, everything changed.

I didn't want to lose these people. I spent each day consumed with pain and was partaking of as much ibuprofen as was medically advisable, but I wasn't thinking about the suffering. Instead, I was spurred on to catch my friends at the next break, to hear one more joke, to get to the campsite we all were aiming for. At every break, I knew someone would be there to cheer me up or cheer me on.

So far, I'd opted for the warmth of my tent or the ease of the lean-tos, but one clear night, I scouted for a place to sleep outside. I found a cozy, piney spot not far from the shelter, but far enough that Hercules' snores would retreat into a dull roar. As I unpacked my sleeping bag, I marveled at this simple day of walking, eating, and laughing. I laughed with these people in a way I never had with my freshman-year dormmates.

In my later college years, I had strong friendships with my sorority sisters, but those relationships had taken months or years to build. I'd known Jurnee, Algae, Paranoid, Hercules, and Slow Buffalo for mere days, and yet we had formed an instant connection. I knew relatively little about their "real" lives off the AT, but I didn't need to know. Our relationships weren't defined by whom we used to be. Instead, we offered ourselves to each other freely and openly, because this life was the only one that mattered.

I cozied into my bag, settling down. When I'd been in New Jersey, I'd imagined doing this, lying on my back, looking up through the dark branches into the forever stars. Tiny twinkles sparkled through the empty trees, and I watched for shooting stars and satellites.

With thoughts of satellites, a popular Dave Matthews Band song drifted into my head and I thought about when I'd first learned about DMB. A friend in college had given me a mixtape with "Ants Marching" on it, and I fell fast and hard. I bought an *Under the Table and Dreaming* CD and played it endlessly, every word and note piercing right into the core of who I was. The more miles I walked on the AT, the more I saw that trail life mirrored those basic emotions Dave sang about, and the more I felt that DMB was perfect trail music. There was even a song about sleeping outside. And here I was doing it! I dozed off as the glittering stars and planets high above blurred and "Satellite" circled my mind.

In the morning, as I stuffed my gear into my pack, Paranoid came over and handed me a Hershey bar.

"What's this for?" I asked.

"It was really brave to sleep out," she said.

Sleeping outside had been more fun than brave, but I could feel Paranoid's respect and accepted her kind gesture, stuffing the candy into the top of my pack.

That day, we reached the 100-mile mark, a tiny measurement on a walk of more than 2,000 miles, but still significant. We all stopped together and passed around the chocolate bar, some M&M's, and the usual trail snacks. KC and Cleo came along at the same time, surprising me by joining the celebration and giving a few bagels to the gathering.

"We need some nachos," I said.

"I'd prefer a beer," Hercules said. "Anyone got one?"

"I've got something just as good," Algae said, reaching for her water bottle.

"Water for everyone on this momentous occasion!" Jurnee decreed with a flourish.

"Party on," Slow Buffalo deadpanned.

A short distance farther down the trail at the rickety bridge at Rock Gap, we found something a little more exciting to drink. A note was taped to the handrail offering congratulations and a cold drink for completing 100 miles. A trail angel had left a few six-packs of soda cooling in the stream. The others moved on, but Slow Buffalo and I eagerly popped one open and enjoyed another break in the sunshine.

The delights of the day continued when I descended into Winding Stair Gap and found Brad and Colin, whom I'd last seen atop Blood Mountain. US 64 passed through there, and they had just returned from Franklin. Their buddy Kurt had left the trail, but they'd decided to keep hiking with their newly earned trail names, Carolina Kid and Pooh Bear. I listened to their stories about Franklin as they shared some Crunch 'n Munch and a Cadbury Egg.

The mileage that day was my longest yet, and when I arrived thirteen miles from where I started, I could not bear one more step. My body had become slightly more conditioned, but my pack still bore down on me with uncompromising torture. My blisters continued to pierce my heels and though my knee had improved, I still felt a twinge of pain with each step.

Jurnee and I were the first ones at camp and were setting up our tents when Slow Buffalo strolled in. Buffalo always made backpacking look easy somehow. His pack was compact and, unlike me, he didn't shrink under the weight of it. He almost walked like a normal human being, rather than a fool with fifty pounds on their back. Buffalo dropped his gear and promptly dug out a package of Reese's Peanut Butter Cups, thrusting them at me with a small grin. I didn't know where he'd gotten them, but I reached out and hugged him.

I'd heard the term trail magic and knew it was an unexpected, often food-related gift, but the Hershey bar, soda, and candy all showed me that trail magic was more than just a treat. It was an offering of support, of trust, of friendship from someone I barely knew, or in some cases, I might never know. It came without expectations, without conditions. It acknowledged that we were all the same out there, and the least we could do was spread a little love.

When the evening's discussion turned to religion, I realized Slow Buffalo and I were more alike than I'd guessed. Both of us had been raised in Protestant churches, and both of us had turned into adults who questioned organized religion. Buffalo was studying Buddhism because he liked its teachings more than the Christian ones. He told me that Buddhists believe that every animal is a sentient being, worthy of its own life, and that humans, with their greater intellectual awareness, should be kind to and protect every creature, even the insects.

"That's exactly what I already believe!" I exclaimed. "When I was a kid, I ran into the street in front of my house during rainstorms to save the earthworms from being run over. I hated seeing them squished in the roads."

"I know." He nodded. "I feel guilty just walking on this path every day. We're killing all kinds of stuff."

Jurnee snorted nearby. "I'll kill them," he said. "When I'm the first one out in the morning, and there are all those spider webs crossing the trail and sticking to my face, I'm happy to smack any of the little buggers I see."

Buffalo and I exchanged an amused glance. Not everyone could be as enlightened as us, I figured. It was rare to find someone else who cared in the way that I did. When Buffalo later told us he'd been in the Coast Guard for a few years, I was surprised. He was the least likely military man I'd ever met. Could you be Buddhist in the military? Maybe that was why he left it.

The boys and I finished our dinners as night fell. Algae, Paranoid, and Hercules hadn't arrived yet, and I began to worry. The girls were probably just dawdling somewhere along the way, but Hercules had been struggling. He was tough, but he was also old. He'd never said his age, but I guessed he was close to sixty-five. If hiking was this painful on my young body, I had to imagine the AT was thrashing him even harder. And for anyone, regardless of age, arriving in darkness made camp chores all the more difficult.

"Do you think he's okay?" I asked Slow Buffalo.

"Yeah, he'll get here," he replied. "He always does."

"You wouldn't worry about me if I didn't make it to camp," I joked.

"Of course, I would," he said. "We've got to take care of each other out here."

I looked at him in the fading light. He was serious. He really would care if I didn't show up. I was taken aback. But how could I worry about Hercules, without acknowledging that the others would equally worry about me? The question was solidifying in my mind when we heard a loud howl. I couldn't tell if it was a cry of distress or elation until I saw Hercules appear with a grin on his wrinkled face.

"What was that?" Jurnee asked.

"I made it through another day," Hercules said. "That deserves makin' some noise."

Buffalo and I looked at each other, then howled back.

My relief that Hercules had made it safely was cut short by the news he brought with him. As he set up his sleeping gear in the shelter, he relayed that Algae's feet had gotten worse, and the girls went to Franklin to find a doctor. They didn't know if they'd return to the trail, and if they did, if they'd be able to catch up to us.

Hike your own hike. I had heard others use that saying, and I knew that Algae and Paranoid needed to follow their own path, and I needed to follow mine. Still, I felt a wave of disappointment realizing that just as I had found my group, a part of it had broken away.

•   •   •

The next twenty-five miles traversed the balds of North Carolina—a unique phenomenon of mountains that rose from 4,000 to 5,500 feet but with nary a tree atop them. Instead, the trail cut across vast open fields covered in amber grasses. No one farmed or mowed these grass-topped peaks, and mostly they were not encroached upon by the surrounding forests. Everyone had a different theory on how the balds came to be. Some said they resulted from prehistoric human activities. Others compared these heights to corresponding elevations in the Northern Appalachians, which would be in the alpine zone, suggesting maybe this was a warmer, southern equivalent. Whatever the reason, the wide expanses allowed for sweeping views across the whole range, and I stopped often to rest my eyes on the far horizon.

At the lower elevations, the trail returned to forests, shrubs, and deep gaps thick with rhododendrons. The rhodies still wore last year's growth, and I relished walking through corridors of shiny leaves. It wasn't warm enough for flowers yet, but I was looking forward to seeing the bushes covered with vibrant colors. Some segments of trail there had switchbacks and when my lungs could keep up, I sang whatever songs came to mind, often Dave Matthews or Sarah McLachlan. Some annoyingly appropriate songs, like James Taylor's "In My Mind I've Gone to Carolina" and "Walking Man," got stuck on endless repeat.

Jurnee, Slow Buffalo, Hercules, and I were surrounded by a cohort of thru-hikers moving north at generally the same rate. We'd leapfrog past each other, throughout hours or days—one stopping here, another stopping there—each time, sharing information, jokes, or stories. I had gotten to know Cameraman, who informed me he'd hiked with Melissa. I hadn't seen her since Standing Indian and wondered what became of her until Cameraman told me a friend of hers had died and she planned to leave the trail. There were two Greybeards, both gray-haired men close in age to Hercules, one of whom I repeatedly commiserated with over our blistered feet. Cleo and KC also remained in the area, and I'd had to revise my original perception of them as they more often reached out with friendly gestures.

Having the cohort around, while reassuring in case of injury or bear attack, also felt stifling. Though I was walking through wilderness every day, I didn't go more than an hour without crossing paths with a thru-hiker or day hiker. The shelters, which generally could sleep six to ten people, were always full, often with additional people tenting in the vicinity. Our human presence dominated the landscape with the clanks and thuds of camp gear, snores, and loud chatter late at night or early in the morning.

Inevitably, there were some hikers I didn't like much. Buffalo read my mind when he said that Repartee, a young woman with whom we had shared several shelters, had a "bad aura." I'd tried to strike up a conversation with her when we first met, but she'd answered in monosyllables and quickly walked away. I wondered how she'd gotten her trail name. Perhaps it was meant to be ironic. Repartee hiked with a guy named Seth, who I guessed was her boyfriend, but none of us were really sure because he didn't talk to us either.

"I think I'm gonna get some water and move on to find a tent site," I said to Buffalo and Jurnee when we arrived at Wayah Shelter. The area was filling up with hikers, and I wanted to find some space.

"Yeah, I'm up for it," Slow Buffalo said without a pause.

"Well, if you guys are going, then I'll Oompa Loompa along behind you," Jurnee added while adjusting his glasses. Jurnee had recently likened himself to one of the orange creatures from *Willy Wonka and the Chocolate Factory* and informed us he often sang the Oompa Loompa song as he walked. It seemed fairly appropriate, though he was finally shedding his extra teddy bear weight.

In shelters, there was little concern over bears. With so many human noises, bears rarely tried to infiltrate the area. But where we stopped to camp, several miles from Wayah Shelter, bears were a very real possibility. I knew the theory of bear bagging: hang your food bag at least ten feet in the air, at least eight feet out from any tree trunk. I'd only set up a bear bag a few times, but after dinner, I dug out the purple length of climbing cord with a carabiner tied to the end and began searching for a good tree.

"Over here!" Jurnee hollered. I walked in his direction to find him struggling to throw his rope over a branch twelve feet above our heads. After numerous throws, he finally got it over.

"Ha-ha!" He shouted with triumph. He clipped his food bag to the rope and hauled it up.

"Um, and what about that nice log that's leaning up right behind your bag?" I asked. "It's a perfect ramp for a raccoon or a bear."

"I didn't notice it, so they won't either," Jurnee responded. Then he let go of the rope, and the food bag dropped with a thud. "Well, where are you putting yours?"

"I've got a perfect spot," I said and led him back to a tree near my tent. I threw my rope over the branch with ease. I smirked with superiority and gave a tug on the rope. With barely any pressure, the branch snapped and crashed down on my head.

"Nice one!" Slow Buffalo laughed from nearby.

"Let's see your skills, then," I said, pulling twigs out of my hair.

Buffalo tied a rock to the end of his rope and with a strong throw, the rock arced around a branch above. It quickly unraveled from the rope, and once separated, came swooping back and nearly hit him in the head.

"Damn!"

"Perhaps we should just keep our food in our tents?" I suggested.

Hours later, when I awoke in the darkness to a sound I couldn't identify, I regretted we hadn't tried harder on the bear bags. There was a thump. Then another thump. Hard, hollow, like something hitting a tree.

Shit. My food bag was just outside my tent door. And now the bears had come for us.

Then the hissing began. Another animal joined in, farther off. They were encircling us. It sounded more like a cat than a bear. I rationalized that all I had in my food bag was dried pasta and CLIF Bars. No self-respecting bobcat would go for vegetarian food. Jurnee had beef jerky and peanut butter. I could hear Jurnee snoring, a dozen feet away in his tent, unaware of our impending doom.

Then I heard a hoarse whisper from the other direction. "Jurnee?"

I stayed quiet. When no response from Jurnee or the animals came, I ventured a whisper.

"Buffalo? What was that?"

"I'm thinking a couple of deer," he answered. "Maybe bucks."

"Not bobcats?"

"I don't think so."

But what did he really know, anyway? Like me, he'd grown up in the suburbs.

Then Jurnee's snoring stopped. "Huh? What's happening? We got company?"

"I think they moved away," I said through my tent wall into the darkness. "Some help you'd be if we were under attack."

"Well, it was probably my snoring that scared them away. You guys owe me. Can we go back to sleep now?"

I heard Buffalo chuckle. The thought crossed my mind that it was possible we were about to be eaten by bears or wolves or bobcats, and yet, somehow, I felt safe. The fear and unease from my first days had subsided, and I hadn't even cried anytime recently. I knew that our time together could end, abruptly—Algae and Paranoid had disappeared without even a chance to say goodbye—but I didn't want to lose Buffalo and Jurnee. They already meant too much.

• • •

Walking into the Nantahala Outdoor Center in Wesser, North Carolina was like entering a beer ad; scantily clad, beautiful people frolicked through a strategically picturesque backdrop, merrily preparing their red and yellow kayaks, rafts, and life jackets for hours of outdoorsy fun. The Nantahala River rushed through the gap between the mountains as people loaded into vans to be transported up river, while others who had already raced back down the water were unloading onto the shore. The NOC was a regional center for river rafting and kayaking and a hub for outdoors people of all kinds. The trail meandered through the complex that included an outfitter and rafting shop, several restaurants, a motel, a laundromat, and a bunkhouse. After days of moving two miles per hour, the intense noise and bustle of the cars zipping by and the river thoroughfare were disturbing.

The boys and I arrived in the morning, after only one mile. The day before had been my longest at fifteen miles. The first part of the day included no less than eight extreme ups and downs, each one rising steeply to a bald, then descending just as sharply to a treed gap. I'd been ready to stop at Wesser Bald, leaving six miles into NOC this morning. But Buffalo bribed us with an offer to buy Ben and Jerry's ice cream if we pushed on. Not one to turn down free food, plus the fact that we'd have a whole day off in this outdoor recreation utopia, I pushed my body to the limit.

After claiming a bed at the hiker hostel, the next order of business was food. The River's End Restaurant was an impressive, barn-like building, situated parallel to and almost hanging over the edge of the Nantahala. Inside, we found a long room full of wooden tables and windows offering views over the wide river. The thick smells of breakfast floated through the dining room, and I urged the boys to our seats and began scanning the menu. There were too many choices, so I ordered several vegetarian options: a chocolate milkshake, pancakes, and the house specialty called Hashbrown Delight. By the time our food arrived, so did Cameraman and Melissa. They pulled up chairs to our table and marveled at the vast array of choices on the menu.

"If you don't like anything here," Jurnee said, "I've got some extra packages of dry oatmeal back at the bunkhouse." When he was met with several groans of disgust, he added, "What? They've got little freeze-dried cranberries in them."

Melissa turned to me after placing her order. "I still want to hike with you through the Smokies," she said. "But I've gotta shave the ounces. I might get an ultralight pack."

"Cameraman told me you were leaving," I said. "I'm sorry to hear your friend died."

"No, ma'am, I ain't leaving." She shook her brown hair back and forth. "Ida gone home if you said you wouldn't hike with me. But I'm staying. Don't care about getting back to college. And don't care what Mama says."

"Do you always call people sir and ma'am?" Jurnee asked. A Northerner like me, he was equally fascinated with Melissa's accent.

"Yes, sir," she replied to Jurnee. "Mama taught me to always be polite."

The two of them got to talking about packs, and I was glad he changed the subject. I wasn't sure that I wanted to hike with Melissa through the Smokies. I planned to stick with Jurnee and Buffalo, and I didn't quite know how to tell her that.

After breakfast, everyone dispersed to take care of their various chores. I needed to do laundry since I would be stopping in the next town, Fontana Dam, thirty miles away, for only a brief trip to the post office for my mail drop. Once in the Smokies, it was one hundred miles to another town; it would be nice to start with clean clothes.

In the bunkhouse, I stripped everything off and pulled on my rain pants and jacket. The pungent smell emanating from the small pile of clothes resembled a well-used locker room filled with moldy cheese. The sweat stains and ground-in dirt would never come out, but maybe I could eradicate the stink. The plasticky fabric of my rain gear stuck to my bare skin as I did an awkward duck walk over to the laundromat.

As my clothes spun, I sat in a hard chair, alternately writing in my journal and gazing through the windows at the river scene outside. Every so often, another of our hiker cohort trekked into NOC. Cleo and KC, Seth and Repartee, and Pete, who now went by Walks Like a Pregnant Possum, all arrived and piled into the bunkhouse alongside the rest of us. Hercules arrived, and I had to adore him even more after he showered, combed his thin white hair to perfection, and donned the church-ready khakis and button-down shirt he reserved for town wear.

Once I had changed into my fresh hiker clothes and visited the River's End again for a giant plate of nachos, I headed to the outfitter to see if my boots had arrived. At the Blueberry Patch, I knew I needed to ditch the Montrails and had asked my mom to send me my backup boots. Sure enough, a box neatly labeled with my mom's handwriting was sitting behind the counter alongside a dozen other boxes. She had visibly marked it "HOLD FOR THRU-HIKER" as I had instructed her. Inside laid my unmarred, light brown, ankle-high, EMS boots. I'd broken them in over the winter, but only on soft trails and sidewalks. They were still stiff as I slipped one foot inside. Tight, but significantly better than the Montrails, which I promptly packed into the box to ship home.

Slow Buffalo kept his promise, and I took a pint of Ben and Jerry's Chocolate Chip Cookie Dough out of the store's freezer while the boys shopped. I sat on the bench by the parking lot, curving my tongue over the creamy vanilla. The cold exploded in my mouth as I watched the cars speed by and the people pull into the parking lot and hurry to the office to buy rafting tickets. None of them noticed me; I felt like the proverbial fly on the wall. I, however, couldn't ignore them. They were so clean; their t-shirts didn't have sweat stains under the armpits, their shoes were not caked in mud or taped up with duct tape, and their hair was styled and shiny. They would spend the day on the river. Then they'd get back in their cars and head to a hotel where they could shower and put on a different set of clothes for dinner. It was as if this brief foray into nature was just a distraction, an escape. I wondered if they were happy with their busy, mechanized, technology-driven lives.

I scooped another spoonful, digging out three big chunks of cookie dough. I knew I was being self-righteous, judging them. But only because I had once been like them. Even now, I thought I should be doing something else, joining the activity, hustling about. Sitting quietly and eating ice cream wasn't enough. In college, I'd always had a million things to keep track of at one time: reading, studying, taking classes, going to work, and keeping up with friends and family. On the trail, there were very limited options. Life had been boiled down to walking, eating, and sleeping. Mix in collecting water, journal writing, the occasional campfire, and a daily stop at the privy, and that was it.

Am I happy? Have I ever been happy?

Happiness had been fleeting as a child. I could be enjoying a book, climbing a tree in the yard, or playing with the dog, and it would all come to a halt when my father struck one of his moods. "What do you think you're doing?" He would demand.

"Eating ice cream," I replied casually. I was about thirteen years old, sitting with my friend Marsha in the sunshine on the deck, each of us with a bowl of chocolate chip cookie dough in our laps. Looking up at him, I realized he had sought me out to reprimand me, and I regretted my words.

"Don't give me that attitude."

I felt my own anger rising. I didn't have an attitude, he did. But I tamped it down and didn't respond.

"You opened the new box of ice cream. You ripped the lid and ruined it!"

"Oh." If I contradicted him to explain that the lid worked just fine when I put the box away, he would completely detonate. It would be wise to say nothing, even though I hated letting him think he was right.

"You need to stop being so irresponsible and childish! If you don't know how to open an ice cream box, you shouldn't be having any ice cream!"

"Okay," I said, sinking into my lounge chair, not wanting to look at Marsha.

"You should learn to be more careful and not break things!" I could feel the weight of his glare. "Well?" he stood there, waiting.

"I'm sorry."

He turned and stomped back to the kitchen, slamming the door behind him. I took a breath as the air settled. Marsha asked, "Is he always like that?"

"Uh, sometimes." I didn't want to talk about it. "He's stressed about work and stuff."

"It's just an ice cream box," she said.

"Yeah."

I didn't want to tell her that this was a small one on the Richter scale of his earthquakes. It had lasted mere minutes, but it had sucked the joy out of the ice cream, out of the day. With every explosion, I'd stuff my feelings further down. College had given me space, but my hurt feelings snuck out in an unending sadness. It wasn't until I'd returned from my semester in Australia, after I'd had a break from the sorrow, that I finally saw my early college years for what they were, a severe depression.

Now, I took another scoop of my pint. My tongue was just about frozen, and my throat was clenching up from the cold.

"Hey, Tamarack, how's the ice cream?" Slow Buffalo appeared out of the store.

"It's perfect," I replied. "Thanks again."

"You earned it." He smiled underneath that thick beard, but I could barely see it. I wasn't attracted to Slow Buffalo, but I suddenly wondered what he looked like clean-shaven. "I'm happy to make you happy," he said softly.

"Um, cool." I paused and looked away from him. "Did Jurnee pick out a pack yet?"

"Nah, he needs to look at them for the rest of the day and contemplate. I wouldn't call him quick on his feet. In any sense of the phrase."

"Well, you should talk. Did you find some poles?"

Buffalo's knees had been hurting him on the downhills, causing him to slow down considerably compared to his usual pace. He had gone to the outfitter to find a set of trekking poles, hoping for some relief. In general, though, his pace was much faster than Jurnee's or mine, and he could have easily been doing higher miles at this point. I guessed he had slowed his hike to stick with us.

"Yep," he said, holding up a set of dark blue poles. "I'm ready to tackle the next mountain."

I scraped the bottom of my pint, getting every last lick of ice cream. I would be ready too, tomorrow. For now, sitting there, doing just one thing was quite enough.

•　　　•　　　•

The next morning, as I helped myself to bananas and cantaloupe that someone had donated to the free box, Melissa found me and said she was going home after all. She had resigned to her reality of doing what her mama demanded. I hugged her, sad to see her give up what she wanted so badly. I hoped she'd be able to find her way back to the trail someday.

Despite the moist, cool morning air, I overheated quickly on the long climb out of the valley. My new boots reopened a somewhat healed blister on my right heel, so I rested at each of the rocky outcrops overlooking the Nantahala River. We weren't headed far, only seven miles, and I tried to focus on the beauty of the land rather than my aching feet. Despite the scenery, I was glad to arrive at Sassafras Gap Shelter.

Slow Buffalo and I had decided at the NOC store that we needed to liven up our first evening out. We combed the shelves for something we didn't normally eat and discovered the perfect item. We'd agreed that I would buy it and he would carry it.

"If you can't have nachos in the woods," I said as the sun set on our campsite, "there's always Jiffy Pop!"

Buffalo pulled the silver package out of his pack in an exaggerated display. "Ta-da!" He waved it in the air. He started to pull off the paper lid, then said, "Damn. Uh, Tamarack, it says right here. Do not use over open fire."

"No way. How did we miss that in the store?"

"Because your stomach was bigger than your eyes, Chowhound," said Hercules from the shelter, using his new nickname for me. "As usual."

"Ha ha." I feigned a laugh. "We're making it anyway." I was already getting a fire going in the rock ring in front of the shelter.

"What could possibly go wrong with you two, a fire, and an explodable metal cooking device?" Jurnee commented.

"We're still making it anyway," Buffalo repeated. He reread the directions and gripped the handle, ready to put it on the flames.

At first, we reveled in the sizzle of butter inside the package. But it didn't take long for the heat to travel quickly up the short metal handle and for Buffalo to scream and drop it in the fire. I shrieked, and lunged for it, at the last second realizing that unless I was magically fire resistant, it would be too hot for me, too. I grabbed a stick and poked the burning metal until I could drag it out of the flames. The side was charred, and the top had not even started to puff up like in the TV ads. Buffalo had some duct tape and taped the handle to the stick, allowing him to put the aluminum pan back into the fire from a safe distance. Resting on the burning logs, the lid encouragingly puffed up a bit. All was not lost, until the heat melted the tape, causing the pan to keep sliding sideways off the stick. Finally, we agreed that the popcorn was probably done enough and pulled it from the fire.

Jurnee was laughing at us. Hercules was shaking his head. I had a sudden thought of my father. He would have been having a fit. We were not following the rules, not adhering to package directions, and most definitely destroying this perfectly good popcorn.

Buffalo cut open the half-puffed lid and searing steam burst out. The popcorn inside was partially popped and scorched, but it had a salty sting and a marvelous crunch. As we dug in, exclaiming how tasty it was, loudly enough for Jurnee and Hercules to hear us, I couldn't imagine being much happier than this.

THE SNOWIES

Walking into Fontana Dam Village was the complete opposite of walking into NOC; it was like entering a ghost town, as if everyone had gone to a funeral and no one stayed to staff the stores. The village, technically a resort community, sat nestled in the Nantahala National Forest at the edge of the Great Smoky Mountains National Park, two miles off the AT. The sky glowered gray and foreboding, and a drizzle fell as I slugged along the road away from the trail. My energy drooped; my mood sank. Two miles was an unthinkable side trip, but no cars came for a hitch, so my feet suffered the hard pavement for a long half hour.

The large Fontana Inn sprawled across a wide hillside, and the empty hotel from *The Shining* sprang to mind. The quaint village also boasted a hiker hostel, a restaurant, and thankfully, in a flat-roofed brown building near the Inn, a gear shop. My PUR water filter had broken the night before, and I was stuck with iodine-treated water, which tasted like bitter dirt. I dumped my pack at the front door, dug out my filter, and walked inside, causing the doorbell to jingle.

An employee named Tracy listened to my water woes and tested the filter to assess the problem. Eventually, he suggested we call PUR. I meandered the shop wondering if I should invest in more iodine, which was far cheaper than a new filter, while Tracy made the call.

"Well, how about we give you a new filter, Tamarack," Tracy said, returning to me several minutes later. "I told them I had a thru-hiker here with difficulties, and they said they'll take the old one back and you should get a new one."

"Wow! Really?" I gaped at him. When I'd worked at EMS in New Jersey, we had a similar ethic of helping customers, but I'd never been able to support someone in need so quickly and unquestionably. "Thank you."

"No problem. We're glad to help a thru-hiker."

I unboxed the new filter and gave Tracy the packaging, along with my broken filter. I thanked him profusely, then headed down the hill under a darkening sky.

The post office was nestled into a long building with a covered front porch and stone pillars and had that classic, dark brown, National Park look about it. The building also housed the grocery store, ice cream shop, and laundromat. There, I found Hercules, Slow Buffalo, Jurnee, Seth, and Repartee and all their gear. Spread across the benches, tables, and chairs were grimy stuff sacks, drying socks, Ziploc baggies of dry goods, granola and candy bars galore, and piles of dirty clothes. This was our living room for the afternoon.

At the post office, I picked up my food box and a handful of letters. There was also a second box, from Tish, my parents' next-door neighbor in New Jersey. I opened the box to the sweet aroma of sugar and chocolate, discovering a double batch of chocolate chip cookies inside.

"Dang, Tamarack," Jurnee said, "people must really love you!"

"I told everyone they'd better write," I said, handing him the box. "I didn't expect cookies, though. That's Tish for ya."

"I'm definitely hanging out with you at mail drops from now on," Jurnee mumbled, his mouth now full of cookies.

Ignoring him, I opened my food box and poured out packages of pasta, rice, beans, oatmeal, dried potatoes, my dehydrated fruits and veggies, and Balance Bars and CLIF Bars. I hoped it was enough to get me through the Smokies, but with my appetite larger than ever, I worried. And yet, the overflowing food bag made me feel like a pack mule, and I could not stuff in one more grain of rice. I felt nauseous at the prospect of hauling this load across the porch, let alone two miles back to the trail or up a mountain. I didn't think I could do it.

The weather didn't help. Even though spring was breaking through in these lower elevations, it was still winter in the higher mountains. The weather report at the post office confirmed my hunch; a cold front was coming.

The mail, the conversation on the porch, and an ice cream cone had cheered me, but my mood dipped again as the boys and I bid good night to Hercules, who decided to stay at the hiker hostel. Tomorrow we'd traverse Fontana Dam and enter the Smokies, but tonight we headed to the free hiker shelter known as the Fontana Hilton. The Hilton was a typical dirty, three-sided, wooden lean-to and held no resemblance to a real Hilton. It was, however, near the park visitor center which had showers, bathrooms, and a pay phone. I was disgruntled further when we got there to find a couple of male hikers I didn't know smoking inside. They talked loudly and seemed unconcerned that other people needed space. I slid some of their stuff out of the way and set up my sleeping gear. I was glad Jurnee and Buffalo were there, but the gray day, the road miles, the prospect of a heavy pack through a rugged range took me from grumpiness into full-on homesickness. I missed my family, my cat, my car. I didn't want to sleep in a crummy old not-real Hilton; I wanted comfort.

I traipsed over to the visitor center for a shower and to call my uncle Tommy. Months ago, we'd planned for him to join me for a few days, and now we needed to finalize our meeting spot. I loved Tommy enormously, and talking to him, my homesickness lightened. But another stress emerged.

I was much stronger than I had been three weeks ago, I could hike between ten and fifteen miles a day. Tommy wouldn't be able to keep that pace, and when he arrived, my whole routine would have to change.

On the phone, we both studied our maps and agreed on a spot for April first. If all went well, I would have enough days to walk there, while he drove from Wisconsin and got shuttled to the woods. We'd then hike as far as we could for about five days until we needed to hit the highway and drive to Nate's graduation. When I'd agreed to this, I hadn't known that leaving the trail for even such a short time meant that you might never see the same hikers again. I hadn't known that I would become so attached to people. I hadn't known that it would mean I wouldn't be hiking with the boys anymore.

I pushed the thought aside as I hung up. It was a week away; there was no use worrying over it now. The Smokies held plenty of challenges to distract me until then; Wingfoot's guide spelled out a long list of regulations to follow within the park. Thru-hikers needed a permit that allowed us free passage, but also directed that we would remain on the AT route, not stay more than one night at any shelter, and not take more than seven nights to traverse the park. The only place to sleep was in the shelters, which were available on a first-come first-served basis, and hopefully wouldn't be filled with troops of Boy Scouts. Once we got up on the ridgeline, the AT straddled the border between Tennessee and North Carolina for 300 miles until Virginia. The park contained the highest point on the AT, Clingmans Dome, which measured 6,643 feet. It would be the highest mountain I'd ever climbed, if I made it that far.

·   ·   ·

I kept my head down, pushed against gravity, and focused solely on maintaining the movement of my feet. My mood hadn't improved since the previous day, and I found the morning climb out of Fontana up Shuckstack steep and unpleasant. The boys took off ahead of me, and I grappled with the reality of battling another mountain.

When a noise ahead broke through my labored breathing, I looked up. Two white-tailed deer meandered across the trail. We paused and looked at each other. I didn't want to scare them. I stopped and quieted my breath. I'd seen hundreds of deer in my life. They proliferated in the New Jersey suburbs; herds of them passed through our yard every week. These looked the same as all the others, tawny brown pelts, long graceful necks, and big ears sticking up, rotating, listening for any changes around them. They probably saw lots of hikers passing through, and I wondered whether my tall, purple-clad form with a massive black lump on its back appeared any different to them than all the other humans. Perhaps the only information that registered was my humanity, and thus the fact that I presented a threat. They flicked their tails, waiting to see what I would do. My breath caught up to me, waiting to see what they would do. After a time, they seemed content and walked on. With ten miles before me until liberation from the backpack, so did I.

The last two and a half miles to Mollies Ridge Shelter were straight uphill, and way more than two and a half miles. When I stumbled up to the stone shelter in the late afternoon, I was desperate to drop my too-heavy pack. I walked around the front to glimpse inside and see who was there, only to find the front completely fenced off with metal wire. The fence door opened on the left end and Jurnee came out, headed to the creek.

"Welcome to bear country, kid," he said, grinning.

The fenced shelter looked cold and unwelcoming. I didn't feel particularly excited to sleep in a closed-up, jail-like hut. Were we keeping the bears out or locking ourselves in with the mice?

"Hey, who's here?" I asked before Jurnee got too far away. I hadn't seen another woman all day and wondered if I'd be in the shelter again with only men.

"Everybody."

"Are there any nachos?" I asked longingly.

"Not for many more days," Jurnee replied. "Sorry, nature girl."

Inside, indeed, everyone was there. The two levels of sleeping platforms were packed with men in various stages of camp chores. Someone had started a fire in the stone fireplace and socks lined the hearth, steaming as they dried. I looked around, thinking I'd much rather put up my tent outside, but not wanting to break the rules on my first night in the Smokies, I found a spot on the lower level next to Buffalo.

The difficulty of the day hadn't worn away my sadness. I needed space to think, privacy. But space and privacy didn't exist in a drafty hut in Great Smoky Mountains National Park. Instead, in a room full of men, I set about replacing my sweaty layers of clothes with dry things. Trying to maintain some measure of modesty, I left on my damp undergarments, which I would have to change later when ensconced within my sleeping bag.

I usually started my camp chores by getting water, and eager to try out my new filter, I followed the sign down to the spring, passing Jurnee on his way back up. The pump drew and expelled water quickly, and my Nalgene began to fill with the icy creek. After only a minute or so, I heard a snap and the flow of water shrank to a dribble.

"Dammit," I swore loudly. I struggled for a few minutes with the device. I didn't know if it was the same problem as last time, but I doubted I could figure it out. I had plenty of iodine to treat my water, but getting through the Smokies without a filter was one more challenge I didn't want.

I climbed back to the shelter frustrated, angry, and thirsty. "My filter broke again," I growled at Buffalo, flopping onto my sleeping bag. "Another week of iodine water ahead."

"The new one?" he said. "That sucks. Here, you can have some of mine."

He poured some of his already filtered water into my bottle and offered me the use of his filter if I wanted to return to the spring. Like we had talked about days ago, he was taking care of me. But I suddenly felt annoyed. I didn't need a man taking care of me. I was absolutely capable of doing this hike on my own.

As I drank his filtered water, I told myself to relax. He wasn't offering me water in a man-taking-care-of-a-woman-because-she-can't-take-care-of-herself kind of way. Rather, he was being a friend. How many times had we shared food or made each other laugh? At some point, the others would need my help, and I'd give it freely.

A few more hikers arrived at the fenced lean-to, and finally at dusk, the door opened and Hercules stumbled in. Before any of us could greet him, he said "I'm too tired to howl." Then he dropped his pack on the platform and lay down.

· · ·

The gray sky fulfilled the Fontana Dam post office's weather report, and when I awoke the next morning, a white sheet covered the forest. Peeking out of my sleeping bag through the fence, I thought the scene looked like a postcard-perfect wilderness wonderland. I reconsidered the beauty of winter, however, when I abandoned my warm bed for the frigid air. The cold was startling, and my body clenched. I needed to move to keep warm, but when I bent down to the floor, I found my boots frozen solid. I crammed my feet into what were essentially ice blocks, my socks offering scarce padding against the hard leather. The only remedy was to wait for my feet to thaw them.

When I stepped outside to find a spot to go to the bathroom, I discovered another downside to winter in the woods. For some unknown reason, there were few privies in the Smokies, and people had simply walked into the woods a short distance and shit right on the snow. Brown plops melted holes in the snow all over the area. The near-frozen ground made it impossible to dig a hole, but I wanted some other option. I broke a stick off a tree and did my best to unearth some superficial rocks and clumps of grass to cover my own waste. So much for the old motto, take nothing but photos, leave nothing but footprints.

By the time I began walking, the sunlight had peeked through the trees and was glittering on the mat of snow. Its meager warmth brought the temperature up to freezing, and the three inches of snow melted and softened. Here and there, clumps of white fell from overhead branches, causing faint thuds. I again felt awed to be immersed in such gorgeous scenery.

I quickly discovered that walking in wet snow was not good fortune, but torture. On each step forward, my boots could not gain traction and slipped half a step backward on the greasy snow. Each jerky skid surprised me, and my muscles tensed in response. Numerous times, one foot would slide out from beneath me, and I'd lose balance and stumble to the ground onto my pack. All the slipping and falling slackened my already pokey pace, and my irritation grew with the futile endeavor.

The wet cold swirled thick around me, almost seeming to add weight to my pack. It clung to my face and hat, cooling my skin. I wiped the dampness off my cheeks with my gloves and realized that there was nowhere to go indoors to get away from this.

For my whole life, I could bundle up to go sledding or take a walk through a park or go out to shovel snow, and there was always a home, a dorm, or at least a cabin with a wood stove to return to. Now, here, for 100 miles ahead there were no warm kitchens or living rooms, no cafes with hot coffee, nothing between me and this icy air. Blood Mountain had reminded me I was a small and very inconsequential piece in a very big puzzle. The Snowies, our nickname for the Smokies, were reinforcing that notion.

I paused only briefly and occasionally throughout the day, knowing that if I stopped too long, I'd freeze. At least my ice block boots kept my feet dry, but they weren't cut out for this gripless terrain. After hours of slogging uphill, I didn't think I was either.

I arrived at the shelter hungry and tired, needing some space and food to recover from the brutal day. When I pulled open the fence door, I was assailed by humanity. By testosterone. Both bunk levels were full. Gear hung from every corner. My boys were there, along with many others I knew, Mike the Wandering Taoist, Cameraman, Pooh Bear, and Carolina Kid. And still others I had only just met, Hillbilly, All Downhill from Here, and Flusher. Repartee and Seth were off to one side, so at least there was one other woman, but she and I didn't speak all evening. In total, thirteen men and two women packed into the shelter for the night.

"Anybody have an extra water bottle?" Came a male voice from a few sleeping bags over. "I don't want to get up to go pee."

"Jesus, Hillbilly," another male voice responded. "We're not all guys in here."

"Yeah, so? I don't want my dick to freeze off."

Enjoying the laughter from all sides, the hiker named Hillbilly went on. "I know. I'll eat a PowerBar and that will soak the pee right out of my fucking bladder. Those suckers will dehydrate your insides."

More snickers. I exhaled an irritated sigh, shaking my head.

From the other side of me came a different voice, speaking quietly. "I'm with you on that, Tamarack." It was All Downhill from Here, settling into his thin, very-lightweight-looking sleeping bag. He grinned and rolled his eyes, as unimpressed by Hillbilly's crudeness as I was.

I smiled in return, then turned and put my journal away. I tucked deeper into my heavy bag, tightening the head flap around my ears, to keep out both the cold and the male noises.

What am I doing here?

I was trapped inside a frozen stone box, my body coated with days of accumulated sweat and grime, beaten down by snowy exhaustion and irritation, surrounded by stinky men with no manners. Perhaps this was what it was like to be one of the boys.

I'd never wanted to be one of the boys. What I'd wanted was a boyfriend. Yet, for most of my life, I was fairly sure that something was wrong with me because that hadn't happened. I first kissed a boy at a friend's thirteenth birthday party while playing spin the bottle. The ensuing two-week relationship included talking to each other once on the phone, which involved many long, awkward pauses, and dancing together for a few songs at a school dance where the boy tried to kiss me again, after which I promptly dumped him. After that, I returned to my obsession with movie stars.

I didn't fare much better in high school, where most of my classmates did what I thought was normal teenage behavior— according to the John Hughes movies—of going to cool parties, making out, and falling in love. I'd had crushes on a couple of boys, including my only male friend, Don, which were never reciprocated. So, I hung out with my girlfriends and wondered when I'd get to meet a movie star.

I attended prom because that's what we did in the suburbs. But I lived for months beforehand in anxiety over who might ask me. When no one did, I asked an acquaintance, trying to ignore the pathetic role reversal of a girl asking a boy out. Doubly pathetic since that boy was shorter than me. I was also embarrassed making such a big production about a fancy dance where I had to wear pantyhose, but I played along, hoping some boy would see me all dressed up and suddenly fall in love. That's how it happened in the movies.

By college, I was convinced that I was definitely defective. I was unattractive for sure. Perhaps I was gay and everyone knew it but me. I went on a few first dates, but as soon as a guy started to show interest, I fled, never returning his calls. They had to be losers, for what could they possibly see in me? My lack of a boyfriend only added to my depression, reinforcing my unlovableness. In the sorority, we hosted a lot of date parties, which I loathed, because I didn't know any boys to invite. I'd ask a roommate to set me up, or I'd go alone, always unsure of why I even signed up for these things. The epitome of my awkwardness was the one Winter Formal I attended with yet another male acquaintance I'd asked out of desperation. Surrounded by my infinitely more self-assured sisters, I ate dinner and danced clumsily, as unsure of what to say to him as I had been to my eighth-grade boyfriend. I didn't have to worry about him trying to kiss me though, because during our jaunt to a coffee shop afterward, I'd embarrassed myself by promptly spilling a mocha down the front of my purple, satin dress.

In the dark shelter, the last flashlight beam struck the ceiling above me as someone adjusted their gear. The chatter had died, and the men around me rustled in their sleeping bags, farted, and snored. Surrounded by their sounds, I realized this situation was one more aspect of hiking the AT that I hadn't imagined when back at my parents' house. Sharing space with so many men was not something I would have chosen a few years ago; I'd been scared of men. Until my senior year when I'd started making out with random guys at frat parties. Until Chad.

"Togue Pond, clear," the deep male voice clicked across the Baxter Park radio. Working in the visitor center each day, I heard rangers all over the park checking in with each other, but the voice at the entrance gate with the wicked Maine accent was adorable, and I knew I had to find that guy. When I met the dark-haired, fit, and attractive Mainer, Chad finally validated that I was not a loser. From the moment we met, we were together. Chad and I hiked, drank beer with the other summer rangers, and went skinny dipping. He knew he was good-looking, and I figured he'd had several girlfriends before me, but he was also kind and generous. Some nights, I slept at his cabin, and we became intimate in ways I never had before, and for a moment, I believed I was beautiful.

I thought I loved Chad. And I wanted him to love me back. He did, as much as he could. I went with him to his hometown an hour away to meet his parents where we hung out with his high school buddies. He went to bookstores and out to eat with me even though he didn't have a lot of cash. We spent a sweet weekend in Acadia National Park, playing on the beaches.

We broke up when he went back to college in Arizona. I was mad at him for not wanting more, for deciding to go on with his life without me. But I also knew we weren't well-suited in anything but our attraction to each other; I didn't like his buddies, and he didn't like my bookstores.

Standing in front of his parents' house for the last time, he gave me a nonchalant goodbye. "Catch you on the flip side."

I kissed him, tears running down my face. As I climbed into my car and waved goodbye, my heart broke at the same time as relief washed over the sadness. I was scared of boys until Chad. Dozing off in the dark with thirteen male hikers, I wondered if I was still.

•   •   •

"I wish I had some hot nachos right now," I said.

"Well, if it makes you feel any better, it's all downhill from here," said All Downhill from Here wryly.

"You always say that, don't you?" I asked.

"Yes, but this time it's true."

We were standing with Slow Buffalo at the snow-covered circular observation tower at the top of 6,643-foot Clingmans Dome. Another two inches of snow fell the night before, but the sky had cleared, and the view was vast. Tennessee in one direction, North Carolina in another. Though the white snow contrasted beautifully against the blue sky, the sun did nothing to warm the icy wind that whipped across the peak, and I remained thoroughly bundled up in most of my clothes.

"Yep, and once we get out of the Smokies there'll be a nacho stand every mile," added Downhill.

"That would be great," I replied. "I'm starving."

After we took photos of each other, Downhill left. I expected Buffalo to take off, too. But he waited for me. I had wanted to stay up there alone for a few minutes. It had been a while since we'd had any clear days with such a spectacular view, and I wanted to soak it in. But I felt awkward with him standing there, so I heaved my pack and followed him.

Buffalo stuck with me, and a short while later Jurnee caught up. Since it really was downhill from there, for the next few miles at least, the three of us moved down the mountain together, complaining about the snow and imagining the next town stop.

"Wow, Tamarack," Buffalo said from behind me, "Your socks really do reek."

He referred to my wet socks from the day before, which I had tied to the outside of my pack to dry. "They probably do," I replied. "But yours aren't any better!"

"Phew, maybe not," he said, "but seriously, yikes."

"Let's change the subject. Do you guys ever sing when you're hiking?"

"Yeah," Jurnee replied. "I always sing the Oompa Loompa song. It's pretty much constant."

"I've had Jimmy Buffet stuck in my head lately," I said. "We should sing 'Margaritaville' and think about someplace that isn't covered in snow."

"Sure," agreed Buffalo.

"Okay, what are the words?" Jurnee asked.

"Um." I thought, but the only thing that came to me was the thrumming beat of the Oompa Loompa song. "Wait, I know it. Um, wasting away again…"

I did know it; I'd been singing it to myself for days. The words were there just beneath the surface of my awareness, but sloshing along, focusing on my steps with Jurnee in front of me and Buffalo behind, I couldn't come up with any lyrics.

"Well," Jurnee said after a few minutes of silent walking, "that was fun."

I doubled over, almost falling again into the snow as laughter leaped out of me. In the absurdity of the moment—the mountains, the snow, the faulty filter, the constancy of being surrounded by men—the tension broke. The trail was a taskmaster that was forcing me to give every ounce of myself if I wanted to survive. It seemed that hilarity was the only way I was going to get through it.

•   •   •

Tourists packed the large parking lot where a road crossed through Newfound Gap. The road to the peak of Clingmans had recently opened, and visitors were stopping there to use the bathroom or look at their maps before driving up. I thought that driving to the peak of a mountain was cheating and passed them by with a sense of superiority.

Jurnee noticed a small sign from a hiker named Simply Seeking, directing thru-hikers to his car, parked at the edge of the lot. Simply Seeking wasn't there, but he'd left his trunk open and full of happy choices: oranges, apples, granola bars, and chocolate. Jurnee, Buffalo, and I leaned our packs against his car and dug into the pile of food. I was grateful for the generosity, but it barely touched my hunger.

Krispina and her dad Pyro wandered up as we snacked. I left my pack with them and headed to the bathroom. A real bathroom where I could wash my face and hands was a luxury I couldn't pass up. A middle-aged woman stood over the single sink helping her young daughter wash her hands. I stood to the side so they could finish. When she turned and saw me, the woman's eyes widened, and she grabbed her daughter's shoulders roughly.

"Watch out!" she exclaimed. "She's a hiker!" The woman snatched her daughter away from where the girl reached for a paper towel and pushed her out the door.

I knew I looked ragged and dirty, and I fully admitted the smell of my socks could knock a person out, but I didn't think I yet rivaled Buffalo's hairy Sasquatch appearance. I looked in the mirror and saw a countenance I hadn't seen much lately. My face was pale, but my cheeks glowed pink from the cold. I undid my ponytail and ran my fingers through my thin hair, damp from snow and sweat. *I'm scary.*

I thought about the woman as I hiked, wondering if she'd seen the exhaustion and hunger in my eyes. Perhaps she didn't want her daughter to grow up and get any crazy ideas about becoming a thru-hiker. In a way, I couldn't blame her; this was a painful experience, particularly this section. Walking through the Snowies was like walking through superglue. Through stew. Through a swamp. There was no way to get into a rhythm, no way to gain momentum and use that momentum to push the body forward. Every step required its own individual act of strength.

I stopped for lunch each day in one of the bear-cage shelters, which at least offered a brief respite from walking on snow. But the cold threatened, uncompromising, and even hot ramen or macaroni and cheese did little to penetrate the chill I always carried. It seeped in through the layers of polypropylene I wore underneath my thin blue raincoat.

Out in the frigid air, always battling the snow, I felt like I couldn't breathe. Like those times immobilized on my dorm room floor, restrained from sorrow or exhaustion, all that existed was suffering. After days of slipping and slushing and falling and trudging, the heaviness and pain boiled over the top. I clutched my trekking poles hard and let the anger fill me. I cursed the snow. I opened up to all the madness I could muster and started running, gliding over it. *Why is there so much snow?* The adrenaline poured through me as I raced against myself. My heart thumped loudly in my ears. This was not fun. *Who built this damn trail, deciding to climb straight up the side of these mountains?* I passed Slow Buffalo, also toiling, and pushed onward, funneling the energy of fury into my legs. I hated this trail, this place, this challenge. *I can't do this!*

At this thought, I launched into a final burst of strength that took me another few tenths of a mile. An icy rain set in, droplets splashed on my face and hair. My boots sloshed with each step. Someone yelled up ahead. I came around a bend to find Jurnee on the ground.

"Fuck!" he screamed. He was struggling to right himself using his trekking poles as crutches and in the process was flinging snow all about. He looked like a fish flopping on dry sand. "Fuck!"

I came up beside him, gasping for breath. "I'm sorry," I said. "As sympathetic as I feel for you there, you look ridiculous."

"What the fuck are we doing out here?" he yelled. I gave him a hand and pulled him up. He brushed off his wet pants and coat and readjusted his pack. "And where is the fucking shelter?"

"Ahead. Somewhere."

"Very helpful. Thanks."

We walked together, sharing our misery until eventually, we found the trail to the shelter where we had hoped to stop for lunch; 0.5 miles down a hill. Not wanting to expend the energy to get back up the hill later, Jurnee and I stopped to sit and eat at the junction. I leaned against my pack as the cold soaked through my pants and froze my butt. At least the icy rain had ended.

Soon, Buffalo caught up, and we regaled each other with tales of the morning. The boys hated the snow too, though I didn't think they were questioning whether to stay on the trail as I was. We shared our concern about Hercules, who had recently fallen behind. As we discussed his abilities, along with our own, out of the corner of my eye I saw Jurnee raise his arm to point at something above us. Buffalo was looking down, but I looked up just in time to see a huge clump of wet snow crash directly onto Buffalo's head, snow scattering all over his shoulders, pack, and food.

Buffalo flinched under the crash. Time stopped for a second, and there was a sharp intake of breath. As Buffalo opened his eyes widely looking at us, Jurnee and I exhaled into laughter.

"I totally saw that coming!" Jurnee said.

"And you didn't warn me!" Buffalo demanded, with both annoyance and amusement in his voice. He shook his head and shoulders like a dog getting water off his fur.

"You gotta admit," I said, "that tree has amazing aim."

As I spoke, I looked up to see another clump of snow falling gracefully through the air. I raised my hand and spluttered a warning, but not before the snow hit Buffalo squarely on the head. This was too much for Jurnee, and he fell over on his pack, chortling and clutching his stomach. I hoped he didn't choke on his GORP. I wouldn't be able to haul both a frozen Buffalo and a choking Jurnee out of the forest.

"Maybe that tree doesn't like you," I said.

"Come on," Buffalo said, standing up and packing up his things. "Let's get out of here before the whole tree falls on me."

The lunch break had eased my distress, and I again took up my slow, slipping pace. Buffalo and I walked together for a while, talking about our siblings, hometowns, and things we hadn't already covered in the past few weeks. The distraction of our stories made the slushy walking more bearable.

"So, are you dating anyone back home?" Buffalo asked.

I tensed. Thus far, none of the men I'd met had asked me about relationships or my history. Somehow, I'd known Buffalo would be the first to ask.

"Uh, I broke up with someone last fall. He went back to college, and I didn't want to follow him around. It was okay. We had some fun together, but he was kind of a jerk." Not wanting to go into more details about Chad, I turned the question back to Buffalo.

"I recently broke up with someone too," he said.

"I'm sorry." I wasn't sure whether I was supposed to ask questions, but as we walked, he unwound the story of his last girlfriend. They'd dated for several years, and he'd been deeply in love.

"But she was dating this other guy on the side." When he'd found out about the cheating, he tried to convince her to stay with him. They lived in a limbo relationship for months, with him waiting on her to dump the other guy. She never did.

"Wow, that sucks more than this snow," I said. If my boyfriend cheated on me, I would have no problem walking away. Buffalo was a gentle soul, but this was too gentle and passive. He sounded like a wounded puppy as he told me minute details of the betrayal. I was glad to listen and be supportive, but his revelations made me think he needed a therapist, not my uneasy ear. I wondered if he was telling me all this because he was interested in me.

He dropped the topic when we got to Charlie's Bunion, an exposed rocky knob that would have had great views if the sky had been clear. Jurnee was there, reading a large caution sign which warned us to "Closely Control Children." He suggested we take pictures of ourselves clinging to the side of the icy cliff and send them to our parents. We took several photos, with big smiles and laughs, capturing one more ridiculous moment on film.

Despite my new questions about Buffalo's intentions, the boys were the antidote to the constant struggle of the snowy Smokies. I had no romantic inclinations toward either of them, but I had definitely fallen in love with the fun we were having. Trail life was going to change. I could feel it coming already, but for now, I had their friendship.

•   •   •

The end was in sight. Tomorrow I'd leave the Snowies, and the day after that, I'd meet up with Uncle Tommy. Today was one of those days where the cold air swirled about, but the sunlight blasting down from a bright blue sky offered a tinge of warmth that broke through the icy wind. I'd made a sudden decision to take the half-mile side trail to Mt. Cammerer. This was a distinct change from my regular policy of not straying from the AT, but I'd asked myself when I'd ever have the chance to see the world from the top of Mt. Cammerer again. Likely never.

The trail was a river of mud, and it had been a slog to get there. Luckily, I'd been powered up by some trail magic from Pappy Bill, a section hiker and local trail maintainer. He'd come by Cosby Knob Shelter at lunchtime with a basket full of homemade, hot apple turnovers to share with starving thru-hikers. I practically lunged at him when he showed me his goods and wished I could have eaten a few more. Instead, I joyfully scarfed down one turnover while I talked to him about his life, thanking him several times before leaving.

I took my time on Mt. Cammerer, feeling like Rip van Winkle waking from a long sleep into a new world. Birds darted through the trees. The dark green rhododendrons dripped with snow melt. The mountainside flashed with life.

Everyone else was zipping through these last snowy miles to get to Davenport Gap and Mountain Momma's store and bunkhouse. I didn't want to spend money on what I'd heard was a sub-par hostel when there was a free shelter on the trail. I'd be alone for the night, but after a week of constant men, I welcomed it. When I got to the Davenport Gap Shelter, however, Slow Buffalo was there, waiting for me.

"I thought you were going to Momma's?" I asked, dropping my pack.

"Nah," he said. "I didn't want you to be alone here."

"Oh, well, I'm fine if you want to go."

"And miss out on the last fenced-in shelter? No way!"

Buffalo and I were the only ones in for the night. He offered to make a fire if I wanted one and filter water for me. I declined both. We played hangman and the dot game on my journal paper, as we often did in the evenings, but I turned away from him early, wanting to be alone. I didn't own this space, but I felt irritated that he had encroached upon it. I was going to miss the boys once we parted ways, but maybe a separation would be good for a while.

•   •   •

After a week in the Snowies, April first dawned sunny and warm. I had five miles to walk until the road where Tommy would meet me at six o'clock. The boys planned to hike a full day. They dawdled all morning, as reluctant to leave as I was for them to go.

"Hey, you guys, I need to get your addresses," I said, "so we can connect again after… well, later." I didn't want to get too sappy; they'd call me on that immediately.

"What are you gonna do all day?" Jurnee asked.

"Well, I've got to write out our Oompa Loompa song lyrics, for one," I said. The past few days we'd taken Jurnee's favorite tune and come up with our own version. I intended to write it out in the shelter register for the entertainment of all future hikers.

"Oompa Loompa doompadee day, I climbed another mountain today," Jurnee began.

"Oompa Loompa doompadee day, I ate another spider today," I joined.

"Don't forget the chorus line," Buffalo said. "Mars bars, Reese's, Nutrageous too. Nothing but the best of Snickers for you. CLIF Bars, PowerBars, Balance Bars too. Another long day in the privy for you."

I couldn't stop myself, I had to say it. "It's been really great hiking with you guys." I swallowed back the giant lump forming in my throat. I would not cry.

"We're going to miss you, too," Jurnee said. Buffalo nodded, offering a sad smile. "But we're going to see you again soon. I'm sure you'll catch up in Hot Springs."

"Yeah," I said. "I'm sure." Even though I wasn't.

I hugged them each, thinking of Dorothy bidding her companions goodbye as she prepared to travel with the wizard in the hot-air balloon back to Kansas. The past month had been like being in Oz—a magical world of kind people, wild animals, and towering forests. The AT was the furthest thing from a flat, golden brick road, but both paths served the same purpose of leading its walkers to the promised land. I only wished we'd seen a few flying monkeys because if we had, I'm sure my boys and I would have laughed heartily at them.

"Now, get out of here," I said. "The smell of your socks is killing me."

THE GOOD OLD DAYS

A Jeep sped up the dirt road and slammed to a halt, causing dust to billow in a cloud around me. The driver emerged and introduced himself as Dan Gallagher, owner of the Bluff Mountain Outfitters in Hot Springs. From the passenger seat, Uncle Tommy climbed out. "Amanda K!" he hollered.

"Fancy meeting you here," I replied. I embraced him with a smile, slightly incredulous that we'd managed to find each other at a random spot in the middle of a North Carolina wilderness where neither of us had ever been before. I pulled back to look at him; thinning hair and pale skin, but pretty good shape for a guy in his fifties. He'd listened to my warning not to wear cotton and was ready for the woods with his quick-dry pants and red polyester t-shirt. The green pack he pulled out of the vehicle was an appropriate medium size, since I would carry the tent, stove, and still-broken water filter. He also had a sturdy-looking pair of brown boots, which I hoped he'd broken in.

"Come on, I'll show you our camp." We thanked Dan and headed down the slope away from the road.

My mom's older brother was one of my favorite people on the planet; the adult who sat on the floor and played games with the kids; the first to jump up and dance to a groovy song, no matter whether in the living room or the grocery store; the person people always respected because he respected them first. Growing up, I'd spent a lot of time with Tommy, particularly at our family cottage in western Michigan. Most summers, we gathered at the cottage with my grandparents, Tommy and his kids, and my mom's sister Barbara, her husband Rick, and their kids. We didn't have a TV there, and the rural village offered little to do, but we devised our own fun with family talent shows, trips to the library, and exploration of the vast surrounding farmland.

My mom's side of my family also owned a one-acre island in a remote lake region of Ontario. My grandfather had bought the almost inaccessible property with some of his fishing buddies forty years previously. Though my parents weren't interested in going there, I loved that pine-covered wilderness and was able to go with Uncle Tommy, Aunt Barbara, and Uncle Rick. With no electricity, no plumbing, no heat or air-conditioning, my aunt and uncles showed me how to thrive in and enjoy the most secluded place I'd ever been to. There was even less to do at the Canadian cabin than at the Michigan cottage, but I relished it. We filled our time in the deep woods with swimming, playing cards, and canoeing the lake in search of loons and beavers to photograph.

I hadn't been to either family retreat for several years, however, with college and summer jobs taking precedence. But walking through the woods with my uncle down to our AT campsite, memories from those times flickered under the surface of my thoughts.

Tommy began to unpack his gear and pull out some of the food he'd brought. I hovered over him like a mosquito waiting to land on her next victim.

"Don't you eat out here?" he asked, watching me devour his goods.

"I just finished my pot of mac and cheese when you pulled up," I said. I took a scoop of oily hummus and then placed a slice of a beautiful, red tomato on top. "Basically, all I do is walk and think about food," I added. "I hope you brought something for yourself." Then I sliced some of his fresh Wisconsin cheddar and laid it atop a piece of pita bread with more tomato, taking a bite.

The food was a welcome treat after a long afternoon of anxiously sitting around. The sun had shone warmly all day but had inched across the sky. I'd written in my journal, studied the maps again, and said hello to many fellow hikers walking by including Carolina Kid, Pooh Bear, and Hillbilly. All day I'd wondered how far the boys were hiking.

We put away the food and looked around for a bear-bagging tree. When I suggested Tommy get his bed set up in the tent, he pulled out a giant air mattress.

"What are you going to do with *that*?" I asked, stifling a skeptical laugh.

"You said to bring a mattress, so I did. I'm going to blow it up."

"By the time you get that thing blown up, it'll be morning!" I realized I had failed to tell my uncle the difference between a five-inch-thick traditional air mattress and a half-inch backpacking Thermarest or Ridge Rest. I couldn't control my amusement as over the next forty-five minutes, he lay on his back with the air mattress on top of him. Puff by puff it grew until he finally capped off the opening and squeezed it into my small tent. It took over most of the space, covering half of my narrow Ridge Rest.

"Not much room for you in there," he said, throwing in his sleeping bag. "So, what are we going to do this evening? Make a fire? Play cards?"

"Uh, we sleep."

"What! It's seven-thirty!"

"Yeah, we mostly just sleep at night. Then get up early. I don't make fires when I'm not at a shelter. Too much trouble."

Night came and with nothing to do, we squished into the tent together. We drifted into one of those profound conversations full of rambling and philosophical thoughts. We'd had these kinds of conversations before. After my sophomore year at college, I lived in Madison with Tommy for the summer and worked at a local bakery. In my off time, I hung out with my cousin Emily and got to know thirteen-year-old Paul, Tommy's newly adopted son. Even though Tommy was busy with his own work, he always made time to have thoughtful conversations with me.

In the tent, we discussed trail names, and after I explained mine, he said he wanted to go by Tucker J. He simply liked the name but had also contrived it to include the first letter of each of his kids' names:

Tim, Emily, Rodrigo—a Rotary exchange student from Brazil whom he'd hosted and had become like one of his own—and J for Paul's middle name, Jason. I told him about Blood Mountain and my knee injury. Then about Slow Buffalo, Jurnee, and Hercules and the fun we'd been having. I told my uncle lots of things, but as I talked, I found it hard to explain what life on the trail was all about. I didn't know why I was obsessed with nachos or why we had long existential debates about pizza. My days on the trail were a strange mix of difficult and absurd, and I wasn't sure how to capture the essence of it. But I told the stories anyway, and he listened.

"I'm really glad you're here, Uncle," I said. We talked until sleep took us both.

•   •   •

With an endless goal of ticking off more miles, there wasn't much use for lingering around camp in the mornings. Each day I dressed, ate oatmeal, filled water bottles, stuffed the sleeping bag, and took down the tent without thought in about twenty minutes. On Tucker J's first morning, I arose and busied myself as usual, completing each chore quickly.

"Which bandana do you think I should wear?" Tucker J asked.

I stopped stuffing the tent into my backpack and looked over at him as he pulled all his clothes from a plastic bag. His gear littered the campsite, mattress deflating, granola still in a bowl. I recommended Tucker J choose the green bandana and sat down next to my pack. My usual routine no longer applied. We might as well take our time.

And he did. An hour and a half later, after a slow, deliberate organization of his pack and the donning of his canvas hat, Tucker J was ready. We had all day to go seven miles, a distance I could have done before lunch, but I readjusted my expectations and told him to go his own pace.

Our campsite was just below the summit of 4,629-foot Max Patch, two-tenths of a mile uphill. Max Patch was the first bald we would cross in the next few days and with the clear weather forecast Tucker J had brought with him, I was looking forward to showing off my beautiful trail.

"Are we there yet?" Tucker J whined from behind me, using a mocking tone that I undoubtedly used at some point as a child on a long car ride.

"Yep. This is it," I replied, as the trail continued upward.

Awe replaced the joking when we emerged from the rhododendron forest onto an open, grassy field the color of honey. Mountain ranges extended in all directions. To the north, I could see more balds poking up above the budding greenery and thought that we should have camped up here last night. It was a remarkable spot.

"So, this is what you do all day?"

"Pretty much," I replied. "Easy climbs to spectacular three-sixty views, perfect weather, and lots of fresh food."

We took a few photos in the warm sunshine, then looked to find the route north. With no trees, a sporadic row of wooden posts painted with white blazes stretched across the field. We puttered past them on the grassy path, descending Max Patch over a long downhill.

We walked slowly throughout the morning, taking turns in the lead. Talking sometimes, sometimes not. The trail flattened considerably, and I wanted to speed along, but Tucker J moseyed, pointing out bird calls and spring flowers alongside the trail. There was so much nature I hadn't noticed while I was looking at my feet, balancing the weight on my back, and thinking about my friends. Tucker J was reminding me of a different kind of hiking, the kind I had thought I would do when I had started this trek. I relaxed, enjoying having my own hiking partner for a change.

We stopped for a long lunch break at Roaring Fork Shelter, where we met Robocop, QT, and the couple Woodcutter and Woodpuppy. They were all older than Tucker J, closer to Hercules' age, and I'd seen their names in the registers. We chatted for a few minutes, but after lunch, I wrote in my journal while Tucker J napped.

Thinking back to Georgia, I could have napped on most of those early days. But I'd been so anxious about reaching my destination before dark that I rarely stopped for longer than it took to catch my breath. Once I made it there, I couldn't have walked an extra step even if a paving truck had just driven by flattening and clearing the path ahead of me. So, I was surprised and pleased when Tucker J and I reached our planned shelter for the night, he agreed to go another two miles. He refused to sleep in a shelter because of the mice, so we needed to find a flat tent site. We pushed ourselves up and over Walnut Mountain and arrived at Catpen Gap, where there was an open area and a spring. By then he was spent. I left him on his back to blow up his mattress while I filled our water bottles and treated them with iodine.

•   •   •

Hot Springs, North Carolina was a perfect trail town because the AT went right through the main street. It also offered every amenity a thru-hiker might need; laundromat, cafe, post office, outfitter, inn, and a bar. Thoroughly exhausted after a long day pushing to get to town, Tucker J and I made our way to the renowned Sunnybank Inn at Hot Springs, affectionately known as Elmer's.

The huge, white Victorian house sat up on a hill. Wide porches sprawled on each side of the house and porch swings swayed in the breeze. It looked far too fancy for the likes of us, but as we approached, I noticed dirty backpacks, hiking clothes hanging on the line, and a lineup of worn boots by the door, and knew we were in the right place. On the front porch, I barely recognized Carolina Kid, all clean and freshly shaven for his girlfriend, who had come to visit for the weekend.

Despite some obvious wear, the inside of the house equaled the grandeur of the outside. The hardwood floors gleamed under faded Persian rugs. The oak furniture, bookcases, and antique hat rack covered in antique hats made me think Sherlock Holmes might step out from the drawing room at any moment. A piano, several guitars, a didgeridoo, and a banjo silently awaited players. I arranged for a room with the young man working there, and he gave us a tour of the rest of the house, including details for signing up for the vegetarian dinner and breakfast each day. The massive house would have served as a perfect setting for a Victorian-era murder mystery. And when we climbed the ornate stairway to our second-floor room, we learned perhaps it had.

"The fellow said this room is haunted," Tucker J said as we assessed the well-kept space. The rickety beds were antiques, but I couldn't wait to sleep on a soft mattress, no matter the age. "Maybe we'll get a visit from the ghost."

"Well, I'm the thru-hiker here," I said, dropping my pack with a thud, "I don't care who visits us as long as I get the double bed."

"You're no thru-hiker," a deep voice said from behind us.

I whipped around to find Slow Buffalo standing in the doorway, his black hair washed and combed back, his sweat-stained blue shirt as clean as it could get, and a big grin beneath his black beard. I raced over to him for a hug.

"Man, you stink," he replied.

"Good to see you too," I said. "Where's Jurnee?"

After Buffalo assured me Jurnee was there too, I introduced him to Tucker J. We spent a short time catching up, promising to talk more at dinner after we'd gotten settled and showered.

Tucker J and I had pushed to get there in time for dinner, and when I entered the dining room and saw the long table already piled high with bread and butter and eggplant parmesan, I was glad. Ten other hikers took their seats around us to partake in the vegetarian feast. The tradition at Elmer's before the meal could begin, however, was that guests had to introduce themselves and answer a question. That night's question was: *If you could be anything, other than yourself, in the springtime, what would you be?* I sat impatiently listening to everyone's introductions as I ogled the food. When my turn came, I answered *a daffodil* and was soon released to dig in. I ate three bowls of bean soup with crackers, a fresh salad with tahini dressing, a serving of eggplant parmesan, another serving of vegetable lasagna, and homemade focaccia bread with olives. I also packed in several pieces of cheesecake with strawberries.

I didn't realize I'd gone overboard until I tried to get up from the table; I could barely move and felt nauseous. I dragged myself to the living room and lay down on the floor, groaning. The boys and Tucker J followed me, laughing.

"This is what it's like to be a stuffed pig." I moaned.

"Geez, kid, you could have restrained yourself," Jurnee said.

"I was hungry." I groaned again.

"I'm glad you're back with us, Tamarack," Buffalo said.

Having them all there with me, eating, joking, just being together, I was too.

•   •   •

I hadn't had a zero-mile day since the Blueberry Patch, but since the next day was Easter Sunday and the post office wasn't open, I needed to wait until Monday to pick up my mail drop. Tucker J thought this was a fine idea because it meant a day off to rest his aching body and prepare for more mountains. The boys had been in Hot Springs for a day and a half already, but when Tucker J and I told them our plan, they both decided to stay.

My now athletic body had easily metabolized dinner overnight, and by morning I was eager for the next meal. Elmer's breakfasts rivaled its dinners, and I joined the group for huge plates of vegetarian biscuits and gravy, cantaloupe and honeydew melon, grits, and cheesy scrambled eggs.

With my appetite sated, I called my parents from the house phone to fill them in on our progress. Though Mom didn't say it, I knew her fears for my safety persisted. I could practically feel her relief radiating through the phone wires knowing that her brother was there to keep me safe. I asked her for directions to Jane and Bill's house, about an hour's drive south of Hot Springs. Jane and Bill were old friends of my parents from their Air Force days, and they'd offered to host Tucker J and me when we left the trail in a few days. The plan was perfect because Jane and Bill would also be driving to Mississippi for my brother's pilot training graduation, and they'd agreed to give me a ride back to the AT with them after the weekend celebration.

On a sunny day with nowhere to go and nothing to do—except laundry and eating—I lounged for hours. Tucker J, the boys, and I passed an enjoyable hour of trying on the numerous hats in the living room and practicing appropriate accents to match them. Later, Tucker J joined me in testing every porch on the house. We had a tiny porch off our bedroom, which was cozy and quaint. We visited Buffalo and Jurnee's bedroom porch which overlooked the driveway and budding trees beyond. We liked the view from the porch swing on the side of the house and sat there for a while.

"We've done some fun stuff together, haven't we?" I said to Tucker J. "And I don't mean all these porches today."

"Indeed, we have. That time I took all you kids to Canada," he said with a smile, "and customs thought I was abducting you all." He'd been the only adult on that trip, taking Tim, Emily, my cousin Roxanne, and me across the border. "They took you each into separate rooms and questioned you."

"Was that the time with the trash?" I asked. "Now that was funny."

He chuckled, but it was a forced laugh. Midway through that week at our cabin, Tommy wanted to row back to the car and take out some of our accumulated trash. It had been a beautiful day for a paddle, and Emily and I went along to help. Halfway to the car, we pulled over at the shore to readjust our seating. As Emily climbed out of the canoe, I leaned the same way, and we tipped over, dumping Tommy into the lake, along with all the trash. The wind didn't take long to disperse the floating tin cans and bits of plastic wrap across the water.

"You didn't want us causing any more damage," I said, smirking, "so you left us on the shore with the canoe, and swam across the bay collecting the trash."

"Emily was what, eight?" he asked. "You were about thirteen."

"Man, those were the good old days," I said with a sigh.

"No, Amanda, *these* are the good old days," he said, stopping the swing, suddenly serious. "*This* is what you'll look back on and reminisce about someday. Appreciate it. Now."

As often happened, some Dave Matthews Band lyrics wafted through my brain. I had sung the song "Stay" again and again last summer after the new album, *Before These Crowded Streets,* came out. At the time, I related it to my relationship with Chad. Now, months after he and I had parted, I could feel my memories of him fading. But this experience, this trail, was burrowing into me. Day by day, step by step, I had walked 270 miles, on a trail I hadn't even known about a year ago. Tucker J and Dave were right. *I will miss these things.* But there was no holding on to time.

During our philosophizing, my stomach told me it was getting close to dinner time. We switched to the front porch where we happily welcomed Hercules to town. He was exhausted and looked significantly skinnier than he had before. I trusted that a night or two at Elmer's would fix him right up.

New faces joined the dinner table and introduced themselves as the food was placed before us. That night's question was: *If you were to have someone write your life story, whom would you pick?*

"Shakespeare, of course," I said. "Oh, and I'm Tamarack."

"You're Tamarack?" said a round-faced, blond woman sitting across from me. "We've been reading your shelter register entries every day. It's so great to finally meet you!" The woman and her boyfriend both had southern accents and went by Biscuits and Gravy. "But I'm still not used to the names," she said when she introduced herself. "I'm Alison. He's Chris."

"But we're trying to go by our trail names," Biscuits chimed in, more invested in the names than Gravy. He was dark-haired and skinny; the trail had already slimmed his slight frame. "You can remember which is which because B is for boy and Biscuits, and G is for Gravy and girl."

I held myself back that night at dinner, not wanting to explode my stomach again. I only had two bowls of cauliflower potato soup, two plates of salad with dressing, and a broccoli-zucchini-cheese calzone. I saved room for chocolate cake with ice cream for dessert. After giving the cook my greatest compliments, I returned to the front porch again. The boys, Hercules, and Tucker J came out, and we popped open the bottles of beer that I'd bought earlier.

"You guys ready to leave town tomorrow?" Jurnee asked.

"Yes." "No." Buffalo and I said at the same time.

"I want to stay and continue watching these leaves grow," I said. "Seriously, you guys, these leaves are bigger than they were this morning. I have literally been watching leaves grow today."

"You'll never get to Katahdin if you stay here, kid," Jurnee said.

Katahdin. She had slipped from my mind. I remembered I was on a journey to somewhere, for some reason, but the end was far off. Each day was full of other mountains, other challenges. I knew she stood waiting for me far north, but here on this cozy and warm porch, it was hard to believe she even existed. I knew I'd get there eventually, but for the moment, I was doing what Tucker J and Dave Matthews suggested—living in the now.

·   ·   ·

Monday morning came and with it a flurry of activity. Amidst packing up our gear, Tucker J and I enjoyed another large breakfast in the dining room. I ate as much as I could of the nut granola, date muffins, melon, and fried potatoes with cheese.

I visited Dan Gallagher's outfitter shop, and when he couldn't figure out my broken filter, I talked with a representative from PUR, trying to explain the problem that I'd had twice now. I was frustrated that I'd been hiking all this time without a functioning filter, and though the man offered to send me a new one in Erwin, I asked for my money back, and he reluctantly agreed. I bought an MSR filter, which pumped more slowly than the PUR, but if it didn't break, I would be happy.

I then made a trip to the post office, where I received my food box along with eleven letters from friends and two small boxes. One box was from my parents' New Jersey friends, Bob and Marilyn, who worked for the M&M Mars Corporation. They sent a large bag of M&M's which Jurnee cheerily offered to help me carry. When I felt how heavy the package was, I agreed. *Who knew M&M's weighed so much?*

The second box came from a college friend who was spending a semester in Australia, as I had done. She had sent me a package of Tim Tams, my favorite Australian cookies that were not available in the US. One bite of the creamy chocolate-covered biscuit launched me back in time, and I could almost smell the salty beach air. I would gladly share the M&M's, but I planned to hoard the Tim Tams for myself.

After group photos on Elmer's front porch, Jurnee, Buffalo, Tucker J, and I said goodbye once again to Hercules, who was taking a zero-mile day. By noon we were climbing out of Hot Springs. I felt crummy, perhaps because of the big breakfast or the weight of the pack. Perhaps because the day turned into the hottest yet; the thermometer spiked up to sixty-eight degrees. I struggled on the long, gradual climb, realizing that stopping in town was refreshing, but leaving was getting harder and harder each time.

Ahead, the trail traversed several 3,500-foot mountains before rising to some 5,000-foot balds beyond that. We would pass those, then Tucker J and I would be picked up again by Dan Gallagher and brought back to Hot Springs. I worried we would move too slowly for the boys, but in some places, Tucker J was stronger than all of us. He'd clicked with Buffalo and Jurnee; they all had a similar light-hearted attitude which made the days and miles speed by.

We fell into a rhythm where we each climbed the mountains at our own pace, then waited at the top for the others to share in the views. One afternoon I rocketed ahead of them all, making it to the top of the rise and another open view across a bald.

"I don't want to be goin' to Carolina in my mind anymore," I complained to Jurnee when he arrived. "I can't get James Taylor out of my head."

"Think about The Jetsons," Jurnee suggested.

"Meet George Jetson," I sang.

"Jane, his wife," Jurnee sang, adding the do-do-do tune that followed Jane's introduction.

"I can do better than that," Buffalo said, coming up over the rise. He belted out, "Conjunction junction, what's your function?!"

"Oh, yeah," I said, "that's a good one to get stuck in your head!"

We pondered TV show tunes as we waited for Tucker J to catch up, adding theme songs from *Three's Company* and *Cheers* to the growing list. Later, when we met up with Carolina Kid and Pooh Bear, we mentioned our playlist. They eagerly added the songs they had been replaying, particularly proud of the apropos "Straight Up Now Tell Me" by Paula Abdul. A little nugget that lodged into my brain ready to play on every uphill to come.

On our last afternoon together, I moved uphill through the sunshine with Tucker J close behind. There had been several rocky outcrops, and I hoped for a good view at the top of this climb.

"This has been a great hike, Tamarack," Tucker J said, his labored breathing causing him to speak in gasps. We were both aware of our last miles on the AT together before leaving for Mississippi. Again, the reality of leaving the boys brought up a deep melancholy, but I focused on my uncle and this time together. I could tell that Tucker J had begun to understand the essence of trail life that I had been trying to explain to him on his first night.

I slowed my pace as we neared the crest of the ridge. Tucker J went on, "I'm so glad I got to do this with you." He stopped walking. "But let's promise that we'll never let each other climb Mt. Everest."

I exhaled a chortle. "I'm with you," I replied. "One hundred percent."

We paused where the trail leveled out, looking for cliffs. Wingfoot mentioned that peregrine falcons lived there, and sure enough, we came across several side trails to overlooks where handmade signs warned hikers to keep back from the ledges where falcons were nesting.

We found Jurnee's and Buffalo's packs at one intersection. Tucker J and I dropped ours as well, grabbed our water bottles, and followed the path through the laurel. The boys were sitting on large rocks, looking out over the great expanse of ridgeline after ridgeline. Mountains upon mountains extending into forever.

"Breathtaking," Tucker J said.

A falcon floated above, sailing on the wind. Two buzzards drifted by, calmly scanning the area. This seemed to irritate the falcon, and she started swooping at them.

"I hate to quote a beer commercial," Jurnee said, "but it doesn't get much better than this."

No one said anything for a while as we drank our water and munched on snacks. The falcon soared lazily, having scared off the buzzards, never straying too far from the cliffs.

Last week, I'd fretted about leaving Jurnee and Slow Buffalo when I'd waited for Tucker J. Now I would be off the trail for three and a half days. It would be unlikely I could make up time and catch them again. I told them I didn't want them to wait around. Hike your own hike. That was the rule. But sitting on the cliff edge with them, looking across the limitless earth together, I knew it would be hard to leave. Or rather, it would be hard to come back and hike without them.

I thought back to my first week on the trail and how I'd felt so uncomfortable with all the men drinking beer and smoking pot. I hadn't found a place to fit in until our group coalesced that night at Standing Indian Shelter. Through days of battling these mountains, we'd become family. We'd been bound together, if not by DNA, then by laughter, tears, and swear words. We had a connection I'd never felt with boys before. Certainly not with Chad last year, nor any of the vague male acquaintances I'd had in high school or college. Jurnee and Buffalo were different. Perhaps I was different too.

In a sudden shift, the falcon turned on edge and fell to the earth, head down, blasting through space like a rocket. I wanted to gasp, or sing, or climb over the edge to see where she went as she sped behind the mountains and out of view. What was she after? Something had caught her eye. Something I couldn't see. Once she was gone, only the endless mountains remained.

"These gnats are wearing down my Buddhist principles," Slow Buffalo said, breaking the silence. He swished his bandana in front of his face for the thousandth time. "Can we go?"

We all agreed it was time to move on.

•   •   •

For the past month, my life's pace had equaled the speed of water trickling into a cup, snowflakes falling, leaves growing. Speeding along the highway toward Columbus, Mississippi, my senses couldn't comprehend the rumble of noise and blaze of color. My eyes couldn't adjust to the confusing blur outside the windows, so I turned to the journal on my lap. Since Tucker J had joined me, I'd spent more time at camp talking rather than writing. So, while he drove us across the country, I filled in the unwritten days.

We'd spent a lovely night at Jane and Bill's house nestled in the North Carolina woods. They were gracious hosts, offering us a huge meal, hot showers, and warm beds. Jane was a quilter and Bill a painter, so we passed the evening telling stories and looking at their artwork. After a big breakfast, we'd set out in our separate cars, agreeing to meet again at the hotel in Columbus. My emotions were all over the place. I was grateful to Jane and Bill but homesick for the trail. I was excited for Nate to graduate but sad that this meant the end of my time with Tucker J. I was looking forward to seeing my parents and extended family but I wondered if it was my real family that I was leaving behind.

Tucker J drove the whole way, and we stopped often to fill our bellies. It wasn't easy to find vegetarian fast food along the interstate, but Waffle House and McDonald's sufficed. We made a pass through Taco Bell, where we laughed like hyenas when they gave us an order of beef tacos instead of bean burritos.

I couldn't help but think of my father, who had never been fun to go anywhere with. The summers we drove to Michigan, my father did most of the driving, though sometimes he let Mom drive. Unfortunately, always used to being the one in command, he didn't do well in the role of copilot. One evening my mom was driving on the highway as we neared Aunt Barbara and Uncle Rick's house in Ohio. I sat in the front seat of the Caravan with Dad studying the map in the backseat next to Nate. He noticed too late that she'd missed our exit.

"Dammit, Laurie!" he exclaimed. "That was it!" He raised his hands and waved the map with vigor.

I flinched.

She apologized.

"Now we have to go all the way to the next exit and double back," he yelled. "It's going to take an extra twenty minutes."

"Chill out, Dad," Nate said.

I spun in my seat to look back at my brother. *What is he doing?* Now that Nate was a teenager, I knew he was pushing the limits more, but we weren't supposed to say things like that. Nate knew that would provoke him.

"What did you say?"

"She made a mistake. It's not a big deal."

I sank further into my seat. I wanted out of the car.

"I'll tell you what's a big deal. This jerk who should butt out when I'm talking to my wife."

"Nate, it's okay," Mom said.

"You're not talking," Nate said, raising his voice. "You're overreacting."

The explosion came in milliseconds. Swears, insults, yelling. I turned to see Dad's hand reaching for Nate's neck. In the small space of the backseat, they were practically on top of each other, their faces grimacing, their arms extending around the seat belts.

"Steve!" Mom yelled, looking in the rear-view mirror while attempting to stay on the road.

"Don't 'Steve' me!" he yelled, gripping one hand around Nate's throat. Dad's face was fire red. "He's an insolent, ungrateful punk. He needs to learn he can't talk to me like that."

Nate was on the school wrestling team and quickly grabbed hold of Dad's wrist and pulled it away from his throat, twisting it. "But you can talk to *her* like that?"

Shut up!

Dad let go of Nate's neck but reached around with his other hand to smack him. They scuffled in the back of the van for a few minutes, Dad trying to hit Nate, and Nate pushing his hands away. Both were breathing heavily and scowling at each other.

"STEVE," Mom yelled again. "Stop it!"

Dad finally pulled back and didn't strike again. With further words about Nate's "attitude," Dad gave his final comment, "I'll deal with you when we get there."

No one responded, for which I was glad. Though the yelling stopped, the anger didn't dissipate; it hovered in the crowded space, waiting for one more wrong move so it could stab again. What exactly Dad meant by dealing with Nate later, I had no idea. Certainly, there would be more yelling. I guessed they would have a fistfight. I thought of the wolf packs I had learned about in science class. There was always that one highest-ranking male wolf, but when the younger males matured, they started challenging the leader to try to take over. Maybe that's what was going on here. Otherwise, I didn't understand why Nate had talked back like that.

When we arrived at Barbara and Rick's house, no one spoke as we got out of the van. I was terrified, but I tried to focus on the two golden retrievers who came rushing outside to say hello. I walked with them to stretch my legs as they bounded around the yard.

Before I could even go inside to use the bathroom, Barbara and Rick told me we were going out for pizza. Almost as an afterthought, they added that we'd bring some home for Mom, Dad, and Nate. My aunt and uncle acted as if nothing out of the ordinary had happened. But never had we arrived at their house only to have them swoop in and rush me back into the car.

First, we went go-karting. It was fun after the long car ride, my aunt cheering me on as I raced past my uncle. Then we went to the pizza place, where we sat in the restaurant waiting for our pizzas, eating mozzarella sticks and onion rings. All in all, it was a fun outing, and I wished I got to do more stuff with them. After a final stop at the grocery, we returned to their house.

When we walked in, all was quiet. My parents and Nate were on the sofa, watching TV. Mom had even gotten out plates and napkins for the pizza. Everyone ate, the adults talking and joking around the table. I felt an empty ache inside, trying to understand why they were acting as if we had just arrived and the last few hours hadn't existed.

But I knew those hours existed; my stomach was still full of mozzarella sticks. There had to be some clue as to what had happened while I'd been out go-karting. I looked at Nate closely, willing him to tell me what happened. I had never seen anyone win a fight against Dad and wanted to know if he had pushed back against our father and somehow come out okay. But he avoided my eyes.

Nate and I didn't bond together against our father. He was four years older and always seemed out of reach to me. I didn't think he saw me as an ally, just a burdensome little sister who got in the way. We lived in a troubled house together, but he didn't come to my aid, and I didn't go to his. We were each fighting our own battles against our father.

Whatever had passed between Dad and him that night in Ohio, Nate betrayed nothing of it to me. And as always, no one ever spoke of the conflict again. It was like it had never happened, and the next day, after the pizza and mozzarella sticks were all gone, I wondered if it really had.

•　　　•　　　•

Aunts, uncles, my cousins Emily and Paul, Jane and Bill, one of Nate's former teachers, my parents, Nate, and I all packed around a long table in a restaurant in Columbus, Mississippi. The food and drinks kept coming. Along with the questions. "What do you eat? How far do you walk every day? Where do you sleep? How are your feet holding up?"

"On that one, let's just say it's a good thing my dress shoes aren't open-toed," I answered. "You don't want to see my feet." I was overwhelmingly happy to be sitting with my family, happier than I'd expected.

"Seriously, though, how is it?" Nate asked.

"It's great," I replied. "It's hard. I've never done anything so hard."

"Aren't you scared to be out there alone?" This one came from Aunt Missy, one of my dad's sisters. She almost shuddered as she asked.

"Not at all. Tommy can tell you. I'm rarely alone. And I wouldn't have made it this far without my friends." I thought of the boys and wondered where they were camping tonight.

"Tell them about the bear," I urged my uncle.

"Oh no!" Mom exclaimed. "Where? What happened?"

"Ah, yes, the bear," Tommy said, wiping his mouth with a napkin and pausing for effect. "Well, I got up one night around midnight to pee. Off the clearing by our campsite, I saw a huge black bear just standing there, watching me."

"He barely made it back to the tent alive," I said, smiling. My mother gave me a puzzled look, confused why we hadn't mentioned a dramatic bear encounter earlier.

"In the dark, it was a bear," Tommy went on. "In the morning, it was a tree stump. But in the middle of the night, I tell you, *it was a bear*." They all laughed, relieved to think that such a risk was only imaginary. I wanted them to understand the goodness of the trail, allay their fears and misconceptions. Maybe our brief stories could somehow show them.

The next day was the graduation. Nate walked across the stage, shook a general's hand, and got a piece of paper. Dad got choked up. Mom cried. The rest of the family clapped. Mom had brought me at least three different outfits for the various events, and I changed in and out of clothes several times. I drew the line at the attire for the fancy banquet and refused the pantyhose. I could barely squish my swollen, black and blue feet into dress shoes, but thankfully, no one was looking at my feet.

The more remarkable event took place when Nate took us all out onto the tarmac near the hangars. It was a breezy, warm day, and the sun hid behind some high clouds. I climbed up the ladder to look in the cockpit of the two-seater training plane—a long, bluish-gray jet that looked like all the others to me. Nate explained the dials and knobs, and I nodded as if it all made perfect sense now. I couldn't have said the difference between this plane, an F-16, and one of Orville and Wilbur's inventions, but I expressed as much interest as I could muster.

I was more bewildered by the fact that other than the air I was breathing, nothing about this place held any resemblance to the Earth I knew. From where I stood, all I could see was black asphalt. There was not a tree, a flower, or anything living within sight. The world I had been immersed in for the past month could not possibly have been more different than this one.

Occasionally, a jet would take off or land, its engines searing the air. Nate kept his eye on those planes, and when an F-16 went by, he'd point it out to us. It reminded me of when we were kids. Perhaps it was due to our father's time in the Air Force as an F-15 pilot, or perhaps it was just in his nature, but Nate had always been obsessed with planes. He built model planes, flew remote control planes, and in high school learned to fly a Cessna. Nate had always had his eyes turned to the sky. He'd dreamed of becoming a fighter pilot his whole life, and here he was on the verge of it. Despite this weird, nature-free, gray world he was ensconced in, I was happy for him.

In front of the training jet, Dad clamped his arms around me and Nate, both of us almost as tall as him. My tiny mother joined us on one side, smiling as the camera clicked. *Picture perfect.*

All my life, the definition of family had been people who yelled at each other, then pretended nothing had happened. I knew there were other options; I saw how Tommy raised his kids and how my friends' parents treated them. All families were fraught with difficulties, but mine felt particularly troubled, thanks to the man squeezing my shoulder. The reality was that I felt a lot closer to my trail friends than these people I was posing with. On the trail, I was myself. I was a girl who ate as much food as she could stuff in, who loved all nature, who liked to sleep on the ground and not shower for days. Here, I was whom they perceived me to be, whom they wanted me to be, and whom I used to be.

At the same time, I loved my parents and brother. When my dad pinned a special badge onto Nate's uniform, his eyes had shined with a paternal glow of pride. I wanted that too. I wanted them to see that I wasn't just the annoying little sister or the rebellious daughter who refused to conform to their standards. I wanted them to see me for the strong, smart, independent woman I was becoming. This was the family I had been given, and I couldn't change who they were. But I wondered if they would ever see who I was.

This strange side trip had been worthwhile, but the contrast had shown me exactly where my place was, and I was eager to get back to it. Dad hugged me and Mom cried as I headed to Jane and Bill's car. I wouldn't see my parents again until I made it to New Jersey. Nate said he'd try to meet me on the trail for a few days when I was in Virginia before he headed to his next base. When I said goodbye to Tommy, he handed me a bag of bright red apples.

"In case you end up with an order of beef tacos while you're on the road," he said, pulling me in for a long hug.

"Thanks again for hiking with me, Tucker J. I'm going to miss you."

"Just remember, Tamarack," Tommy said, looking me in the eye, "*these* are the good old days." I nodded and gave him one more hug before I left.

ON MY OWN

According to the maps, I had 150 trail miles from where Jane and Bill dropped me off until Damascus, Virginia. Wingfoot called Damascus "the friendliest town on the Appalachian Trail" because the community was accommodating of hikers in both lodging and kindness. I was eager to get there, where I hoped I might catch up with Slow Buffalo, Jurnee, and Hercules. But first, I had to face four major mountains: Big Bald, Unaka Mountain, Roan High Mountain, and the Humps, all between 5,200 feet and 6,200 feet in elevation. Also ahead were a dozen smaller peaks ranging from 2,000 to 5,000 feet, and countless knobs, gaps, and hollows.

My feet pounded the trail. My healing blisters pinched, and I could feel the pressure against my toes, which felt more squished than usual. After being free from boots for four days, my feet rebelled against the return to confinement.

The sky was as gray as tarmac and getting darker. Rain had started spitting when I'd left the car, then had let loose in squalls all morning. Jane and Bill had walked a short way with me, impressed to see me shuffle under my massive pack. I was amazed too. Had I really walked from Georgia with this thing? It pulled at my shoulders as a sense of nausea hit me. I wondered what about this I had missed so much while in Mississippi.

The readjustment wasn't just physical; I felt disquieted and out of place. I had told my family that I was never by myself out here, but this time, I was completely alone. I had become dependent on Jurnee and

Slow Buffalo; they were what kept me going through the ridiculous pain.

And now they were gone.

I don't want to be here. There would be new people, but they had all started at Springer days or weeks after I had, and it would take time to get to know them if any of them even went a similar pace to mine. I almost felt as if I was back on the Approach Trail.

The climb up Frozen Knob was 1,500 feet in two miles, steeper than I would have liked after four days of rest. The clouds hovered low; the wind burst up in surges. The higher I climbed, the foggier the world became. There was no hope for a view in this weather, and when I reached the wet summit, I found a fully treed peak anyway. A man wearing all blue rain gear sat on the ground next to the trail with his stove out, cooking lunch.

"Hey there, hiker," he called out. "Great day for it, eh?"

I paused in front of him, catching my breath, and watching him open packages of ramen. His round face was stubbly from several days of not shaving, and based on his appearance, I wasn't surprised when he said his name was Grubby.

"How're you liking the trail so far?" Grubby asked.

Before I could answer, a wind gust blustered up. The trees above us rattled and released several large splats of water, which plopped directly onto Grubby's head and into his soup pot. We looked at each other and laughed, not needing words to understand how we each liked the trail so far.

Grubby wiped his face with a bandana. When the wind died down, I told him about my venture off the trail into the foreign military world.

"My aunt asked me whether I was scared to be alone out here," I said. "I thought it was an odd question."

"Yeah, I've been alone," he said, then paused, thinking, "pretty much never."

"I'm not really scared, but I do miss the guys I was hiking with before."

"I bet you'll make new friends by the end of the day," he said with a smile.

I didn't know how I'd do hiking without Jurnee and Buffalo, but Grubby was a cheery chap, that was for sure. I hoped he was right.

•   •   •

I spent the night at Low Gap camping with Grubby and a man named Tim who had a chocolate Labrador named Alta. Tim was twenty-four, from Connecticut, and one of the top two cutest guys I'd met on the trail. We passed the evening sitting around a fire comparing stories and gear, laughing as the gales blew the smoke in our faces. I still wondered where Jurnee and Buffalo were camping.

Overnight, the wind geared up for a long assault on the mountains. Several times I woke to the creak of trees overhead. My tent walls bent against the pressure, sometimes compressing to inches from my face. It seemed inevitable that the poles would snap.

My tent held strong, but the wind didn't calm down the next day. Instead, it increased. I was headed up to 5,500-foot Big Bald, aptly, if not unimaginatively, named for its bald top. The chilly wind dominated the forest on the climb, but when I stepped out into the open meadow, I felt as if I'd entered a wind tunnel testing site. I'd always wanted to experience wind strong enough to counter gravity. I leaned into it, letting the weight of my pack pull me backward. The wind held me up, and I laughed out loud. The immense power was exhilarating.

The thrill faded when I looked across the top of the bald. The trail meandered, but there was nothing to block the wind for a very long stretch. Like other balds, this one had wooden posts with white blazes to mark the trail, and even these seemed to be struggling to hold up in the wind. I gripped my poles and tried to steady myself, my body cutting sideways against the gusts.

Mountains and balds spread out before me with a breath of spring green painting their sides. I noticed the view as I walked, but couldn't stop to appreciate it without being blown off course. After twenty minutes of pushing against this battering ram, I wondered if wind pressure could cause bruising. Every muscle felt strained and beaten. I pushed myself harder to get off the mountain.

Eventually, back in the forest, the trees cut the wind's power in half. The canopy far above me took the brunt of the assault. I paused to readjust my askew pack and disheveled hair and took a quick look at my map before moving on.

A few miles later, I sensed someone approaching from behind and turned to find not a human, but a beautiful golden retriever padding toward me. When I said hello, she spun and ran away.

I wondered how that golden retriever and Tim's Labrador, Alta, had managed across the bald in that wind. Both wore saddlebags, but they were low to the ground, so perhaps the wind didn't trouble them as much. The retriever came up again behind me. I stopped. This time she trotted over, sniffed me, and let me pat her head for a moment before she dashed off.

I'd grown up with a golden retriever named Peaches. My aunt Barbara and uncle Rick bred their dogs, and when I was nine, my parents agreed to keep one of the puppies. Peaches was a sweet dog, always available for cuddling or playing dress up. I loved all animals and had hoped to be a veterinarian someday, but Peaches was more than just a pet. She was my best friend. She kept me company in my bedroom after fights with my dad, her big brown eyes solemn as I cried into her furry mane. Sometimes, I felt like she was the only one who listened to me.

The third time the retriever approached me, she started walking at my heels. She stayed with me until I heard human footsteps behind me. Her person, a short man wearing a white t-shirt with cutoff sleeves and a red bandana tied over his hair, sped up to join us.

"Sorry, I hope ya don't mind dogs. She's always runnin' ahead to see who else she can hike with," he said. He spoke with a slight accent I couldn't place. "She kept coming back to tell me to hurry up. I think she likes you."

"Well, I like her, too. What's her name?" I petted her again, though this time she pulled away, heading up the trail. She was perturbed that we'd stopped walking.

"Sundog," he said. It was a perfect name; she was as blonde as the sun was bright, especially compared to how auburn Peaches had been. "And I'm Full Moon."

When I introduced myself, he said, "Tamarack! I've been wanting to meet you." He explained that he'd been reading my register entries for weeks and loved all the quotes I'd been writing, particularly the Dave Matthews ones. "I think we're going to have a lot in common."

•　　　•　　　•

Over the next couple of days, I crossed paths with a lot of people. In addition to Grubby, Tim and Alta, and Full Moon and Sundog, I met Waterboy, an older man who kept to himself, Bud from Oregon, a very tall fellow with a shaved head, Bee, a young woman about my age, and her dad Old Blue, a retired cop. I also met the hiking trio Nuge, Jamie the Kid, and Charlie Hustle. I was surprised to catch up to Charlie and Mom still plugging away. Charlie had changed names a few times and was now called Thor.

One man in running shorts told me he was doing twenty-six miles a day because, he said, "Anybody can do this trail in six months. That's no challenge!"

I glared and walked away. I was suffering through long days of walking through wilderness, being nearly blown off mountains, and missing my boys so much I cried. My body was being held together by peanuts and noodles. My feet might as well have been tree stumps. I didn't need some jerk telling me that my experience was easy.

When I made it to the road crossing for Erwin, Tennessee, a blond woman in a pickup stopped for me. As I climbed into the front seat next to her tiny white dog, she offered me a Mountain Dew and then chattered nonstop as we drove the four miles to town. Erwin was a metropolis compared to other places I'd stopped. While the movie theater, restaurants, and motels all sounded inviting, I had to resist. There were many miles ahead, and I couldn't stop again. I planned to get my mail drop, make a quick run to the hardware store for gas, and return to the trail by evening. At the post office, Full Moon sat on the front stoop next to a sleeping Sundog. I greeted him and dropped my pack before heading inside.

"You got a lotta stuff there," Full Moon said as I joined him a few minutes later with a stack of letters and boxes. Sundog's eyes opened as I sat down, and she prodded my arm to see if I had brought her anything good.

"Yeah, the mailman was happy to meet me," I replied. "Said all the workers were impressed. I had a new piece of mail come in almost every day." I opened a box from Marilyn and Bob, the M&M friends, and handed Full Moon the giant brown bag inside. "I have friends in high places."

He chuckled, opening the bag and dumping a bunch of M&M's onto the map spread open in front of him. Sundog thrust her nose toward the pile, but Full Moon pushed her head away before she was able to suck up any chocolate pieces.

"If I go vegan, I'll have to give these up," he said.

"Are you even vegetarian?" I asked, surprised.

"Of course! I would never eat an animal," he said. "The best thing that humans can do to slow our inevitable destruction of our planet is to stop eating meat." He rattled off some statistics about how much energy it took to produce a field of corn to feed one cow, versus how many people could be fed directly by that same field of corn. I listened to his data, but he didn't need to convince me. I had studied this stuff for years and was well acquainted with the problems humanity faced.

"I know," I said. "We're in big trouble if people don't start changing their behavior. Why don't people understand that?"

"Cuz people are idjits," he said, with an exaggerated accent. He let out a hearty laugh. "Nah, not really. They just aren't informed."

"I'm amazed that there's someone else who thinks like I do," I said. "No one I know cares much about animals or the environment. Or if they do, they're not willing to *do* anything about it."

"Tell me about it," he said, pulling his red bandanna off his head. I saw that his scraggly brown hair was bleached at the tips. "I'm from western Pennsylvania. I work at a fucking rib joint. Nobody there gets it."

"A vegetarian who serves ribs," I said. "Nice."

He shrugged, and I turned back to my food box, suddenly proud of my little baggies of dried veggies and fruit.

"Hey, will you watch Sundog while I hit the grocery?" Full Moon asked. "I hate leaving her tied up outside."

"Of course! I'd love to babysit." She sat alert next to me, ready for action should any M&M's or other tidbits lose their way when moving from box to food bag. I scratched her head as Full Moon tossed me the end of her leash. I was indeed happy to spend time with Sundog, but I felt a nudge of something else. Full Moon was pretty cute, though far too short for me. He probably had a girlfriend back home anyway. Still, he was unlike anyone I'd met before, and I wanted him to like me.

As Sundog and I sifted through my food, Grubby, Tim, and Alta wandered up. Alta and Sundog greeted each other, no doubt exchanging their own hiking tales. Tim and Grubby spread out on the porch nearby, and we chatted until Full Moon returned. Our empty stomachs sent us around the corner for lunch at the brand-new Erwin Burrito Company.

The colorful restaurant was an excellent stop, particularly since they offered a variety of vegetarian fare. I scarfed down a plate of nachos as I waited for my bean and cheese burrito.

"Having just arrived in town," Grubby said, between mouthfuls of his burrito, "I would appreciate a night off. You all should stay, too."

"The Holiday Express was awesome," Tim said with a drip of sarcasm. He, along with Full Moon and Bud from Oregon, had spent the previous night in town. "I'm into staying again. With the four of us, it's like fifteen bucks each."

"I could be convinced to stay over again," Full Moon said.

"Tamarack?" Grubby looked at me. I had told him of my fixation on nachos, and he used the information wisely. "Think of all the nachos you could eat tonight."

I was tempted. But I felt the tug of more miles.

"I can't let the Erwin vortex suck me in. I was just off the trail for four days. I think I have to keep going."

"You sure?" Full Moon asked. "You can have one of the beds in the room. I'm happy to be on the floor with Sundog."

"Aww, thanks. But no. I have to go."

As soon as I got back to the trail, I regretted not staying in Erwin. These three amazing guys had invited me to join their club of coolness. Grubby was so kind, Tim was so cute, and Full Moon was a kindred spirit. And I'd said no. *What was I thinking?*

Jurnee and Buffalo—that's what I was thinking. At every shelter, I read their register entries, checked their progress, and estimated how far ahead they were. Jurnee and Buffalo weren't hiking together anymore, according to the letter Buffalo had left me at the post office. He called it a "spat" over politics. We hadn't ever talked about politics when we were together; I wondered what brought it up now. I also wondered if I was the glue that had held our little group together. Now, we were all apart; Buffalo was four days ahead, Jurnee three, and Hercules one.

It was an impossible task to hike fast enough to catch them. They were hiking with new people. I needed to do the same. Maybe I was nervous. Scared of getting to know Full Moon, Grubby, and Tim too well, and liking them too much. And then being disappointed when I lost them, too. Maybe I just missed my friends. Maybe this whole damn thing was too hard. All I could do was keep walking, unsure of anyone else, knowing only that I was on the Appalachian Trail headed north, adrift.

•   •   •

A massive stand of red spruce covered the summit of Unaka Mountain. After days of hiking through rhododendrons and hardwoods, and across vast, windy balds, the evergreens were a welcome change. It reminded me of a northern forest, a rust-colored layer of needles coating the ground. High above, the dark green canopy blocked out sunlight, while at my feet, vibrant mosses circled the bases of many trees.

I shed my pack and stood off the trail, soaking in the silence. Nothing stirred. The place radiated magic; I imagined gnomes or fairies hidden behind the fallen logs and in the broken snags. I felt lucky to be able to visit such a place. More so, happy to know that this still existed and had not been decimated by human arrogance. I wanted to stay longer, but the sun was high, and I needed more miles. So, I pressed on, leaving the enchanted forest behind.

The days blended together, punctuated by moments of stunning scenery and nights of camping with a variety of people. I'd been overtaken by a dense cohort of hikers and reconnected with Biscuits and Gravy, the southern couple I'd met in Hot Springs. They often stayed toward the edge of the crowd, content with each other's company, but I was enjoying getting to know them.

The day we hiked up Roan High Mountain, Gravy caught up to me, and we walked together for a stretch. She told me about her hometown in Tennessee and her time in design school at the University of Georgia. It was drizzling most of the climb, making the trail mucky and slippery, and the wind had picked up again. Like when I hiked with Buffalo, Jurnee, and Tucker J, hiking with Gravy made the rocky trail, the nasty weather, the physical pain fade to mere background noise. She was the first woman I'd met who I thought could be a real friend.

We arrived at the summit of Roan to discover there was also a road to the peak. The clearing around the parking area and picnic tables was trashed. Plastic soda bottles and food wrappers littered the area. Cigarette butts. A stuffed garbage bag laid ripped open, raided by wildlife. Chip bags cartwheeled in the wind. Anger surged in me, displacing the joy and gratitude I'd felt on Unaka. *People are such assholes.*

Coming up to Roan High Knob Shelter didn't make me feel any better. The structure was a dark stone hut, with a roof that looked like it might be about as effective at stopping rain as a kitchen colander.

Plus, it was packed. Wet hikers and gear took up the entire shelter, with barely an inch of free space to drop my bag. I shoved someone's stuff out of the way and forced my gear into a damp corner where I knew it would never dry out.

The rain clouds moved on, and the sun peeked out as it sunk to the west. The trees dripped, and the cool air that smelled like sweet watermelon was far more welcome than the musty haze inside the hut. Gravy and I went together to the spring with our water bottles and filters.

"There's a lot of testosterone in that little hut," I said, sitting on the ground and unpacking my filter. "You know every guy is ogling you, right?" She was definitely the prettiest girl on the AT, and if she wasn't hiking with her boyfriend, the vultures would have gotten her by now.

"It's not like I'm anything special," she said modestly, underestimating her blond beauty. "They're all just missing their women back home. I am glad I've got Chris, though."

"I'll bet. Are you going to get married?"

She laughed. "Oh, golly, I don't know! I s'pose if we can survive the AT together, we can handle marriage."

"I would think so!"

"He's somethin' else, sometimes. We're always together. *All the time*." She paused in her water pumping. "It must be nice to be on your own."

Her comment surprised me. "Yeah, I guess." I'd been spending so much time missing Jurnee and Buffalo, I'd forgotten that I was doing this hike for myself, not anyone else. I had the freedom to stop whenever I wanted. To sleep in or stay up late. To not coordinate with anyone but me. My schedule, my days, my choices were all mine, with one single objective: walk north.

Over the next few days, when the trail aggravated me or I sank into loneliness, I tried to remind myself of this freedom. I paused for expansive views, spent a long afternoon in deep conversation with a southbounder, and came eye-to-eye with a songbird. Gravy was right, it was nice to be on my own. For all I didn't have, I did have a lot.

•   •   •

Bob and Pat Peoples ran the quaint Kincorra Hostel in Dennis Cove, Tennessee. The quaintness evaporated, however, when twenty-two hikers packed into the log cabin bunkhouse. This large number was because Bob offered a slackpacking service. Bob drove hikers to the AT trailhead north of Pond Flats, which was not flat at all, but rather a six-mile, 2,000-foot climb and corresponding descent. From there, people could hike back to the hostel without their backpacks. Slackpacking still counted as doing the trail miles but was a luxurious treat without the heavy pack. Most people spent two nights at the hostel, so there was a constant overlap of hikers.

At Kincorra, I caught up to Hercules. He had been hiking on and off with Old Blue and Bee, Robocop, and another older man, Diamond. I also met Seiko, a man who claimed to know every mile on the Appalachian Trail. That evening, many hikers sat around the small living room fixing gear and playing Trivial Pursuit, while Seiko convinced Bee to play a data game with him. She'd name a shelter or town, and he'd say how many miles it was from Springer. She'd double-check it against the Data Book, usually finding his numbers accurate. Perhaps he had a photographic memory or he'd walked the trail a dozen times, but I didn't care. I found his little display of superiority obnoxious. Instead of listening to him brag, I turned to Bud from Oregon.

Bud and I had leapfrogged past each other several times over recent days. He was an unlikely friend, not someone I would have ever crossed paths with in the real world. He was about thirty-five and based on the way he spoke, kind of an old hippie. Back at Apple House Shelter, I'd just finished my first dinner when a trail angel named Superfeet walked up with some beers to share. As we popped open a bottle, Bud showed up too.

"Hell yeah, man, I'll take a beer," he said. "Right on, man."

Then there was his name, Bud from Oregon. Though I had zero experience with pot, I was pretty sure that it was common out there in the Pacific Northwest. I never actually saw Bud smoke, and I didn't know how or where he got it out here, but it didn't matter, because like Gravy, the more I talked to him, the more I liked him.

Trivial Pursuit dragged on all evening, boring everyone by the end. I joined Full Moon in the kitchen where he was making a pan of brownies to share. I asked him more about his vegetarianism. He showed me an essay from a musician I'd never heard of, which I skimmed. It seemed to be about our screwed-up societal values. Full Moon pointed out a part of the essay where the writer listed some alarming facts about the killing of animals for food.

"We humans are horribly out of sync with the earth," Full Moon said, pouring a huge bowl of chocolate batter into a pan. "That's why I'm vegetarian."

"Vegetarian?" Know-it-all Seiko demanded from the far side of the room. "What the hell you eat out here?"

"Anything but meat," Full Moon responded, with his hearty laugh.

"That's crazy. People are supposed to eat meat," growled Wee Willy the Prince of Wales. "We got those sharp teeth and all."

Wee Willy reminded me of Jabba the Hutt, only hairy. He wasn't even a hiker; he was what we called a yellow-blazer. He hitched rides from town to hostel to town, where he'd eat, sleep, and pretend he had exerted himself to get there. I'd never met him before, but I'd heard of him and his crowd and didn't want to be near him.

"We also have flat teeth for grinding vegetables," I said, feeling heat rising to my face. "And even if we're *supposed to* eat meat, that doesn't mean we have to."

"It's not healthy being vegetarian," a hiker named Cracker jumped in. Full Moon and I had struck a chord. These men were full of the usual arguments. "Our ancestors ate meat. We should eat meat."

"Now, hang on, man," Bud said. "Let's hear what reasons they have for being vegetarian. Sounds like it might make some sense."

"It's not healthy torturing animals, either," I snapped. I didn't want to get into a fight over this, but I was starting to feel like I had on Roan Mountain, pissed at human ignorance.

"The meat industry is not at all healthy," stated Full Moon. He was keeping his cool and responding as if we were talking about flower gardens rather than a controversial topic. He launched into his facts on factory farms, water usage, and crops. "Eighty percent of chicken-factory meat inspectors have stopped eating chicken. What does that tell you?"

Cracker and Wee Willy continued their insistence that a vegetarian diet and vegetarians themselves were just plain wrong. I became flustered under the weight of my ire. Like during so many of the fights I'd had with my dad, in the face of attack, I lost my own composure. The cloud of frustration made me forget the facts and how to make my arguments. So, I shut my mouth and let Full Moon carry the conversation.

"You show me one reputable book that describes how meat eating is healthy for the planet, how they treat the animals well, and how it's good for the body, and I'll reconsider," Full Moon said logically. "In the meantime, read John Robbins' *Diet for a New America*. Then we'll talk more."

My mom cooked all kinds of meat when I was growing up: pork chops, beef stroganoff, meat chili. I relished all of it, especially salty beef jerky and fried meatballs, until I took Mr. Streko's Environmental Science class during my freshman year in high school. I loved pets like cats, dogs, and gerbils, and I respected wild animals like wolves, whales, bears, and the animals that we studied in class. However, I didn't know much about farm animals; I'd always been told they lived on idyllic, green farms where they were cared for with kindness until the sad but necessary day came when the thoughtful farmer would butcher them humanely. Like in *Charlotte's Web*.

But Mr. Streko enlightened me about factory farms, the overfishing of the oceans, and the destruction of wildlands for cattle. These animals in cages had faces, beating hearts, and breathing lungs, and they were being abused for human consumption. One day during that freshman year, it dawned on me that if I loved animals, I couldn't eat them anymore.

It was the first major personal decision of my life, and I was determined to stick to it. My family, however, didn't make it easy. Mom with her nursing background was concerned for my health. "Where will you get your protein?"

Nate and his best friend delighted in one more way to harass me. "Mmm, good hamburger, Amanda," they teased through mouthfuls of meat. They reached across the table to shove the burgers from their plates right up to my face.

Dad, of course, got angry. "She's not going to eat the meals you cook for her? Well, what *is* the spoiled girl going to eat?"

In consultation with a big vegetarian cookbook, Mom and I figured out some recipes. Once Nate left for college, though, family dinners around the table came less often, and fast food more often. In elementary school, a trip to McDonald's for a Happy Meal, with its perfectly folded box and that big yellow M that doubled as a handle, the toy inside, and the activities and jokes on the outside, filled me with joy. By the time I was fifteen, though, Happy Meals were a thing of the past, and the vegetarian choices at McDonald's were limited: French fries and salad. So, that's what I ordered one evening when my parents and I walked up to the brightly lit counter.

Dad and I filled our cups at the soda fountain and walked to the seating area to pick a table. The whole restaurant reeked of grease. My feet slipped on the slick tile floor.

"What kind of oil do you think they use to fry the French fries?" I asked.

"Who knows," Dad said. "It doesn't matter."

"It matters to me. I don't want to eat something fried in pig lard. I told you about how smart pigs are and how they kill…"

"Yes!" Dad barked. "We know."

Mom came to the table with the tray of food and began setting each item out.

I flipped open the salad's clear plastic lid. A light green bed of iceberg lettuce, shredded carrots, cheese, two cherry tomatoes, and little squares of ham and flecks of bacon sprinkled all over the top.

"Oh no!" I said. They both looked at me. "It's got meat on it."

"Oh, dear," said Mom, her shoulders drooping. Dad shook his head and took a bite of his burger.

"I can't eat this. I didn't think a salad would have meat on it. It's a *salad*."

"I bought you that salad," Dad said, his voice deepening. "You're going to eat it."

"But I'm not eating meat anymore."

"Eat your dinner! Now."

"But…"

"EAT IT!"

The one other family in the restaurant turned to look at us. I hunched my shoulders, turning my face away from them as my eyes welled with tears. Some pig had suffered to end up in this plastic container. I would suffer too if I didn't eat it. Or if I did. I put a bite in my mouth, my gag reflex intensifying. I didn't know if I could swallow.

• • •

I woke to the smell of bacon cooking. The sky was still dark, but the old guys—Robocop, Diamond, Old Blue, and Hercules—were all early risers. The bunk room was situated over the kitchen, and every sound and smell traveled like wild horses thundering past. I pulled my fleece sweater over my head and tried to doze. When I heard others stirring in the room, I gave up and began to prepare for my day of slackpacking.

Full Moon had slackpacked the previous day and was itching to get to Damascus. As we packed up in the bunkroom, I asked him how he stayed so calm last night during the debate.

"They don't know what they're talking about," he said, tying on what seemed to be his signature red bandanna over his hair. "You can't get angry at people for ignorance. We need to lead by example, be open to their perspective, then educate them. People will come around."

"Sounds like a Dave lyric," I said with a grin.

"Ha. Probably is. Keep the essay. Give it back to me when we meet up in Damascus."

Full Moon and I had loads more to talk about. I could have sat with him for days to learn all he knew. I hoped we would get the chance.

The morning was sunny and warm and walking up Pond Flats without a backpack was like floating up the mountain on the tail of a kite. I carried only my fanny pack and a water bottle, leaving everything else at the hostel. I spent the whole day with Hercules, who still walked even slower than I did. One of Herc's best friends had recently died, and he spent a long time telling me stories. We reminisced about Hot Springs and the amazing meals at Elmer's and laughed about his crazy howling. It was fun to be with him again; I was reminded of what a sweet and sensitive man he was. The climb over Pond Flats was easy for me, but I sensed he might be losing steam for the trail and wondered if this might be the last time we hiked together.

Along with Bee and Old Blue, Robocop, Joe Cool, and a young couple called Peanut Butter and Wraparound, Herc and I stopped for lunch at Laurel Fork Falls, where a gorgeous waterfall, white and rushing, slipped down the side of the mountain. Wingfoot noted that this rhododendron-filled gorge was one of those idyllic places "that you imagined when you first dreamed of hiking the AT." Indeed, it was. As our slackpacker group posed for a picture together with the water gushing behind us, I noticed I felt more peaceful than I had in a while. It was so simple, being in the woods, talking with a friend, walking.

Hercules decided to stay at the hostel again that night, but I wanted to get a few more miles under my belt. I bid him goodbye, assuring him we'd meet in Damascus. After a quick stop at the grocery where I ran inside to pick up a pint of Ben and Jerry's Chocolate Fudge Brownie, Bob Peoples dropped Peanut Butter, Wraparound, and me back at the trail north of Pond Flats. The ice cream would stay solid enough in my pack over the two flat miles around Watauga Lake. That evening in the shelter, I would enjoy a tasty end to an easy, sweet day.

From Watauga, it was fifty miles to Damascus. I felt tougher than I had since returning from Mississippi. Over the next two days, I walked the trail alone, stopping infrequently, camping by myself, and pushing myself to do twenty-mile days. The ache in my feet and thighs never subsided, but I pounded on, dreaming of pizza, beer, and friends. I didn't know whom I would find in Damascus. My old friends, my new friends, both, or entirely new people altogether. Whomever was there, I would be glad to see them and share a beer or two. They were all a part of this tale called *hiking my own hike*.

•   •   •

The trail passed through Damascus on a flat bike path called the Virginia Creeper Trail along the south of town. I cut north and made my way through the village. My first guess for where to find people, Quincey's Pizza, was a good one. Sundog was tied to the bike rack out front, and she greeted me like a long-lost relative, wagging her whole body.

I stumbled into the restaurant, sweaty, hot, and exhausted, and found Full Moon, Grubby, Waterboy, and some other guys I didn't know in one of the shabby booths. They welcomed me to my fourth state with cheers and smiles and pulled up an extra wooden chair. Within seconds a beer was in front of me, and I took a long appreciative swig. I ordered classic Quincey's fare: a giant calzone, packed with veggies and oozing cheese.

"I'll go ahead and put in a chocolate cake order, too," said the waitress with a wink.

"Slow Buffalo has been here for four days, Tamarack," Grubby said, tipping back his beer.

"What? Wow. Why?"

"He's been waiting for you," he said with a raised eyebrow.

Like Erwin, Damascus had its own inescapable vortex, and hikers were known to stay for long periods. But four days? That was too long.

My calzone and cake devoured, I left Quincey's to search out a hostel called The Place. I turned a corner and ran right into Jurnee and Buffalo. I let out an uncharacteristically girlish scream and grabbed them both for a hug. They turned to walk back to the hostel with me. I had missed them so much, but something had shifted. A hesitation arose. We'd been apart for a long time. Had separate experiences, made separate friends. I'd figured out how to truly be on my own. Now that I was there with them again, I wasn't sure things could ever be quite the same.

THE SOUND OF FREEDOM

Damascus spun me around in a whirlwind of food, beer, and laughter. While I was there, the sun shone continuously, making it feel like summer might actually come. The small town offered all the amenities in a walkable, hiker-friendly layout, and I bounced around between the post office, the laundromat, the restaurants, and back to The Place hostel.

I was delighted to have found Jurnee and Slow Buffalo again, and we hung out at Quincey's and caught up on our time apart. Happy as I was, I tried to ignore the niggling feeling that the shine had dulled. Buffalo, however, basked as if I was the sun. Wherever I went, whomever I talked to, he rarely left my side. Instead of returning the attention, I found myself drawn to Full Moon, Bud, Grubby, and Tim, who now went by Dogman. Full Moon and Grubby had visited the barber and gotten haircuts with an AT symbol shaved into the back of their heads. Grubby also opted for a mohawk, and proud of his ridiculousness, he strutted through town showing it off. I enjoyed the mellow camaraderie of these guys.

Dozens of other hikers were in town: Biscuits and Gravy, Carolina Kid, Waterboy, Robocop, Jamie, Nuge, Charlie Hustle, Joe Cool, Peanut Butter and Wraparound, Bee and Old Blue, and Diamond. I also met some new hikers. Kaybek was a very attractive college guy from Quebec. He spoke little English but was learning as he hiked the trail. He'd chosen his trail name because he wanted Americans to pronounce the name of his home correctly. Megan was twenty-eight, from

Ashville, North Carolina, and though I didn't think her quite as beautiful as Gravy, she was making waves with the men. She claimed to have a boyfriend back home, but without his presence here, many guys were vying for her attention.

Blisters and Pizza Guy were two late-twenties buddies who were a classic odd couple; Blisters was organized, barely a scuff on his boots, while Pizza Guy was scruffy, his one shirt already in tatters. They invited me to join in my first-ever game of hacky sack. I kicked my feet up, missing the hack three out of four times. When I did make contact, it was only to shoot the hack far from any other player. Despite my pathetic skills, I decided I needed a hobby and invested in a red, yellow, and green striped hacky sack and planned to perfect my skills in the coming weeks.

Arrival in Damascus meant the completion of nearly one-quarter of the trail, a fact which resulted in much celebrating at Quincey's and Dot's, the two most popular drinking establishments in town. After dinner and beer at Quincey's, some hikers planned to walk the Virginia Creeper Trail the few blocks to Dot's. One round easily became two, then three, as friends came and went. I'd always liked Carolina Kid but drinking with him was even more fun. We recapped our favorite hiking songs, and he reminded me of "Straight Up Now Tell Me;" one I'd attempted to cut from my mental playlist. He was cute, in a clean-cut, Boy Scout kind of way, and I wished he didn't have a girlfriend back home. Still, she wasn't here, and I didn't see the harm in flirting. I wondered if Buffalo had a problem with it though because he sat in a corner all night sulking and staring at me.

It had been ages since I'd gotten drunk. My senior year in college, when I finally loosened up and decided to spend more time drinking than studying, I'd always gone to the bar with my sorority sisters. Though we mingled and flirted, I was there with the girls.

There, at Dot's, it was completely different; I was with the guys. I knew I wasn't one of the pretty girls on the trail, like Gravy or Megan, but I reveled in the increased attention I was getting. Whether it was the alcohol, the flirting, or just delirium from walking 450 miles, my whole body vibrated with glee. We'd spent weeks slogging through mud, snow, and rain, climbing impossible mountains, cramming into tiny, dirty shelters with strangers. For what? Adventure, entertainment, self-torture? I didn't know why anyone else was hiking the trail, but I knew I wasn't alone in the experience. The beer goggles illuminated the fact that I was a part of a large group of very crazy people. And I loved it.

•   •   •

The trail traversed 500 miles through the state of Virginia, a daunting amount. The first night out of Damascus, I camped with Jurnee and Slow Buffalo by a small pond. Back together again, I hoped we could recreate our goofy, laughter-filled group and was particularly glad they were nearby when a hailstorm dropped icy pellets on us. But my feelings had changed. We were in a cohort of hikers who I also liked; I didn't want to restrict myself to being only with Buffalo and Jurnee. I guessed Jurnee felt the same, but after all the doting in Damascus, I wasn't sure that Slow Buffalo did.

I felt awkward as the boys and I packed up the next morning. Was I supposed to wait for them, walk with them? I'd gotten used to doing my own thing, moving at my own pace and on my own schedule; I was suddenly unsure. The three of us had walked out of Damascus together the day before, moseying down the delightfully flat Virginia Creeper Trail for a mile before heading into the woods and dividing into our separate paces. But now what?

I didn't have to decide because Jurnee left first. By the time I was ready to go, so was Buffalo, and he followed me out of camp. We walked together through the rhododendron lowlands for several miles toward the first challenge of Virginia: Whitetop Mountain, 5,080 feet. When we arrived at the base of Whitetop, the trail steepened, and I slowed, Buffalo at my heels.

"Go ahead." I stepped to the side of the trail.

"Oh, it's okay, I don't mind being behind you."

Well, I mind.

"You're always faster than me, you'd better go on," I urged, feeling irritation percolating.

"Okay, well, age before beauty," he said with a grin and moved past me.

My stomach lurched. *Is he serious?*

I waited until Buffalo disappeared around a bend ahead. Then I slogged up the mountain, my feet aching, my brain settling on "Straight Up Now Tell Me." I cursed Carolina Kid for getting that stuck in my head again and Buffalo for being so clingy.

As I crested the peak, I saw Buffalo sitting near the summit sign.

"How ya doing?" he called out.

"I'm fine." I gasped. "As I always am after climbing thousands of feet with fifty pounds on my back." *And with my friend not giving me any space.* My lungs could barely get enough oxygen, and I was beginning to feel like Buffalo was smothering any air I had left.

The trail skirted the peak of Mt. Rogers, the highest point in Virginia at 5,729 feet. I skipped the one-mile round-trip to the summit, preferring to stick to the vast views I'd already had and knew were coming up. Jurnee, Buffalo, and I spent the night at Thomas Knob Shelter with a couple of weekender guys from Pennsylvania. I found them very entertaining and laughed a lot as we cooked our suppers at the picnic table in front of the two-story shelter. Jurnee joined in on the joking. Buffalo, however, sat apart from us and remained quiet throughout the evening.

I'd heard that the trail through Mt. Rogers National Recreation Area and Grayson Highlands was spectacular and was glad when I woke to see that the night's fog had lifted. I was also pleased when Buffalo left the shelter before the rest of us, not waiting for me. I wanted to enjoy the day at my own pace.

I savored the meandering trail as I left the shelter, trying to look at more than just my feet. Spring unfolded over the land; green shaded every shrub. The terrain was like the balds farther south, wide open with only sparse tree cover, like the wild plains of Patagonia. But it was unique too; the Grayson Highlands undulated with craggy rock outcrops jutting up all over. The Forest Service had taken over this grazing land back in the 1970s. Locals wanted to prevent reforestation and retain the mountaintop meadows and gorgeous views. So, they introduced ponies, built fences, and let them run wild. The ponies didn't rely on humans for their survival, but humans did control the population by giving health checkups and selling off a dozen or so each year. I'd heard that the herd was large this year, and I was looking forward to seeing them.

I hadn't walked far when I caught up to Buffalo sitting on one of the outcrops. He said he was enjoying the morning solitude, but quickly jumped back on the trail behind me when I walked on, shattering *my* solitude.

The day had turned warm, and the sun was bright behind high gauzy clouds. We met up with Jurnee at the metal gate where we would enter Grayson Highlands State Park. He was chatting with a group of teenagers who were amazed that we'd hiked there from Georgia. They offered us fresh oranges and directed us to where they'd seen some wild ponies.

Inside the gate, the trail morphed into a one-foot-deep rut that the ponies had forged into the soft, loamy soil. More crags protruded out of the earth in jumbled rock piles. I paused when I heard voices ahead and looked up to see several horses fifty feet from the trail. In varying shades and patterns of chocolate and tan and smoke and silver, they grazed carelessly in the open meadow. They were not as large as domesticated horses, their fur wasn't as sleek, and some of them had long, scruffy manes covering their eyes, but I wasn't prepared for how striking and charismatic the feral ponies would be. Some of them stood grazing in the middle of the trail, stoic and indifferent. Others came trotting over when they saw us, obviously having been trained by previous hikers to expect food.

Jurnee, Buffalo, and I meandered together through Grayson Highlands, navigating past dozens of ponies. Three miles later, when we shut the gate behind us, I wanted space. I felt a surge of strength and took off ahead of the boys. With the wild ponies on my mind and DMB on my lips, my legs felt light, my feet felt sure, and I cruised down a long descent away from the meadows and back into the budding deciduous forest.

•   •   •

"Are two pizzas enough?" I asked Jurnee, Buffalo, and Megan, the pretty woman from Asheville. We were sitting inside Partnership Shelter, considering our lunchtime options.

"I want a calzone," Jurnee said. "Count me out for pizza."

"More people are gonna show up. Someone will eat it, right?" I asked.

Partnership was thus far the best shelter on the AT. It was a fairly new, two-storied building that had a small side room with a warm shower. It was also next door to the Mt. Rogers National Recreation Area Headquarters, which had a pay phone. And to this pay phone, a nearby pizza shop delivered.

That morning we had only walked ten miles with every intention of moving on in the afternoon. But as we waited for the pizza, my friends kept taking things out of their packs and settling further in to the clean and cozy space. The morning's mist turned into rain, and no one wanted to go back out into it.

"Atkins is only twelve miles away," Megan said, looking at her guidebook, "Let's stay here today and speed over to Atkins tomorrow to stay in the hotel."

"I'm with her," Jurnee said quickly. Of course, he was. We had sucked Megan into our little group, for the moment, and Jurnee was unable to hide his adoration.

"What do you think, Tamarack?" Buffalo asked.

"Yeah, sure. If we stay, I can blow dry my hair on the bathroom hand dryers again."

To my ears, Megan's words sounded more like a decree than a suggestion. Megan had a domineering, yet magnetic personality. She made decisions, and people followed. With her long, brown hair, thin face, and bright eyes, it was easy to see why she attracted attention; I was sure she had been one of the popular girls in high school. Despite being a little annoyed at and jealous of her, I liked Megan, too, and was glad to have another woman to balance our group dynamic.

The rain didn't let up the next day, but we forced ourselves to leave the comfort of Partnership. Megan carried a tiny backpack that allowed her to move fast. Hoping some of her coolness might rub off on me, I pushed myself to stick with her all morning. Despite the squish of soggy ground and the rain dripping off the shrubs down my legs, I managed to keep up.

When Megan and I walked across the road toward the Village Motel in Atkins at lunchtime, we met Grubby walking out with two scruffy dogs and his usual optimistic Grubby attitude. He said he'd found them as strays and was considering keeping them. It seemed like a huge burden to hike with two dogs and carry all their food, but he didn't seem daunted. For a moment, I missed having unconditional dog love in my life and wondered whether Grubby might want to give one of them to me, but as he hiked off with the pups into the dreary rain, I let the thought go.

The motel was nothing more than a strip of dirty rooms next to a truck stop. But it had beds and showers and was across the street from a diner. Megan and I paid for a room, and after Slow Buffalo and Jurnee arrived, we headed out for food. At the diner, I played most of Dave Matthews Band's *Before These Crowded Streets* on the jukebox as I consumed two grilled cheese sandwiches, mashed potatoes, and a giant chocolate milkshake.

After an evening in front of the TV watching *Beverly Hills, 90210* and *Party of Five*, melodramatic shows I despised but eagerly devoured in my pop culture-deprived state, I noted the weather to my companions. This time when Megan decreed we stay put in Atkins, I agreed that this was a brilliant idea. Thus began a thirty-six-hour stint of true sloth.

The room Megan and I shared became headquarters whereby we passed time with the *Rosie O'Donnell Show, ER, MacGyver,* and

Jeopardy, interspersed with a wide range of made-for-TV movies. We made periodic trips to the diner and grocery store, resuming our places in front of the TV as quickly as possible. I forced myself to make a trip to the post office, where I collected my mail, another box of cookies from Tish, and M&M's from Marilyn and Bob. I guessed that none of my family or friends would think I was particularly deserving of such treats if they saw me that day.

"You're such a dummy taco stuffer, Tamarack," Megan said as the *Sanford and Son* credits faded to a commercial.

"I know you are, but what am I?"

"What the hell is a dummy taco stuffer?" Buffalo asked, returning to our room with more snacks.

"It's what Fred Sanford calls people," Megan explained.

"And it's what Megan is!" I exclaimed.

"Quit it, kids," Jurnee hollered from his perch on the other bed. "No fighting. I'm trying to work here."

Megan and I looked at each other and laughed.

"What exactly are you working on, old man?"

"Writing in my journal."

"*That's* your journal?" Megan asked, leaning over to look at his paper. "How can you read that chicken scratch?"

"He doesn't write much," Buffalo teased. "He barely knows how to read."

"If you end up writing a book about your AT hike, you're gonna have some problems," Megan said.

"I doubt he'll write a memoir," I said. "But maybe he could do a children's book."

"See thru-hiker eat pizza," Buffalo said.

Jurnee started to chuckle in a way I had seen many times. He was trying to hold it in, but he was about to burst with laughter.

"See thru-hiker walk in rain," Megan added.

"Wait, wait," Jurnee said. He scratched something onto the paper. "See thru-hiker shit in hole," he said and held up a picture of a stick figure person over a black hole.

At that, nothing could hold back the outburst of laughter that overtook the room.

•   •   •

Even though we stopped a lot, our mileage had picked up significantly. Megan hiked as if she had more important places to be than here and now. Jurnee was dead set on sticking with her. I didn't want to be hiking alone with Buffalo, so I forced myself to keep up. And of course, where I went, Buffalo went. It seemed as if during those days he sat in Damascus waiting for me his affection had grown, and now he wasn't going to let me out of his sight. As I walked with Megan one morning, she confirmed that Buffalo had it bad for me.

"What the hell am I supposed to do about it?" I asked her.

"If he's not even willing to tell you, or talk about it," she replied, "then nothing. It's his problem."

"Well, he won't leave me alone. It's *my* problem."

"Do you like him?"

"Of course, I like him! But I don't love him. He's like my brother."

She shrugged. "Just ignore him then. Or hike faster."

She wasn't helping. I couldn't hike faster than Buffalo. He would hike all night to catch me, if I could even get that far ahead. If I slowed down, dawdling behind the others, he slowed down too, waiting for me at every overlook, road crossing, or shelter. I couldn't tell him to leave a campsite, it was a free trail after all. Either he didn't know or didn't care that I resented his constant presence.

The temperature hovered in the seventies every day. Columbine and forget-me-nots and violets bloomed alongside the path. Butterflies and bees rose from the trail as I stomped by. Virginia was a more beautiful state than I'd imagined, but aggravation consumed me. The days passed by at Megan's speed, with Buffalo loitering near me all the time. I wondered whether I was hiking my hike, or theirs. The trouble was, we had fun together, the four of us. At every shelter or stunning view, we'd laugh about some stupid thing. I didn't want to be without them. But I didn't think I could continue to be with them either.

When I made it to Pearisburg, I thought I might be able to break free from the group. Nate was on his way to hike with me for a few days, and I got a motel room to share with my brother when he arrived. Jurnee got his own room. Megan had met up with her grandpa for the evening. And Buffalo, well, he was pouting.

He didn't directly tell me the problem, but I guessed it had to do with the day before. Megan and I had hiked together, stopping at Wapiti Shelter in the late afternoon. Though Megan and Jurnee had planned to hike on to Woodshole Hostel, six miles farther, I had decided to stop at Wapiti, not wanting to spend more money. And because I planned to stop, Buffalo planned the same. But Megan's gift for persuasion won out, and as the sun sank, she and I headed to Woodshole. I wanted to let Buffalo know, so I asked Hillbilly, who was camping there, to tell Buffalo where I was going.

When Buffalo caught up to me the next day on the descent into Pearisburg, he acted aloof and grumpy. I hoped maybe his anger would make him pull away. Instead, he was glowering and surly, acting as if I'd wronged him by deviating from the plan we'd had to camp at Wapiti.

Pearisburg wasn't a hiker-friendly town, and other than the post office and the Pizza Hut, I saw little of it. I hid in my motel room to avoid accidentally running into Buffalo while waiting for Nate to arrive.

•   •   •

"My friends are already calling you Top Gun," I said to Nate as we prepared to leave the motel.

"Dude, I am *not* Top Gun," he replied.

"You're in the military. You fly planes. You're Top Gun."

"That movie was the Navy. I'm in the Air Force." I couldn't tell if he was seriously annoyed or just teasing.

"Why does the Navy even have planes? Isn't that what the Air Force is for?"

He shook his blond, buzz-cut head, clearly amazed that after growing up in a military household, I still didn't understand the military.

"Jurnee!" I exclaimed as we exited our room and met him leaving too.

"Hey, this must be Top Gun," he said. "Great to meet you."

They shook hands, but Nate gave me a snappish look.

I hadn't given Top Gun much direction on what to bring like I had for Tucker J because I thought he was acquainted with wilderness survival and would have decent gear. I realized I should have told him something when he'd showed up with a strange, canvas military pack that carried the weight above his shoulders on a metal frame. Plus, he had standard military equipment: rope, plastic tarps, canned food, a huge knife, and metal water bottles. Still, he was strong and fit. He could fly jets. He'd been through boot camp where he survived by eating ants, for God's sake. Walking a few miles in the woods would be a stroll in the park. I hadn't planned to slow my pace as I had for Tucker J, so the first day, we aimed for fourteen miles.

The hike out of town with a full pack was always a hard one, but this one was particularly steep. Top Gun told me he'd been partying with his buddies the day before and thus wasn't feeling great. He needed to stop, so I told him to drink water, and I'd meet him at the top.

When he caught up, we strolled the grassy and rock-free ridgeline, one of the flattest I'd crossed. The morning sun faded behind the clouds, which began to spit rain by the time we got to Rice Field Shelter for lunch. There, we found Jurnee, Megan, Slow Buffalo, and a thru-hiker named Towhee with her overweight beagle, Ben. Towhee was as tiny and petite as a bird, and I guessed that was where her name came from. She was probably ten years older than I, with frizzy brown hair that seemed like it was challenging to contain. Top Gun and I plopped down at the side of the shelter, unclipping our packs as I introduced him all around.

"He's not liking the trail much," Towhee said about Ben. She was from North Carolina and explained in a southern accent that her husband had recently brought the dog to join her for some hiking. She'd thought he would love the time in the woods. Ben didn't agree. "He just lies down in the trail and doesn't move. No matter what I do."

"That sounds quite funny," I said as I scratched Ben's head. "I don't blame him."

Even though we'd only gone six miles since Pearisburg, Towhee planned to spend the night; she couldn't get Ben to leave the shelter. Jurnee surprised me by deciding to do the same, even when Megan packed up and headed off for twelve more miles. Buffalo looked to see what I was doing, of course. And when Top Gun said he was good to press on, we did.

Thankfully, Buffalo didn't walk with Top Gun and me; I wanted some time to talk just with my brother. The rain dribbled, and I told him about these characters and asked him about the next steps of his training. As we walked along the ridge, the unmistakable sound of a jet quickly came upon us. We looked up to barely catch two dark planes flying low and fast.

"F-15s," he said. I didn't know how he knew but was impressed that he did. "The sound of freedom."

"You're really into this military thing, aren't you?" I said, looking at him as he gazed at the sky. "I'm proud of you."

"Well, believe it or not, I'm proud of you, too," he replied, turning to me. "I think this thru-hike thing might be a lot like pilot training," he said. "It's extremely hard, lots of people drop out, and you'll only succeed if it's the only thing in your life you want to do."

"Wow. Yeah. That's pretty much it."

"I have to admit, Sis, I really underestimated what you do out here. You put in a full day's work. I had no idea."

Despite his weird backpack cutting into his broad shoulders, we made it fourteen miles to a shallow gap in the ridge. I set up my tent as he pulled out his plastic tarps and tried to maneuver a shelter under some trees. The spot was supposed to have water, but all I could find was a mucky trickle that looked like one of the cow patties I'd see throughout Virginia. As I pumped water, my filter clogged repeatedly, and I had to clean it several times.

I scarfed down mac and cheese, and Top Gun ate some crackers and said his stomach wasn't feeling right. Whether it was dehydration, his ridiculous pack, or simply not being fit in the right ways for backpacking, he mentioned leaving in the morning. I couldn't believe it. If anyone could hike this trail, I thought it would be my boot camp brother, but he was totally wimping out.

I didn't want him to go, but after a sleepless night under his makeshift plastic tarp shelter, he had already decided. We had about seven miles across the rest of this ridge, then down to the next road crossing. There, he'd hitch back to Pearisburg and his car.

The morning's hike left me feeling sick in my own way. If he was going to leave, maybe I should leave too. I didn't like Buffalo anymore. I was sick of Jurnee's swooning all over Megan. I hadn't seen Full Moon in ages. And my body hurt. My body *hurt*.

I was weary to my core. I did the same thing every day, slugging uphill, hurting feet, breaking back. Nate was right; this had to be the only thing in your life you cared about if you were going to make it. *Is it?*

We got to Pine Swamp Branch Shelter in the lowlands and met Dogman and Alta there. I almost didn't want to introduce him to Top Gun since my brother was only going to walk two more miles before leaving. But I did, and Top Gun expressed his admiration of us thru-hikers.

Dogman shared bad news: Hercules was off the trail. He'd come down with bronchitis a while back and had finally bailed. My gut roiled. Hercules and I had crossed paths a few times since that nice day we spent together on Pond Flats, but we hadn't hiked together again. Even so, just knowing that tough old man was out there, moving north at his own pace, made me feel happy, better. If he was gone, then anybody could be gone. Including me.

Though I knew Top Gun's decision was the right one for him, I didn't like it. I walked behind him over the last two miles to the road, both of us somber. I tried not to cry. When we arrived at the road, I dropped my pack to get some water and pull out the map.

"Yeah, so, just walk that way a while," I said, pointing to the west, "and you'll eventually get to a bigger road. Someone will pick you up."

"I'm really glad I came," he said. "And I'm sorry I have to go. You're tough. Keep on truckin', and you'll get there. I know you will."

"Thanks." I looked away from him and swallowed hard. "Well, I guess you know what I do now."

He smiled, then hugged me. He heaved his military pack full of canned beans and walked away. As soon as he rounded the bend, my tears came tumbling out. I wanted to run after him.

A 1,200-foot climb up to another ridgeline awaited. I stumbled that direction, coming to a small creek where I stopped and sobbed for a few minutes. I decided I refused to climb this one. I would not do it. I would be like Ben the beagle and just lie down in the trail and not walk.

But what else was there to do? Leave? Go back?

I was lost. So, I did the only thing I could, I took one step. Then another. After only a few minutes the sound of a jet plane overtook me. It rattled the mountainside and sucked leaves off the trees, so close above. It sounded like the ones yesterday. I assumed they were F-15s, but what did I know.

"Fuck the fucking sound of freedom," I mumbled to myself.

I stopped a half-dozen times on the climb, gasping for breath through the crying, wiping my wet face with a bandana. Each stop, I insisted I would not walk anymore. I would stand and wait until someone came and installed an escalator.

Then I would take another step. I wanted someone to come up behind me so I could unload my sadness. But I didn't really want to share my upset with anyone. Certainly not Buffalo. I was alone. Or was I still hiking with these other people? I didn't know. I struggled and fought through the muggy afternoon until finally the Bailey Gap Shelter came into view. I hoped whoever was there would take my red eyes and face for overheating.

I came into the clearing and saw Grubby, oddly, sitting in a lawn chair in the shelter.

"Hey, Tamarack," he said. "How's it going? Where's Top Gun?"

I explained simply that he'd taken ill and decided to leave, trying not to restart my tears.

"Damn, well, just goes to show you can't judge a book by its cover." When he grinned, I noticed something peculiar about his smile.

"What's wrong with your mouth?"

"Oh, this little thing? I broke my front tooth in Pearisburg on a frozen Snickers bar. Stupid really."

"Gee, that sucks," I replied, looking closer. "But, it's kind of still there."

"Oh yeah, I kept it and superglued it back on."

"You what!" I couldn't keep from laughing. After Grubby explained in more detail, I told him about when I broke off my front teeth in middle school. By the time evening came, Buffalo, Biscuits and Gravy, and two southbounders from New Zealand arrived, too. In the chatter of the cooling night, some of my sadness lifted away.

.　　　.　　　.

I kept putting one foot in front of the other because I didn't know what else to do. I didn't, however, know why. My feet throbbed every day. I didn't have the blisters like I had early on, but my leg bones ached from deep within. I could comfortably walk fourteen miles in one day, but after that everything went numb. While the trail's elevation had lessened—we rarely got over 4,000 feet now—the climbs and descents hadn't. We were still doing 3,000-foot climbs and descents every few miles. Lower elevation didn't diminish the views, however, and that light, almost fluorescent, spring green had taken over everywhere. My mood never fully recovered from Nate's leaving, but I forced myself to appreciate the natural world around me as much as I could. One highlight was the Keffer Oak, a 300-year-old tree wider than three people's arm lengths around. With my cheek pressed to the scratchy bark, I hugged it for a long time.

Megan and Jurnee pulled ahead, and I found myself in a lull of hikers with Buffalo. Most others were a few days ahead or behind; I read the registers at every shelter, trying to keep track of my friends. Some days, I found an encouraging note from Grubby or Gravy, other days inspiration from people I didn't even know. Rocky and Bullwinkle, two teachers from New Jersey, wrote, "May you find in these mountains what you came for. May the challenge of this experience in its sweet simplicity enrich your lives and connect you always to this beautiful planet and all that lies beyond. May you, when stripped away from the faces we present to the world, find yourself at the center and be truly glad in that ultimate knowledge. Godspeed."

I wanted to hike my own hike, find my own place. But at every shelter, every overlook, every town, Buffalo was there, waiting. And with every stop, I became angrier, snapping over little things. Sometimes, he just followed me. Sometimes, we made plans together since I felt bad ignoring him. We were together, unspoken and unwelcomed, but together, nonetheless.

On a Sunday afternoon, Buffalo and I hitched a few miles off the trail to a grocery. As I sat outside waiting for him to complete his shopping, a man pulled up in a truck and started talking to me about a homestyle restaurant called The Homeplace. I'd read about it in Wingfoot's book; they served Thanksgiving-style meals all day long, only on Sundays. Since I didn't eat turkey or ham, I hadn't planned to go there. However, the man said they were open for another hour, and the crowd was thinning out. He made it sound delicious, so when Buffalo returned, I said I wanted to go eat. Since he never disagreed with me, we hopped in the truck with the stranger and drove off.

We were offered a table on the patio and within minutes of telling the waitress we were vegetarians, plates of mashed potatoes, green beans, pinto beans, coleslaw, biscuits, applesauce, and peach cobbler appeared. We stuffed ourselves. Though the food was warm and appreciated, sitting with Buffalo, a feeling of deep distress overcame me. My disquiet stemmed not from our pungent hiker smell permeating the airspace or our exceptionally underdressed appearance compared to our fellow restaurant-goers in their Sunday best, rather it came from the realization that I was on a faux bad date stuck in a faux bad relationship.

Buffalo hurried to get me more soda or potatoes or biscuits when we ran out. He left long awkward pauses while I stumbled over my words, not knowing how to talk to him anymore. We had once been such good friends. Now, I couldn't even stand to look him in the eye. I felt trapped. Like I'd felt my whole life.

For as long as I could remember, I'd had an irrepressible wanderlust. I'd chosen the University of Michigan because it was a good distance from home, but I needed to go farther. During my junior year, I'd been allowed to spend a semester abroad in Sydney, Australia. I went to classes at the University of New South Wales, but my real education came from my explorations of the neighborhoods, museums, and beaches. I rode public transit. I joined my classmates in bars where the minimum drinking age was eighteen and I had my first drink. I got a tattoo. I did things that all felt bold and new and not what my parents would have wanted. I loved Australia. There, halfway around the world, I felt safe. And I began to wonder if my need to travel was spurred by a need to get away from my father, from my childhood filled with rage.

When I returned home from Australia, I was aching to leave again. My cousin Emily would be spending a year of high school in Japan through Uncle Tommy's Rotary club. I figured if a fifteen-year-old white girl from Wisconsin could live there for a year, I could go visit for a week. However, I needed permission.

"I thought this might be a good time to talk about Japan," I said to my parents one evening. I leaned against the kitchen counter as Mom cooked dinner.

"What?" Dad asked from the family room, where he was sitting in front of the TV. "What are you talking about?"

I sensed this might not go well; I had to say it the right way.

"I'd really like your okay for me to go to Japan," I said.

"Why do you want to do that?" Dad said, standing up and coming into the kitchen. "You just got back from Australia. Wasn't that enough for you?"

"It might work," Mom said. Trying to hedge, placate everyone. The sound of pasta water bubbling and Mom's kitchen knife slicing through zucchini against the cutting board was suddenly very loud in the deep intake of breath before the eruption.

My father's voice rose. "No. I don't think so."

"You don't have to do anything," I said. He had paid for my college education, including my trip to Australia; I wasn't sure how much I owed him for that. "You don't have to pay for anything."

"And how do you propose to pay for this?" His voice went up again. His face reddened.

Remain calm. "I can stay with her host family."

"You have no money!"

"The flight is practically free. I'll pay you back the fifty bucks for the standby pass."

"They're my passes! I'll say who uses them."

"Steve…"

"She doesn't need to go to Japan!" he yelled, ranting to my mother as if I wasn't in the room. "Does she even know what she's talking about? She can't stay with the host family."

I felt my throat constricting, the tears coming up. He wasn't listening to me. I didn't want to fight. We'd fought so many times, over so many things.

"I'm not a kid anymore." My voice rose. "You can't keep me here forever."

"You're in my house!" he screamed. "You ungrateful brat."

I sank back against the counter, the tears coming faster, bigger. Did he think I was a possession, something he could control?

"I can't do this," I gasped through my sobs. I turned and walked out the door to the garage. I could barely breathe. I wanted to run as fast and far as I could, but it was pouring rain. Where could I go anyway?

I heard him continue to yell. Then he stepped out into the garage to come after me.

"Get back inside! Stop crying like a baby. Let's talk about this like grown-ups!"

I said nothing.

"You can't stand it when someone has a different opinion than you!" he yelled. "I have a different opinion, and you just can't stand that, can you? Didn't you learn anything in college? People can have different opinions!"

"Sure, Dad," I whispered. "You're right. I'm wrong."

"What did you say? You must really want to start a bru-ha-ha with me or something. Don't you? It's always about you. How did I end up with such a selfish daughter?"

I had no shoes or coat, but I had to get out. I was suffocating. I ran out into the rain. My feet slapped the sidewalk. Water drenched my shoulders and thighs. The August evening was warm, but the raindrops hit my skin like shards of ice. I hated this house, this street. I hated him.

I thought of my friend Don, whom I'd known since I was eight. He was also home for summer break and was a mere two blocks away. Down the side street, through the gray evening, I ran, cutting my feet on rocks and splashing through puddles. I banged on his parents' door, still gasping for breath now from the running as much as the crying.

"Amanda!" Don's mother answered the door in surprise.

"Is Don here?"

They were in the middle of dinner, but Don took me upstairs to his room. I was sobbing, soaking wet. He got a towel and wrapped me in it, hugged me, and asked me what happened.

Don's family went to the same church we did. He was funny and nice. Throughout our childhoods, he'd come to our house to hang out with my brother and me, play video games, make snow forts, and climb trees. He'd probably been over hundreds of times, but he didn't know about the anger that ravaged my family. No one did. I'd never spoken of it to anyone. I had to talk about it; I wanted to be free of my father and his control. I sat on Don's bed and poured it out. He listened, and I knew he believed me.

Don offered me dinner, and we listened to music. I had to go home at some point, but I delayed it as long as possible. A few hours later, Don drove me back through the rain to my house.

"I can't," I said, sitting in the car, not wanting to get out. "I can't go back in there."

"You can," he replied. "You can do anything."

He hugged me again. Somehow his encouragement was enough to get me out of the car.

Inside, Mom was relieved I'd returned. She took me aside and tried to explain and defend my father. I'd blindsided him with this topic. I hadn't properly thanked him for letting me go to Australia. I should be thinking about my future career, not traveling. She suggested I apologize.

"For what? What did I do that hurt him?" I demanded.

"Just give him a hug," she said, "and tell him we'll talk at a better time, when he's had a chance to think about it." She wanted me to give up my pride, my stubbornness, my anger. She wanted me—the child—to be the bigger person.

I went upstairs and knocked on his door. I found him sitting in a chair with a book. He didn't look up.

"Dad," I said, "I'm sorry."

"Fine," he said. As he briskly turned the next page of the book, I understood that I was dismissed.

•   •   •

I'd been eager to experience McAfee Knob since I'd picked up Jean Deeds' book, *There are Mountains to Climb*, ten months ago. The spot was a spectacular rocky outcrop, which looked across a ridge of green snaking north and a wide valley of farmlands far below. There were several overlooks in this region, but McAfee, the most famous, featured a long, flat rock jutting out into space. From a certain angle, a person could stand on this ledge and appear to be on a thin strip of rock overhanging nothingness.

I arrived at McAfee Knob on an afternoon dominated by the blasting sun, my blue shirt soggy with sweat. DMB had been swirling through my head all morning, distracting me from my aching legs. I was consumed by Dave's ability to create songs that voiced exactly what was in my heart. Struggling for breath, I sang "Lie in Our Graves" on a continuous loop.

Under a shady tree, I found Ironhorse and Towhee, who had sent Ben the beagle home. Ironhorse was a tall, skinny man, about my parents' age. He had a wry sense of humor and got his name from the ballcap he wore every day with the logo from the Ironhorse brewpub. Both he and Towhee radiated friendliness, and I had shared shelters with them both recently, always glad to run into them on the trail.

As I dropped my pack next to them by a shrubby rhododendron, they inquired about Slow Buffalo's location. As Towhee tried to wrangle her frizzy hair back from her face, she chirped in her southern accent that Buffalo and I were rarely seen apart. He was nearby. I could feel the weight of his expectation, the weight of his need, the weight of all the things he wanted from me that he could not say, that I could not give. If he wasn't there yet, he would be soon. As Ironhorse and Towhee finished taking their photos and moved on, I realized that they, and everyone else, saw Buffalo and me as a couple.

The thought sank me. I was at the most dramatic place on the Appalachian Trail and in the most horrid situation. Because I didn't want to cause a conflict, because I still felt a loyalty to our previous friendship, I had let the unhealthy dynamic with Slow Buffalo go on too long. I wandered onto the ledge with my journal.

Even though I'd never been there before, I thought of McAfee Knob as the epitome of the AT, and the epitome of "Lie in Our Graves." This was the top of the world. And my soul ached to experience it, alone and free, tapping into the energy of this little blue planet I loved so much. Music coursed through me as my legs dangled in the breeze. I felt untethered from the rocky ground, high above humanity, my spirit touching the sky. "I'm blown away," I whispered Dave's words.

I heard Buffalo come up behind me, and I crashed back to earth. I closed my journal, knowing he'd sit by me until I gave him my attention. I asked him to take my picture and watched him walk along the ledge with my camera to get a good shot. Heaviness, not freedom, filled me. I remembered the conversation I'd had with Gravy back on Roan Mountain. She'd said it must be nice to be alone. It must.

I stood up, hand on my hips, gazing at Virginia extending out beneath me. I looked over the edge; there was nothing below me but air. If I'd had a ledge like this when I was a depressed freshman in college, I might have taken advantage of it. Now, I didn't want to go over the edge, I simply wanted my hike back. I had gotten out from under my father's thumb, and I didn't want to fall into a similar trap on the trail. It wasn't fair to be cruel to Buffalo, or ignore him, or resent him. But I couldn't hike all the way to Maine with a doe-eyed disciple at my heels. It was time to be honest.

•   •   •

The morning I was to arrive at the interstate highway town of Troutville, I got up early and left camp before Buffalo. I flew the ten miles in, not letting him catch up. I went straight to the Best Western and got myself a room. I wasn't going to share it or invite him to join me. It was fifty bucks, but I wanted space.

Buffalo arrived and got his own room. I spent the afternoon locked away talking on the phone with my parents and friends. When I went out to the grocery and the various all-you-can-eat buffets, I never went alone with Buffalo. Ironhorse, Blisters, and Pizza Guy were in town, and I made sure they joined us. In the evening, Buffalo knocked on my door.

The moment had come.

"I'm sorry I've been like a puppy lately," he said, running his fingers through his black hair. "I'm cramping your style." He leaned against the door frame, avoiding my eyes. I cringed. Even the sycophantic way he apologized irritated me.

"Well, I think we need to each do our own thing for a while," I said.

"I know I'm bogging you down." He looked at his feet, thrusting his hands in his pockets. In one more of his awkward pauses, I could sense he expected me to deny this or comfort him somehow.

"I'm going to stay here another day," I said instead.

"I can't afford another night in this hotel." I couldn't either, but I'd told my parents about my discomfort with Buffalo, and they offered to pay for a second night, especially if it got me away from him. Despite the struggles with my dad, I appreciated that he came through for me in this way, at a time when I needed help.

"Yeah." I paused. "I know." *Say it.* "Buffalo, we can't hike together anymore."

After every fun experience we'd had, after all the laughing, the caring, the cheering each other up, it had come to this.

I didn't want to be claimed.

I was not his. I was not my father's. I was not any man's possession.

I had come to the trail for myself. And no one else. I turned and clicked the door shut. Then, I walked to the bed, stuffed my face into a pillow, and screamed. *The fucking sound of freedom.*

POOR HELPLESS FEMALE

"I knew from the day we met him that he had a thing for you," Jurnee said.

"You did not," I said as we chose a booth at Western Sizzlin'. I'd heard that their all-you-can-eat buffet wasn't as good as the one at Country Cookin', where I'd eaten yesterday, but I had to test it for myself.

"No, *you* didn't." He chuckled. "I'm not sure how you were so oblivious."

"Well, I wasn't oblivious the past few weeks. God, it was awful. Everywhere I turned, he was there, offering to do something for me, or carry something, or share his food. Felt stalkerish." The waitress came and took our drink order. "What about you? You were pretty obvious about Megan."

"Bah!" He waved my comment away as if it were nothing. "You're crazy."

"Where is she, by the way?"

"Hitched back to Trail Days with Full Moon and Bud."

I felt a tug of jealousy. Trail Days was the yearly hiker party hosted by the town of Damascus. Hikers from across the trail and country came to camp, drink, eat, and parade through the streets en masse celebrating all things AT. I had considered going back but decided to continue my forward momentum. Now, Megan was off with the cool guys I had longed to hang out with before Buffalo had hijacked my hike.

Jurnee and I made our way to the salad bar. "I hope Buffalo hasn't only gone like three miles and is waiting for me again," I said. "I'm glad he's gone."

I'd experienced a similar relief before. As a pilot, my father's job took him on overnight trips all over the country. He would fly to a city, spend the night, then fly somewhere else the next day. It was an irregular and fluctuating schedule.

As a junior pilot, he was often gone over weekends and holidays, and some of his trips kept him away from home for a week. The longer he stayed with the company, however, the more seniority he earned, allowing him to secure shorter and more preferable trips. But no matter how long each trip was, every time he bade us goodbye, the household settled into the respite.

Nate and I would go to school, as usual. Mom would go to her job and be home for us in the afternoons, as usual. We ate dinner, did our homework, watched TV, and played with friends, as usual. But our days were calm and predictable. There was an opening, a feeling I imagined a dragonfly must feel when it climbs out of its life as a nymph in the water and into the new world of the sky.

When Dad's departure came the morning after a fight, there were never apologies. He left angry. We stayed behind to heal. The ache surrounding my heart would loosen, and I could breathe. For a few days.

He printed out his monthly schedule and put it on the fridge for my mom's planning purposes, but it was very helpful for me, too; I liked knowing how many days I had to relax. As the time of his return drew near, the family tensed. Chores, homework, and cleaning were all done to perfection so he wouldn't get mad when he got home.

But no matter how clean or orderly the house was, he often walked through the door and greeted us with an unchecked attack about some small thing, like a pair of shoes strewn on the living room floor or an unclear phone message taken in haste. His colleagues and co-workers didn't know this side of him; he somehow suppressed his anger while flying those planes around the world. But once he was home again, the cork came off. We resumed tiptoeing around, trying not to shatter the fragile glass walls. And every time, as soon as he went upstairs to unpack his things, I went to the fridge to check the schedule. When would he be leaving again?

•   •   •

Escaping town after a day off was like trying to pull a suburban raccoon away from a full trash can. I trudged away from the Troutville mall, motel, movie theater, and plethora of restaurants that had been my home for forty-eight hours. Attempting to bring the town with me, I'd packed all the stuff from my maildrop, along with extra snacks and cookies. The rumble of the highway followed me for several miles, and the constant sound put me on edge.

I'd passed through a lot of fields in Virginia, full of black and white cows or leftover hay bales sagging from winter's weight, and as the highway roar receded, I came to yet another. I paused before climbing over the wooden stile and noticed that the trees were almost completely leaf-covered, such an enormous difference from a few weeks ago. I grunted as I shuffled myself over the ladder, then saw something dash across the field. A fox. No, too big. I froze and glimpsed a gray coyote zip away from me, his gait long and graceful. I wanted to keep watching him, see if I could scrounge up some inspiration from his appearance, but he disappeared into the far trees, leaving me alone.

The ten miles out of town passed in a plod of boredom. My pace slowed as I noticed a twinge of pain in my right leg. By the time I arrived at Wilson Creek Shelter, I was limping. Something in my calf had strained, and every time I flexed my foot, a sharp pain shot up to my hip. It started raining, and I scrambled into the shelter.

Biscuits and Gravy, Jurnee, and a guy named Shaggy and his dog Scooby crammed into the shelter with me to keep out of the rain. Shaggy looked like the genuine *Scooby-Doo* cartoon Shaggy; he was tall, ultra-skinny, and his medium-length, dark hair was always flopping around his face. Scooby was an adorable black Spaniel-Labrador mix.

Her sweetness reminded me of my golden retriever Peaches, who had died when I was in college. I daydreamed about getting my own dog as Scooby cuddled up next to me. I even welcomed her back after she followed Shaggy out into the rain and returned covered in mud.

The rain came down all night, and when a misty daylight woke me, I peeked out of my sleeping bag to see it still pouring. I cozied back into the warmth, vowing to get up soon, when the rain stopped. The rain, however, did not stop. I eventually visited the privy, cooked my morning oatmeal, and thought some more about leaving. When no one else made any move to leave, my motivation sank.

"Man, it sucks to have to go out in the rain to pee," Jurnee said.

"Can't we just pee off the edge of the lean-to?" Shaggy asked.

"No way! That's gross!" I exclaimed. "Go outside. A little water won't kill you."

"At least you're not hiking and soaking wet. And you don't have to stop and take your pack off," Gravy said.

"I don't take my pack off when I pee," Biscuits said. "Do you?"

"Well, it's a bit easier for boys than it is for girls, don't you think?" Gravy responded.

"Can't you girls pee with your packs on?" Biscuits asked, dumbfounded.

"I suppose it's possible." I shrugged. "There'd be lots of adjusting waistbands and hip belts. Then you've got to squat down and balance this huge monster on your back. It seems precarious."

"I think you should try it," Shaggy added. "It really does make life easier."

"Think how badass you'd be if you could pee with your pack on," Jurnee said.

Gravy and I looked at each other, doubtful. Then she answered for us both.

"We'll take it into consideration."

Hour after hour passed with everyone remaining in their sleeping bags, chatting the day away, happy to be under cover from the rain. I had to get to Waynesboro by Sunday to meet my Aunt Barbara, who was coming to hike through Shenandoah with me, but it was so much easier to stay in the lean-to. And so, I did.

•   •   •

Over the next 250 miles, from Troutville to Front Royal, the AT by and large paralleled the scenic Blue Ridge Parkway, crisscrossing back and forth numerous times. Along this stretch, I was never far from tourist attractions, day hikers, or a hitch to town for a scoop of ice cream. In Shenandoah National Park, the Blue Ridge Parkway changed its name to Skyline Drive, but the rest stops, visitor centers, and camp stores continued. What once felt like a remote footpath was now a superhighway.

I followed Slow Buffalo's progress in the registers where he occasionally left me sappy notes and urged me to catch up. The ease I felt without him was liberating, and I hoped he didn't suddenly stop and wait. If he did, he would find both my pace and motivation erratic. Some days I'd push twenty miles. The next day a meager ten. Each day I didn't know how my body would feel with my strained calf and the increasing summer heat, so I listened and followed its needs.

Though Biscuits and Gravy, Jurnee, Shaggy and Scooby, and I were all going the same pace, we didn't function as a group. There were laughs and lunches and town stops together, but I made decisions for myself alone. When Shaggy showed up at Bryant Ridge Shelter with a bottle of whiskey, Biscuits and Gravy and I happily partook, though Jurnee was nowhere to be found. When Jurnee stopped in Glasgow for a night, I planned to press on without him. His promises of restaurant food and TV swayed me, though not Biscuits and Gravy. I was beholden to no one about my last-minute decision to stay.

I was on my own and loving it. My single status, however, stirred up comments from some people. Every day I passed day and section hikers walking southbound. I often paused to say hello and share trail information. If Shaggy or Jurnee was ahead of me, the southbounder would inevitably ask, "You with that guy up ahead?"

They were always ready to answer their own question in the affirmative, nodding their heads before I responded, urging me to confirm their preferred view of reality. If one of the guys was not nearby, the southbounder would acquire a shocked tone and ask, "Are you out here all alone?" Their distress about this possibility formed deep lines on their faces.

"Well, you're just a poor helpless female," Jurnee said as we ate dinner. We were in a shelter with Shaggy and a guy named Mr. B, and I was telling them about the latest rude question from a day hiker. I knew Jurnee was being sarcastic, but the ridiculous double standard pissed me off.

"People don't ask you guys that, do they?" I demanded. I mimicked a high-pitched, day hiker voice, "Oh, you with that awesome, speedy girl up ahead? No, they don't say that! So why do they ask me?"

"I haven't known you long, Tamarack," said Mr. B, "but you don't seem like you need a man by your side to take care of you."

"Thank you, Mr. B. Is it so hard for people to understand that a woman can hike alone just the same as a man can?"

"She needed Buffalo to take care of her," Jurnee said.

"Hardly!" I threw a sock at him. "I'll bet I make it to Katahdin, and you don't. You've got no stamina."

"Hey now!" Shaggy jumped in. "I've got stamina. And plenty of it. Don't be dissing my stamina."

Jurnee doubled over, laughing.

"Oh, for God's sake," I replied. "You men. You're frickin' impossible!"

I couldn't storm away and go to my tent, because I'd sent my tent home in Glasgow. I was planning to buy a lightweight tarp in Waynesboro, but until then, I was sleeping in shelters.

I actually thought it was hilarious to call me a poor helpless female. I knew I was anything but helpless. And I knew these guys were the last people—people who knew exactly how hard this trail was and what it took to hike it—who would put a woman down for not being as good as a man. We were all walking the same miles. There was nothing about the men I had met that made them better suited or more able to hike than me. I could make it to Katahdin if I wanted to, but I felt hopeless to change a society convinced that I couldn't.

I certainly wasn't the first woman to hike the AT solo. That had been Gramma Gatewood back in the 1950s. After her children were grown, she left her abusive husband and headed to the trail with a small knapsack and basic bedroll. In the fifties, society dictated that a woman should be at home, focusing on her husband and family. To depart from that script was to challenge the social standards, and I had no doubt that Gramma Gatewood had faced disapproval.

I wanted to believe that in fifty years, society had progressed and women of my generation faced less scrutiny and had the same opportunities as men. Maybe to some extent that was true, but the day hikers' comments and the flippancy of my male friends' responses stung. For the men, it was a joke. For me, it was the norm. And the thing was, it wasn't just the norm for me, all the women I knew on the trail had stories of inequality or harassment to tell.

•   •   •

The day I climbed 4,059-foot Bald Knob was muggy, and the sun blasted down on my shoulders. I felt like I was walking in hot soup, clashing with everything. When I passed another man who with wide eyes asked if I was alone, I swore under my breath and walked past him.

Jurnee had continued to joke about the poor helpless female, and mostly, I laughed at the irony, but his jests about Slow Buffalo darkened my mood. I resented that Buffalo had sucked up so many days of my hike with his passive-aggressive attitude. He had been one of those guys who thought I couldn't hike on my own. Or he simply hadn't wanted to let me.

The 3,000-foot elevation gain up Bald Knob angered me. I wanted to hit something, shatter something. With each step, I stabbed my trekking poles hard into the ground and let out a swear. I kept my head down, watching my feet move, ignoring the pain in my strained calf.

The sweat dripped from my forehead, leaving tiny dark circles on the gray rocks at my feet. I felt constrained inside the adrenaline and anger.

Climbing this mountain was like being trapped in an impossible battle against gravity. Like being trapped in all those battles with my father: grueling, grim, relentless. My father and his anger had dominated my life forever, and I was still bound to him, to it. I was completely dependent on my parents. I called them at every town stop. They mailed my boxes and gear. I couldn't do this hike without them. I was grateful, yes, but I also loathed their control. Twenty-three years old and still fighting for every little freedom.

I fought upward until the steepness of the trail slackened and the summit of Bald Knob came into view. The undulating mountain range expanded in front of me, but I couldn't see it. Rage throbbed in my eyes. The pressure of every heartbeat pulsed through my temples. I screamed out all the ugly thoughts into the wind. I didn't care if anyone heard me. I had beaten gravity this time, beaten Bald Knob. I was not a poor helpless female. And dammit, if for no other reason than to prove them all wrong, I was going to make it to Katahdin. Alone.

•   •   •

It didn't take much to convince ourselves that a side trip to a grocery in Tyro was a great idea. Jurnee and I stood by the side of the road along VA Route 56 with our thumbs out, watching car after car pass by. It was much easier hitching by myself; together, it took almost twenty minutes.

"I think the Mau-Har Trail sounds rather nice," Jurnee said. "I'm good with blue-blazing." On the other side of this road, the AT went a roundabout six miles up and down over a mountain called Three Ridges. I didn't feel motivated to climb even one of these alleged ridges.

On the other hand, the Mau-Har Trail went past a river, waterfall, and swimming hole over only three miles to the same destination. I'd started the AT as a purist, meaning I intended to hike past every white blaze on the trail. Since side trails were often blazed with blue paint, being a blue-blazer meant taking shortcuts. The Mau-Har Trail did sound nice, but I wasn't sure I was ready to start skipping miles.

As we discussed blue-blazing pros and cons, a pale blue truck that had already passed in one direction came back and pulled over. A young man leaned across the seat and opened the door.

"God told me I have room to take you hikers wherever ya'll want to go," he said with a distinct southern accent. "So, hop on in."

Jurnee and I were grateful that God had spoken and jumped in without a second thought. The kind man introduced himself as Perry. He said he didn't usually pick up hikers, but we looked like we were in need. I told Perry that I was certainly in need. My stomach was off today, my leg was still aching, and I was getting low on ibuprofen. This was all true. However, I didn't mention the fact that really, we just wanted some Ben and Jerry's.

One pint of Coffee, Coffee BuzzBuzzBuzz! and two bottles of juice later, my calf was feeling happier, but my stomach wasn't. We sat on the front porch of the grocery with a hiker named Skid. He was in his forties and had hiked the trail before. I'd seen his name in the registers, but I was skeptical of him. I'd heard he was one of those blue-blazers or yellow-blazers like Seiko and Wee Willy the Prince of Wales, always cutting corners and pretending to be something they were not. Skid was genuine and funny, however, and by the time we left Tyro, I was ready to become a blue-blazer myself.

When we got back to the trail, the three of us dawdled on the grass at the edge of the road, adjusting our packs. As we got ready to walk, Full Moon and Sundog came speeding out of the woods onto the road.

"Oh, my God!" I exclaimed, scratching Sundog's floppy, golden ears as she jumped around me in greeting. "What are you doing here?"

"I got off the trail to visit a buddy for a few days. Just got back from Trail Days," Full Moon explained. "Been hiking with Batgirl and Skid here. I'm hoping to catch up to Grubby."

"Who's Batgirl?" Jurnee asked.

"Oh, yeah, did you know Megan? She's got this crazy new Heptawing tarp, looks like a Batplane or somethin'. I introduced her to everyone at Trail Days as Batgirl. I think the name stuck." He grinned, proud of the name he'd given her.

"That's cool," I said. "It'd be fun to see Megan again. Right, Jurnee?" I raised my eyebrows and gave him a nudge with my elbow. He rolled his eyes in response.

"You must have just missed her; she was literally minutes ahead of me." Full Moon sounded like he too had been smitten by the beauty of Batgirl.

My guts roiled again, and I regretted the coffee ice cream. It was a good day to become a blue-blazer. I slugged along behind everyone, spending a truly unpleasant hour stopping every fifteen minutes to dig a hole and empty my bowels until there was nothing left. I eventually came across the guys on a rock slab by the river, snacking and pondering whether to get into the ice-cold water.

I felt hot and crappy. I wasn't going to sit around and contemplate cooling off. I stripped off my boots, socks, and shirt, and strode over to a small outcrop that stood five feet over a wide pool. I gazed in, assessing the depth. *Good enough.* With a big breath, I launched myself over the side.

Underwater, the cold shocked my skin and shot warning messages to my brain. My limbs began to numb. The air in my lungs threatened explosion. I stopped moving and let the air raise me up. Reemerging into the heat felt like entering a whole new world. One brief moment underwater allowed for a complete reset of mind and body.

"Damn, Tamarack," Skid said when I returned to the rock. "Took a lot of ovaries to do that. I'm impressed."

"Thanks." I wiped my face with a bandana, gasping from the sting of the cold. "Ovaries are a hell of a lot tougher than balls."

•　　　•　　　•

Rusty's Hard Time Hollow was a strange oasis along the Blue Ridge Parkway, as well as my last stop before Waynesboro. Walking up to it, I questioned what I was getting into. The building was the epitome of

Appalachian ramshackle. The one-story shack had a rusted metal roof, with various rickety walls extending from the main house, creating additional rickety rooms. Brightly colored warning and attention signs adorned every space on the outside of the building. They announced notices like not to bother Rusty asking for a ride to town, how to get a bunk, and warned not to touch the gas lamps, which I thought was good advice considering the flammable nature of everything there. Rusty didn't have electricity or running water, but he had a huge barn with many bunks where hikers could crash for free.

The driveway was rocky dirt, but closer to the front door, the dirt transitioned to being covered with flattened aluminum cans. I soon learned that after every soda or beer, the can had to be placed on a post in the driveway and hit with a baseball bat. They would then be walked on or driven over. Years of this practice had turned the driveway into a clinky carpet of smashed cans.

The enclosed front porch, the only part of his house Rusty invited hikers into, was also packed with signs. More striking, however, were the endless rows of Polaroids on the walls and ceiling. He took a photograph of every hiker who crossed his threshold and had them sign their name. Neat rows of smiling hikers from the past years covered every inch. I was astonished to look over the rows, seeing Slow Buffalo, Towhee, Ironhorse, Blisters, Pizza Guy, and many others I had come to know on this journey. It was an incredible catalogue of faces.

Skid had pushed on to catch Batgirl, but I found Full Moon and Sundog, Jurnee, Biscuits, and Gravy all hanging out at Rusty's. Wee Willy the Prince of Wales and some other yellow-blazers were also in residence, claiming they hiked there. Considering that I hadn't once seen Wee Willy actually on the trail, I remained skeptical.

Rusty himself was a true Appalachian Mountain man. He spoke with a thick accent I couldn't always understand, and his sparse white beard stuck out raggedly all over his face. He was boorish and made rude jokes, but he also was generous, cooking dozens of pancakes for us all in the morning. He had a free Hard Time Hollow t-shirt for the one-hundredth hiker of the year, which turned out to be Jurnee, who had signed in immediately before I did. I insisted that the shirt should be mine because if I hadn't stopped to pee that last time I would have been here first. But when Jurnee wouldn't relent, I purchased my own t-shirt, knowing that I couldn't leave the Hollow without a memento.

I played basketball with Biscuits, Gravy, and Full Moon for much of the afternoon. Sundog lay in the shade catching up on her sleep. I flirted with Full Moon and wondered if he saw anything remotely attractive about me. I was not a poor helpless female, and I did not need a man to take care of me, but I wanted Full Moon's attention. When he mentioned he didn't have a girlfriend back home, I realized I would like to take on that role. He was cute and confident, but more importantly, he was making an honest attempt to change the world for good. He was a kindred spirit, maybe a soul mate. However, he was headed back home to Pittsburgh to go to a Dave Matthews Band concert with some friends in about ten days.

"I'm on a quest for Grubby," Full Moon told me as we took turns with the basketball. "I've got to catch him again before I leave."

"But you're coming back to the trail. Right?" I asked. "After Pittsburgh?"

"Yeah, probably. Maybe." He took a shot, then reminded me he had already hiked the northern half of the AT in 1996 with his then-girlfriend. He only needed to make it to Harpers Ferry, the halfway point, to be an official 2,000-miler. "I'm gettin' kinda low on funds. I should work for a while."

I didn't respond but grabbed the rebound and made my own shot. The ball circled the rim, then fell out. Another miss. I suddenly had so much I wanted to say to him. And no idea how to say it.

"Get to Harpers Ferry with me, and you can come to Pittsburgh to see Dave," he said.

"Wow, that'd be awesome," I replied. "I'd love to."

But that was impossible. He'd need to do at least twenty miles a day if he was going to catch Grubby and make it to Harpers Ferry before he got picked up. There was no way I could or would put myself through that. I wasn't going to start hiking Full Moon's hike now that I had gotten back to my own.

Since Rusty didn't allow dogs in the barn, Full Moon slept in the kennel with Sundog. He loaned me his Walkman for the night along with a tape of Dave Matthews Band's *Live at Red Rocks*. I lay in bed, headphones on my ears, thinking about men.

I hadn't come out here looking for a boyfriend. I didn't want a guy hovering over me, but I also didn't want to spend my time pining over one. Maybe I would someday get the chance to spin in Full Moon's orbit, maybe tomorrow we'd leave Rusty's, and he would disappear from my life forever. I couldn't control anything that happened on the trail. For tonight, I cuddled up with Dave, letting the music fill my heart, and hoping that whatever this trail gave me next, I would walk through it to another day.

DANCING NANCIES

With summer's surge across the land, it was time to rid myself of all my cold weather gear and lighten my pack, and the large town of Waynesboro, Virginia was the place to do it. I took off some pack flaps I didn't need and sent them, along with my fleece clothing and my winter sleeping bag, back to New Jersey.

The soles on my boots had worn thin, and I worried about having good traction. Plus, my feet had expanded further and throbbed as if it was the first day I had walked anywhere. It was a risk starting over with new boots, but I hoped the soft Salomons I bought at the outfitter wouldn't take long to break in. I also found an A-frame camping tarp that didn't have a floor or side walls. It assembled using my trekking poles rather than tent poles, making it an ultralight addition to my gear. After all the adjustments, my pack still bore down on my back, but life seemed lighter without all that excess.

I spent a day off hanging out with Biscuits and Gravy waiting for Aunt Barbara to arrive. When Jurnee got to town, he and I went to see *Star Wars: A Phantom Menace*, which had been released a week before. I wasn't old enough to have appreciated the original *Star Wars* trilogy in the theaters, so I was looking forward to experiencing the Skywalker saga on the big screen. It was a relative letdown but sitting in an air-conditioned theater in a galaxy far, far away from the Appalachian Trail for a few hours refreshed me.

Barbara arrived in the late afternoon, exhausted and saying that the long drive had turned her into a "dishrag." I warned her that a long drive was a cakewalk compared to the AT, and by next week she'd have a new meaning of the word dishrag. From her tall height to her bold and uncompromising way of engaging in the world, my aunt was the near opposite of my mother. Where my mother was the demure, proper, little lady, family legend held Barbara as the wild and rebellious big sister. I'd always admired her and been intimidated at the same time.

We spent the night at the Comfort Inn, sorting through her gear and looking at the maps. As had happened with Tucker J, I knew my trail life was going to change now that my aunt was there, but I didn't stress about it as I had in Tennessee when I'd left Jurnee and Buffalo. Everyone would get ahead of me again, and I gave up all hope that I'd make it to Harpers Ferry to go to Pittsburgh with Full Moon. Even so, I was hiking my own hike. And right now, my hike included my aunt.

In the morning, Barbara and I drove Jurnee back to Rockfish Gap and took pictures with him before he sped away. She and I filled out hiker permits, much like the ones in the Smokies, and then set off into Shenandoah National Park.

Not a cloud smudged the sky. The midmorning sun shined through the canopy above, dappling the forest around us in changing patterns of light and dark. The rhododendrons were blooming and around every turn stretched another long corridor of green and pink. The scent of fluffy flowers permeated the air. Beautiful and verdant, the trail here was tame compared to everywhere I'd hiked so far. There were plenty of ups and downs, but they were short and gradual, and I understood why people put in high miles. I could have cruised this section as if on wheels, but our seven-mile walk took much of the day. Like when I had hiked with Tucker J, I found a different kind of walking; I stopped to look deeper and appreciate the natural world.

I couldn't resist teasing Barbara, however. "You sure are slow, Auntie," I said when we stopped for lunch atop 2,885-foot Bear Den Mountain.

"Let's see how fast you hike when you're nearly sixty," she snipped. She wore a white visor to shield her face from the sun and wisps of her graying, brown hair stuck to her sweaty cheeks. She groaned and dropped her pack. "I figured I would slow you down. I was thinking as I drove here that my trail name should be Aunt Tortoise."

I agreed that sounded appropriate and assured her that there was no reason to hurry. Summer was here, and we should enjoy it.

I'd heard that a healthy population of bears lived in Shenandoah and that the park required hikers to use a bear pole to hang food at night. When we arrived at Calf Mountain Shelter, our first destination, Aunt Tortoise and I stood puzzling over the contraption.

In the clearing stood a metal pole about fifteen feet tall with four metal prongs angling upward from the top. We were supposed to use a metal rod with a hook to loop the food bag's cord over one prong. This would leave the bag dangling high above us, theoretically out of reach of a bear. A nice idea, which in practice was almost impossible. The rod bent under the weight of our heavy food bags and it took a dozen tries by each of us and twenty minutes of exasperated laughter to succeed. When we stood back and looked at our work, it was obvious that the bags hung low enough for any determined bear to reach our food easily.

The air cooled that evening, bringing relief from the sultry day. We sat inside the stone shelter, and while Aunt Tortoise sorted her gear, I told her about AT life. She'd brought with her a tiny voice recorder and intended to keep journal entries that way. I thought it was brilliant that she could walk and talk and considered getting one for myself.

Several hikers I'd heard of, but never met, joined us in the shelter that night: Hurdler, Cropduster, Dumptruck, and Sunny P, who was another solo female hiker that guys went gaga over. Aunt Tortoise and I chatted with them, but we mostly turned our attention to each other. As we cozied into our sleeping bags on the hard shelter floor, I hoped that the slow pace, tame trail, and lack of friends wouldn't make the coming week boring.

•　　　•　　　•

The AT paralleled Skyline Drive for most of the scenic highway's 105 miles through Shenandoah. Despite the regular road crossings, the forest blossomed with wildlife. When I paused to wait for Aunt Tortoise, I searched the trees for songbirds. I stumbled across several deer and rabbits scampering away from the trail. I scared up a mother grouse and her half-dozen babies. Everywhere I turned, another creature busied itself with its summertime pursuits.

Aunt Tortoise and I ambled together, coming off the trail to Skyline Drive at Browns Gap. I spotted a trash can by a small parking area and headed that way to dump our trash. As I approached, a loud crash ahead startled me, and I looked up into the trees. A large black blur clattered high above, smacking and cracking each branch on its way downward. I couldn't see its head, but I knew it was a bear.

"Oh, my God!" Aunt Tortoise exclaimed as I mumbled, "Holy shit."

She turned and ran back the way we had come. I froze and watched the animal as it jumped to the ground and galumphed away. It was four times bigger than the garbage can and vastly adept in the woods. I didn't have time to worry whether it would hurt us because it disappeared within minutes of when I first heard it.

"It's gone," I called after my aunt, chuckling at her hasty retreat. "That was cool, wasn't it? That's something to talk about on your tape."

She crept back to the road and stood behind me, looking toward where the bear had been.

"I'm not going that way," she said.

"What do you mean? That's the trail."

"That's where the bear went. I'm not going."

"Barbara, it's gone further up the trail by now." I insisted. "It's not going to come back and eat you."

"It's farther, not further," she corrected me.

I gaped at her.

"Farther is distance, further is time or metaphysical space," she explained as she shook her head. "And I did not come out here to get mauled by a bear."

Aunt Tortoise used to be an English teacher and apparently believed that even in a life-or-death situation, good grammar was essential. I stifled my laughs and did my best coaxing. Eventually, when no bear sounds came from the woods, she agreed to walk in that direction. But over the next four miles to Loft Mountain Campground, my aunt's fear turned her from a tortoise into a roadrunner.

•   •   •

The cohort around us shifted again, and our path merged with new hikers. Jurnee had pulled ahead but kept leaving me notes in the registers. I missed him, but I was happy he was going his own speed. Angel was a blond woman from Germany who couldn't have been more than twenty. She was traveling with a bulky fellow named Plato and his tiny black dog, Sadie. He was in his mid-thirties, and though Angel acted aloof toward him, he was never far from her side. They slept in the same tent and appeared to be a couple, but when I watched their interactions, I got the weird feeling that Plato was obsessed with her. He was constantly touching her and offering to help with whatever she was doing. Maybe I was still recovering from my time with Slow Buffalo, but I wondered more than once whether she wanted that much doting.

Charlie Hustle, Bud from Oregon, Fairweather, and Dogman and Alta caught up. I was happy to hang out with Kaybek again, whose English had improved significantly since I'd seen him in Damascus. His French accent was very sexy, and he was far cuter than I remembered, wearing the same khaki shorts and dark blue t-shirt every day, his dirty blond, rumpled hair held back by a bandana. Like many of the men, Kaybek shaved sporadically, and his disheveled beard attractively framed his face. He was a fast hiker but hadn't been feeling well lately. His pace now matched Aunt Tortoise's, and we shared many stops and shelters with him.

Despite the mice, Aunt Tortoise preferred sleeping in the shelters, so I hadn't yet set up my new tarp. While simpler, the shelters also meant that we were always surrounded by other hikers cooking, snoring, shuffling their gear, and now that the sun set later, arriving late in the evening.

I was always glad to see Bud wandering into camp at dusk, just before daylight evaporated. It was his favorite time of day to walk, and he wrung out every moment of the evening that he could. I learned that his real name was Mitch and began calling him Knight Rider, after the old 1980s TV show. A title he heartily adopted.

At Hightop Hut, Aunt Tortoise and I reclined in our sleeping bags on the lower bunk as others—Kaybek, the Pocono Professor, Bearpaw, Argonaut—filled in the spaces all around us. The sun was down, and I tried to ignore the hubbub. Argonaut, however, was setting up his gear directly above us, standing on the edge of the platform near our feet. As he moved back and forth, carefully avoiding stepping on us, we could only see his legs.

Kaybek, lying next to Aunt Tortoise, switched on his flashlight. "You see, ladies, the beautiful legs of Argonaut," Kaybek said in his prominent French accent, turning the spotlight on Argonaut's legs and moving it up and down. Tortoise let out a hearty laugh, and I spluttered the water I was drinking. Argonaut was an attractive guy and had become known for the ultra-short running shorts he hiked in and his long, toned, and gorgeous legs.

The light went off as Argonaut stepped away from the platform. When he came back, Kaybek shined the spotlight again. "For your pleasure, ladies. For your pleasure," he said, sending us into uncontrollable laughter.

The third time Argonaut stepped up to the bunk and stood there, Kaybek shined the light, then said, "Oh no, ladies, too many times, I do this. I begin to like it myself."

Aunt Tortoise and I couldn't contain ourselves, and I heard Argonaut chuckling as well. He did a little kick with his heels as he climbed up to bed for the last time. It took a long time for the shelter to calm down for the night. When the laughter, rustling, and lights all stopped, I finally dozed off, glad for the hilarity and the camaraderie with Aunt Tortoise and Kaybek.

• • •

Hiking through Shenandoah on Memorial Day weekend gave me a new appreciation for Yogi Bear. The trail was a long corridor of green broken up by car campgrounds, picnic areas, camp stores, and visitor centers, all hopping with vacationers and day hikers. Though my pack was stuffed with regular trail food, I loathed the thought of passing up the sandwiches, fries, ice cream, and smoothies that were available at a moment's notice. Sometimes, I sat on a bench near the store entrance waiting for one of the vacationers to approach me. They were astounded at my trek, my large pack, and my pungent smell. The adoration and amazement made me feel like a cross between a zoo animal and a rock star. As I answered their questions, inevitably, their sympathies would get the best of them, and they would offer food: chips, soda, bananas, and once, oddly, a can of peaches.

The vacationers had strong preconceptions of the AT, and words that always came up in these conversations were *loneliness, solitude, isolation*; words that people often associate with nature. I told them I was rarely alone, and that there were a lot of other thru-hikers. I also wanted to point out the fact that we were sitting in a busy parking lot next to a store jam-packed with people buying overpriced food and plastic crap from China. But I restrained myself, knowing my judgment of them would be off-putting.

And indeed, I was judgmental of their way of experiencing wilderness, as I had been at NOC. They stayed in hotels and RVs, never feeling the press of hot air on their sweaty skin. They drove Skyline Drive, stopping at the overlooks to gaze out from their cars, never feeling their hearts beat fast or their lungs gasp for breath. They lounged in picnic areas enjoying their coolers of beer on mowed grass kept green with herbicides. Society told them that these experiences were nature experiences. But I wanted to scream at them to get out of their cars and away from the pavement. To walk through Shenandoah and breathe in the earthy smells. To *feel* the wilderness. I had to wonder if Shenandoah even counted as wilderness, though, with people, cars, and buildings everywhere.

Aunt Tortoise and I crossed paths with another black bear one morning after we'd left the shelter. It barreled past us, not twenty feet ahead, careening down the hill. It shocked and exhilarated me, making my breath catch and my body go rigid. That bear was wildness incarnate. And yet, it lived side by side with the immense humanity of this park. Was it possible that wilderness and humanity were not mutually exclusive?

The summer days were long, full, and warm. Aunt Tortoise and I traveled companionably along the gentle trail past all the human constructs. We slept late into the mornings, waiting until the others had moved on before making breakfast and packing up. Most days we didn't leave camp before nine-thirty. We puttered through the park, the heat driving us to stop at creeks and waterfalls where we splashed our faces and soaked our bandanas to cool us over the next few miles.

At Lewis Falls, Aunt Tortoise convinced me to trek a steep winding stone staircase down to see a supposedly stunning waterfall. A breeze blew off the water and up the gorge, cooling us where we sat on a stone wall in the shade. It was indeed refreshing, but what we gained from the respite, we lost on the half-mile climb back up the stairs.

When we neared Lewis Mountain Campground, I felt a surge of energy and needed to fly for a change, to burn off the recent days' ice cream and chips. I pulled ahead of Aunt Tortoise, telling her I would wait amongst the RVs and playgrounds. I sped along, my muscles extending with strength, and feeling relief that I could still move fast.

As I approached the campground, I heard the faint clank and clatter of car-camping, then a rhythmic thumping. The rising, sporadic beat sounded familiar; I knew that drumming. My legs carried me faster, and I came within sight of some RVs. I knew that music because I'd listened to it over and over the night I borrowed Full Moon's Walkman. It was "#36" from *Live at Red Rocks* by the Dave Matthews Band. I heard

Dave's voice call out across the campground, "Honey, honey ..." I dropped my pack and began to dance on the trail. It was one of those jam songs that looped around and around as the musicians took turns letting loose on their instruments: violin, saxophone, guitar. I twirled and sang in the sunshine, soaking in the pure joyful song, the synchronistic moment. I wouldn't get to Pittsburgh with Full Moon, but I raised my arms and spun under the green trees, surrounded by rosy rhododendrons, dancing with Dave. Whether this was wilderness or humanity or some blend of both, I felt a deeper connection to the forest, to myself. Maybe there was a place for car-camping after all.

•   •   •

At Pinnacle Picnic Area, Aunt Tortoise, Kaybek, and I found a spot to sit on the meticulously mowed grass under a huge oak tree. My feet ached; my big toenails were still blackened from the previous boots. I couldn't yet tell if my new boots were a positive change or not, but I untied them and slipped on my sandals. We had six miles to Thornton Gap where Aunt Tortoise would be picked up and returned to Waynesboro. The smell of barbecued food floated like smog over the picnic area, and I realized how hungry I felt.

"I really want some potato salad right now," I whined.

"Ah, classic American food, oui?" Kaybek asked.

"Yes. It's what everyone eats on Memorial Day."

"We must get some for you," Kaybek said. He pushed his sunglasses up onto his head, stood, and pulled me up too. "We do this by begging, yes?"

I smiled as we walked away from where Tortoise rested with Angel, Plato, and Sadie who had walked up. "We do look ragged and desperate. Someone's bound to offer us something."

"These people, they all have this potato salad. We ask nicely?" he asked. When I shrugged, he went on. "You are prepared to sell your body for this salad?"

"I can't imagine trading my stinky, emaciated body for potato salad!" I rolled my eyes. "You're insane."

"Then, the money. You get the money, and we buy the salad."

Kaybek never broke a smile, but I could see the laughter in his blue eyes. He had a perfect comeback for everything, a comment on any topic. I, however, couldn't stop laughing as we walked around gawking at the picnickers. I liked Kaybek. He was super cute, as tall as me, and incredibly funny. I'd heard he'd had a fling with Bee a while back. And just the other day Angel had been helping him write a letter to a German girl he knew. He'd been flirting with Angel, which pissed off Plato. He flirted with every girl. He flirted with me too, but I doubted he thought about me in that way since most guys didn't.

Vacationers crowded every grill and table like ants, but we had no luck acquiring potato salad. We didn't return to Aunt Tortoise empty-handed, though, and shared two large pieces of vanilla cake that a friendly family had given us.

An hour later, Aunt Tortoise and I arrived at the Pinnacle, a 3,730-foot-high mountain with an exceptional rocky overlook. After a week of talking and laughing, we sat silently for a while. The valleys of Virginia spread out below, carpeted with summer's warm green. The mountains through Shenandoah were smaller, but the views were just as magnificent. I didn't think I would ever get enough of being thousands of feet high, looking down over the earth. From here, the world was so open.

I had taken my aunt's recorder earlier in the day to narrate the trail for a while and returned it to her now. It would be fascinating to listen to that tape a year from now. I wasn't sure how to say goodbye. We'd moved so slowly through Shenandoah, and yet the time had slipped by too fast. I felt closer to her after this week together and knew I was lucky to have an aunt and uncle who loved me the way that she and Tucker J did, but I didn't know how to fully express my gratitude. A few miles later when we parted, I hugged her and simply said, "I love you."

•   •   •

The day after Aunt Tortoise left, I pushed twenty-four miles, my longest day yet. I wanted to get out of the park, get through the next town, and leave Virginia. Shenandoah made me feel like a slug stuck on a salt pile, and with Aunt Tortoise gone, I needed to move.

I'd been following everyone's progress in the registers. Jurnee, Full Moon, Grubby, Biscuits, and Gravy were all days ahead now. I'd had an awkward run-in with Slow Buffalo back at Big Meadows Campground. He'd come up to me and interrupted the conversation I was having with some day hikers. He was with his mom, who was returning him to the trail after a few days off at home. He introduced us, then stood awkwardly next to me saying little. I was viscerally reminded of how frustrated I got with him and his nervousness near me. I excused myself as quickly as I could. Now, he was only a day ahead, and I hoped he didn't slow down.

Kaybek stuck with me, and that night, we stopped at Tom Floyd Wayside. In the morning, we'd have a short three miles into Front Royal. We sat side by side in the shelter, leaning against the back wall with our journals.

"I've got to get my mail drop. It'd be nice to do laundry, too," I said. As the words came out, I felt very bored with the mundanity of it all. Every town with the same schedule, every mail drop containing the same food. I was closing in on halfway and wondered if boredom might be what prevented me from making it to Katahdin. "What's your plan for Front Royal?"

"Front Royal, oui. I have big plan," he responded, jotting notes in his journal. "I will go to hospital after eating too much food at le buffet."

"You're too much."

"What you write in your journal?" he asked, inching closer to me.

"I don't know. Stuff. Mileage. The funny things you say. I wrote yesterday about my big toenail coming off. That was interesting." His pretty smile lit up his face. "What about you? What do you write?" I asked.

He leaned his journal so I could see the pages. "I write le Français." He grinned.

"Uh-huh. Thanks for that." I shook my head, feeling his arm brush against mine.

Even if everyone else was far ahead, being with Kaybek felt good. It crossed my mind that this would be a good time to hook up if we were going to; we were alone in the shelter. But, we both stank, and the exhaustion of twenty-four miles sent me into my sleeping bag alone.

In the morning, we were up early and did three miles together in less than an hour. At the road, I saw the typical wooden sign indicating trail mileage and information. This sign, however, had a white piece of notebook paper taped to it. I went to inspect it and found the paper labeled *FOR: Bud from Oregon, Tamarack, and Sunny P.*

I snatched it up and opened it. It was from Full Moon and spelled out his plans for getting off the trail and how to get a hold of him if we wanted to go to Pittsburgh. There was a friend's phone number and the date he was leaving. *Today.*

"Oh, my God!" I started jumping up and down. "Oh, my God! I'm going to see Dave!"

"Dave? Who is Dave?" Kaybek asked, looking puzzled.

"Dave! Dave Matthews! Holy shit this is amazing!" I grabbed his arms and shook him. "We're going to see Dave!"

A million thoughts rushed through my mind as we stepped onto the road to get a hitch. I had to call Full Moon's friend Jen and let her know I wanted to go. *Where is Bud?* Maybe in Front Royal, but I didn't know. And I didn't know where Sunny P was.

The diner listed in the guidebook claimed to have good pancakes, and we asked our hitch to drop us there. When we pulled up, the place looked like it had more cockroaches than customers, so Kaybek and I walked back through town, figuring McDonald's pancakes would suffice. There was a pay phone outside the McDonald's, and I decided to call Jen and find out if Bud had called, too. As we crossed the parking lot toward the golden arches, the glass door opened, and Bud stepped out.

I let out a small scream, then charged up to him. "Are you going?"

"Hey, hello," he replied, taken aback at my forcefulness. "Going where?"

"To Dave! Did you see Full Moon's note?"

"No, man. What note?"

I pulled it out and handed it over. As he read, a big grin spread across his face. When he was done, he looked at me and let loose a deep ha-ha, and said, "Hell, yeah, I'm going."

"We don't have tickets," I said.

"We'll get them there," Bud responded. "It's meant to be."

"Oh, my God! We're going to Dave!" I jumped up and down as Bud laughed.

"Who is this Dave Matthews?" Kaybek asked, watching me questioningly.

"Only the best, most gorgeous, most fabulous musician ever!" I said. "You should come with us. It's going to be so fun!"

"We won't hike these days," Kaybek said.

"No," I said, "but we'll be back soon. It'll be so worth it."

While I continued to try to convince Kaybek to come with us, Bud called Jen. Full Moon's friend, Mike, was picking him up right then in Harpers Ferry. We were about an hour's drive south of there, but Full Moon and Mike would swing down to get us.

With the ride arranged, all Bud and I had to do was wait. McDonald's was right next door to Burger King, and Bud, Kaybek, and I spread out on the tiny strip of dirt between the restaurants. The day turned hot, and it was the only spot in the vast range of parking lots with a tree. Fairweather and his dog, Elwood, joined us. Then Argonaut arrived, wearing the big headphones he hiked with, his legs long and beautiful as ever. We all lounged under the shade of the one tree, leaning on our packs, snacking, and doing nothing.

"From the moment I saw that note, I knew I was going to see Dave," I said aloud to no one in particular. I'd thought stumbling across Dave's "#36" playing in a campground was synchronistic, but the note, today, this timing was blowing my mind.

When Mike and Full Moon pulled up in a brown sedan, the door opened and Sundog leaped out. She zealously waggled around Bud and me. I turned to Kaybek.

"Please come. You'll love Dave." I didn't know whether Kaybek would actually love Dave or not, but I urged him anyway.

"Ah, yes, I will love Dave. I go."

With that, we threw our dirty backpacks into the trunk and piled into the car. I had no idea how the next few days would play out, where I'd sleep or eat or shower, but it didn't matter. It was me, four guys, and a golden retriever on a pilgrimage to see Dave.

I'd never felt so free.

• • •

We slept at Full Moon's parents' house that night. But not before a long evening of drinking, smoking, eating, and flirting at the Quaker Steak and Lube, the bar where Full Moon worked before leaving for the AT.

In the morning, we packed up our gear and our serious hangovers and drove to Raccoon Creek State Park Campground near the arena where Dave would be performing. Bud, Kaybek, and I set up our tents together, and a bunch of Full Moon's Lube friends got sites nearby. Instead of tenting with us, however, Full Moon settled into Jen's 1970s, school-bus-orange, pop-top VW van. He claimed they weren't a couple, but with only one fold-down bed inside, the relationship was obvious. I was bummed that nothing was going to happen between Full Moon and me, but the excitement of the upcoming concert and the attention from Bud and Kaybek allowed me to let it go. Plus, it was impossible to dislike Jen, a petite young woman who welcomed and included us all and adored Full Moon.

One party rolled into another when later we piled into Jen's van again and drove to the amphitheater. Pulling into the dirt parking lot, I was stunned to see row after row of metal cars glinting in the sun. People strolled through the dusty heat, meandering along the aisles with plastic cups of beer. Puffs of smoke wafted up from the spaces between the cars. The endless humanity of the place overwhelmed me.

Jen and Full Moon set up their camp chairs next to the van, and their Lube friends drifted over. Jen brought out an astonishing spread of food that she must have worked on for days: burritos, spinach dip, cheeses, salsas, chips, bread, and veggies. When she invited us to dig in, she didn't understand the damage four thru-hikers could do to a table full of food.

Bud, Kaybek, and I still needed tickets, so we went to the box office first. The line was thirty people deep and wasn't moving. We wandered the rows of cars to see if anyone had extra tickets. We found not a single one.

"What if we no get tickets?" Kaybek asked.

"We're going to get tickets," I said. "This whole weekend is meant to be."

"Let's check the box office again," Bud suggested.

It had been twenty minutes since our last swing by, and this time there was no line. We walked up to the counter, asked for three tickets in the lawn seating, and with the swipe of a credit card, it was real. *I'm going to be in the same space as Dave Matthews.*

Back at the van, everyone, Full Moon in particular, had begun to slip into a delirious drunken daze. I'd decided not to drink much, partly because I was still hungover from the night before at the Lube, but also because this was my first time seeing Dave. I wanted to be awake for the experience. Waiting for the show to start, Bud, Kaybek, and I stood between the rows of cars kicking around my hacky sack.

"What's your real name, Kaybek?" I asked.

"Jean-François," Kaybek responded.

"Dude, if you told me six months ago I'd be hanging out at a Dave Matthews concert with a dude named Jean-François," Bud said, "I would have told you, you were insane. But you're pretty awesome, man."

"Well, what kind of name is Mitch? Knight Rider!" I said to Bud. "Even though you're more of a Bud." He stepped back from the hack circle and took a drag off his joint and nodded. "Full Moon is Paul," I went on. "Isn't that hilarious? Come to think of it, isn't it weird that we didn't even know each other's names before?"

"We don't need to know our real names," Bud said. "I mean, Tamarack *is* your real name. The AT is the real world, man."

He had a point. More than ever before in my life I felt like whom I was supposed to be.

"All this shit, these cars, the excess, it's all just a fucking lie. We're just fucking sheep following the herd." He took another hit and handed the joint to me. I passed it to Kaybek. "The AT breaks all those rules."

I didn't know Bud was so philosophical, in a profane kind of way. He presented himself as a tough man with his bald head and harsh words, but I could see past that into the sweet gooey guy inside. After the short time we'd spent together through Shenandoah, I adored him.

"We hack, or we talk about sheep?" Kaybek said, giving the joint back to Bud. Then he tossed the hacky sack over to me. I kicked and sent it flying away from the circle.

When the time came to enter the arena, Full Moon, Kaybek, and the Lube friends were drunk and dawdling. Bud and I left them and dashed inside to find a spot near the front of the lawn. I grabbed his arm and shook it, the giddiness overtaking me despite the lack of drugs in my system. We looked at each other and laughed in anticipation, both glad to be sharing this moment with each other. The others eventually found us and stood nearby.

Darkness engulfed the sky and stage. There was nothing. Then, there was Dave.

A roar came up from the crowd and I heard myself start to scream too. The music began quietly, softly. It built a slow, beautiful cacophony of sounds that streamed out over the heads of thousands of people. Dave sang, "Nine planets…," and my body began to sway.

I let go and enter a world where rhythm dominates, where there is no I, where melody and song resonate inside, and we are all simply a part of sound. The music vibrates through me, and my limbs swing about. I forget time and place.

And I dance.

Every now and then, in a pause between songs, Dave would say something to the crowd. I came to my senses and looked around at Bud and Kaybek. I noticed the massive throng surrounding me, astonished that somehow, the Appalachian Trail had brought me here. Then the music would pick back up, and I would lose myself again and dissolve into the joy, the love, the music.

And I dance.

·   ·   ·

"What did you think, Kaybek?" I asked as we sat around the campground in the morning. Water was heating on the fire for coffee and oatmeal. "It was amazing right?"

"Ah, yes. Good. Dave is good."

"I hope he plays 'Dancing Nancies' tonight," I said, turning to Bud.

"Wait. We go again tonight?" Kaybek asked. "One concert is not enough?"

"Whatever he plays, man," Bud replied, "it's gonna be awesome."

"Of course, we're going tonight," I said to Kaybek. "You knew that, right? Two concerts."

"Ah, yes." He nodded but looked puzzled at our enthusiasm. "What is this Dancy Nancy?"

Before I could answer, Full Moon stumbled over from Jen's van.

"You look like death, man," Bud said. "You didn't see much of the concert, did you?"

"What!" I exclaimed. "Were you too drunk?"

"Dude, it was that last smoke," Full Moon croaked. "I ended up hurling."

"Oh, my God, your first Dave concert, and you didn't even see it?" I laughed loudly. "I can't believe you!"

"Har-har. Laugh it up."

"Okay!" And I laughed again.

The day passed much like the previous: morning in the campground, talking, hacking, eating; afternoon in the parking lot, talking, hacking, drinking. The second concert moved me just as intensely as the enthusiastic band members melded their individual creativity together to make passionate and profound art that poured over the crowd. The previous night's euphoria stretched through the evening. Afterward, as we stumbled back to the van, I slipped my arm through Bud's, and we recapped the setlist. My ears rang. My heart soared. I longed for more Dave Matthews Band.

I was exactly three months from my start date at Springer. Back then, I could never have predicted that I would one day be in western Pennsylvania, nowhere near the Appalachian Trail. I thought about serendipity. About hiking my own hike. About accepting trail magic. But mostly, I thought about these people I had come to know, how I loved them, and what it meant to trust.

VANILLA WISDOM

Sweat ran down my thighs; droplets dribbled past my knees and streaked through the layer of accumulated dirt on my calves. The air was stifling, oppressive, crushing. The days in Shenandoah had been warm, but today was like walking in a furnace with nowhere to hide. Even my chin was sweating. At the end of Virginia came the Devil's Racecourse—an aptly nicknamed section of trail whose elevation profile replicated life in Hell. The ups and downs came in quick, steep, and nauseating succession. The route and heat sucked out every ounce of Dave euphoria I had left. *Misery, thy name is AT.*

Full Moon had dropped off Bud, Kaybek, and me in Front Royal and returned to Pittsburgh, his Appalachian Trail journey complete. It was strange to think of the AT without him on it, but I knew fate would lead us to each other again. He inspired me to do more, to be more, and I trusted our connection would continue beyond the trail.

Kaybek sped ahead, but Bud and I stayed close for a few days and arrived together at Bear's Den Hostel, an old stone building that the ATC had renovated. A handful of hikers lounged on the breezy porch, eating, reading, and staying out of the worst of the heat. The only one I recognized was Thor, the teenager I had met back in Georgia, who was now hiking without Mom. Bud immediately decided to stay when we discovered that the bunk room was housed in the damp, cool basement. I hesitated. I'd only gone seven miles that morning, and the past few days, my mileage had been low—ten, twelve, thirteen miles. We were close to Harpers Ferry; I felt it calling to me, just a twenty-mile skip away. And even though this hostel was inexpensive, I wasn't sure I could keep spending money the way I had been.

Last winter, I'd worked out the average cost of hostels and motels but scheduled in only a few zero-mile days. My work at EMS plus my savings had covered the twenty or forty dollars in traveler's checks I'd included in each mail drop. If that wasn't enough, I'd told myself I would eat leftover trail food and just stay in the woods rather than spend money in town. Sitting in my parents' living room, next to a fully stocked kitchen pantry, I simply hadn't predicted the ravenous chasm that my body would become.

I tore through my mail drop food each week with little but a CLIF Bar and half a serving of oatmeal remaining by the time I got to the next drop. Stops in civilization, and the food that came with them, were vital. Some places, like Kincorra Hostel and Rusty's, suggested optional donations, and I deeply appreciated the generosity of these and other trail angels. The excess of Shenandoah and the trip to Pittsburgh had dwindled my already meager funds. I'd initially intended to use my credit card only as a backup—if I suddenly needed to get off the trail or had an emergency. It was the same card I'd had throughout college, the one with which I'd bought course books, pizza, and the occasional movie out. The one whose bill went to my parents.

I couldn't do this hike without my parents, and I was embarrassed every time I relied on them for money. They had let me live at home while I planned, they had contributed money to the groceries I had bought to fill all my mail drops, and they were also paying to mail all the boxes. They helped with extras, like the second night in the Troutville hotel and the new boots in Waynesboro.

I intended to pay them back, though they hadn't asked me to. I was twenty-three years old; I should be mature enough to support myself. And yet I wasn't. I never had been.

The totality of what I knew about money was how to put it into the savings account I'd had since I was eight years old. My parents had given me the gift of a young adulthood free to focus solely on my college education. But it was also a handicap. I couldn't balance a checkbook, and I'd never paid rent or a utility bill. I didn't understand how credit card interest worked or long-term investments or taxes. It was easier for my dad, and for me, if he took care of it. I was curious about money, but financial topics were taboo. My dad's income was a secret worthy of Fort Knox, and I knew to never interrupt his monthly ritual of grumbling and cursing, sitting on the couch surrounded by piles of bills and papers and a calculator.

Most of what I learned about budgeting came from the time my mom found a twenty-dollar bill in the washing machine as she moved the clothes to the dryer.

"Well, whose is it?" Dad demanded when she told us as we sat down to dinner.

It wasn't mine. I wouldn't have left twenty bucks lying around. Even if it was, I wouldn't have admitted it. Better to take the loss than face Dad's wrath.

"Might be mine," Nate said, approaching the table.

"Might be?" Dad shot back. "*Might* be? How can you not know if it's yours? We give you this money, and you lose it?"

As his voice rose, my stomach clenched. My heart thumped in my throat. If I moved slowly, while his attention focused on Nate, I could escape.

"It's not lost. Mom found it."

"You ungrateful little..." He slammed his fist onto the table in punctuation. I jumped, then turned and slipped into the hall, and dashed upstairs. "Don't you know the importance of keeping your money safe?" he bellowed.

"Steve," Mom said, "it was a mistake. He'll be more careful next time."

"Damn right he will. Get some paper!" he commanded.

"Why?"

"Don't talk to me like that! Get some God damned paper and get over here."

I made it to my bedroom door and crawled into my closet, but I could hear the clatter of dishes and silverware being pushed across the dining room table. Something hit the floor. I couldn't bear to shut the door all the way. I knew Nate was in for it, and I needed to hear what happened if only to make sure Dad wasn't coming up the stairs after me next.

"You are going to keep track of every cent you spend! You are going to make a list of everything you earn, and what's in your bank account, and present it to me every single month."

There was a lull. Maybe Nate was complying. Then a muffled response.

"I'm not angry!" Dad yelled. Another slamming thud shook the walls. "I worked for that money. Did you work for that money? No. I did! And you'll show some respect."

"Steve, calm down."

"I'm fine! I'm calm! I have a right to be angry when my son is disrespecting me."

The acoustics in our modern-style house were conducive to hearing everything that went on because the upstairs hallway had an open balcony that looked down over the main part of the house. I crept out of my closet and into the hallway, inched my head up, and peeked down at my family. Nate was sitting at the table with a pad of yellow paper, pen in hand. Dad hovered over him, pointing and waving his arms about, not able or willing to stop his tirade.

"Are you planning to go to college? Are you? Well, maybe we won't give you any money. Since you don't know how to deal with it. Maybe you'll be fine out there on your own."

Mom tried again to placate him but to no avail. He continued to rant about income and hard work and disrespect. Nate wrote some things down; I couldn't imagine what. Eventually, I crawled back to my closet and shut the door fully. But I could still hear the stomping, the slamming, the deep rumbling of my father's rageful voice.

I stayed tucked in my closet for some time until quiet came and I heard Nate's bedroom door click shut next to mine. My trembling stopped; my breathing returned to normal. I never really knew how to move on from one of the attacks. My insides felt liquified; my very skin felt raw and tender.

Dinner had clearly been canceled, so I ate some of the snacks in my closet. I wondered if anyone had benefited from this incident. Was Nate now going to be a budgeting guru? Could twenty dollars be worth the destruction of our family? It all seemed so pointless. I knew Nate would have to follow through with his budget presentations. And I also knew that life would go on as if Dad's red-hot eruption had not happened. It would melt into the background of volatility that ordered our lives.

At the Bear's Den Hostel, the heat of the day pressed too hard. I went to the front desk and confirmed the price. Twelve dollars. Not even the cost of a fight with Dad.

"One bunk for the night," I said, and handed over my credit card.

•　　•　　•

Along the last stretch of the Blue Ridge, twenty miles to Harpers Ferry, the trail straddled the state border of Virginia and West Virginia. Despite a strange rash exploding on my ankles, despite the gnats dive-bombing my eyeballs, despite my mind's obnoxious fixation on John Denver's song, "Take Me Home, Country Roads," I would walk there today or die trying.

My eyes stuck to the ground directly in front of me. I ignored the green, yellow, and brown shrubbery blurring past as one foot raced to keep ahead of the other. I sang loudly for the country roads to take me home to West Virginia and cruised down the trail until a tan stick two steps ahead twisted.

Then rattled.

A warning shot into my brain, and I leaped into the air and ran backward.

It rattled again.

I backed up farther, watching from a distance, searching to remember how far a rattlesnake could launch itself. My heart raced at my near miss. As I calmed, I imagined the snake giving me the finger for ruining its nice afternoon. I waited as it slithered silently into the brush, then gave it a wide berth and slipped past. I slowed after that, keeping my gaze farther ahead of my steps, but pushed on, pausing only to drink water.

The AT cut left at Loudoun Heights, leaving Virginia behind, plummeting to the Shenandoah River, a marvelous gray-blue swath of liquid pouring past the rocky mountainsides. The river cut a dramatic gap between ranges, and even with my head in a cloud of sweaty fatigue, I noticed the stunning view. After crossing the river on a busy highway bridge, I turned up a steep side trail into the village of Harpers Ferry, West Virginia.

Wingfoot noted in the guidebook that this historic town was founded in 1747. I walked through the quaint, colonial streets feeling like I was on some perfectly painted set at Disney World. Deep red brick buildings with white shutters, petite pink geraniums in wooden planters, and gray cobbled walls. I imagined men wearing knickers trotting up the street on horses and women in long dresses and aprons stepping out from the buildings. The shops and homes were charming. And old. 250 years was an extraordinary amount of time for human constructs to persist.

1,000 miles and three months are equally impressive.

The physical halfway point of the AT was about eighty miles farther north at Pine Grove Furnace State Park in Pennsylvania. There, I planned to participate in the Half-Gallon Challenge, a hiker tradition of attempting to eat one half-gallon of ice cream within one hour. Harpers Ferry, the town that the Appalachian Trail Conference called home, was the emotional and mental halfway point. It was also the highlight of West Virginia's short twenty-eight AT miles. I headed to ATC headquarters to celebrate my success and escape the murderous heat.

I found Kaybek inside, enjoying the air-conditioning. We looked over a large 3-D relief map of the AT together for a few minutes before asking the receptionist to take our photo in front of the building. I leaned against the whitewashed stone by the large ATC sign next to Kaybek.

I walked 1,000 fucking miles.

Georgia was a world away. My old life was a world away, a world in which I had wondered if I belonged on the AT. After 1,000 miles, I knew in my sore, aching, bruised bones that I did.

It was three o'clock, but Kaybek packed up his gear. He was headed another nineteen miles. Amazed at his fortitude, I went back into the air-conditioning to sign the trail register. I wanted my name recorded here forever. If I got to Katahdin, *when* I got to Katahdin, I'd write to this office and give them the details of my hike. There was no burden of proof; a hiker didn't have to describe or justify her hike. But I wanted the next 250 years of history to know I was here today. I wanted the ATC to know that when they sent me that tiny patch that said *2,000-miler*, it was for real.

The ATC had a hiker exchange box where I found Jurnee had left me a letter. "Hey Kid," he wrote. He'd been here a full week earlier. He'd picked up *The Hobbit* in Front Royal and had finished it. I'd once mentioned I wanted to read it, and so he'd left it for me. He concluded his message by telling me I'd better catch up soon, because "hiking without a Poor Helpless Female is boring!" I was delighted to hear from him and get the book, but I knew I couldn't catch him. He had no way to know I'd gotten off the trail.

I also got a note from Slow Buffalo congratulating me on getting to the mental halfway point. It was a sweet, if not expectant message. He commented on how weird it was to hike with "all these new people," but like me, he found most of them to be "pretty awesome." I was happy he was doing well and glad to keep my distance.

Up the street, I stopped at the post office for my food box. My mail had slackened through Virginia; people had gotten accustomed to the idea of me trekking through the woods. The halfway mark, however, had inspired folks, and the postmaster handed over thirteen letters. Perhaps prompted by the thank you card I'd sent a while back, Marilyn and Bob had sent another large bag of M&M's. I wondered how anyone could possibly hike the AT *without* M&M Mars friends to support them!

Aunt Tortoise wrote that it took a while to get back to her truck in Waynesboro, but once she did, had a shower, and recovered with a good night's sleep, she felt ready to hit the trail again. I remembered a similar feeling I'd had back at the Blueberry Patch. She mentioned that her old crony friends back home were proud of her for surviving the trail. I was proud of her, too.

At almost every mail stop, I received a letter from my mom. She also included a note in my food box, so I often got a double dose of Mom. She would tell me the happenings at church, whom she bumped into at the grocery, and the latest health news from various relatives. She was sweet and selfless, asking how life on the trail was treating me, urging me on. As different as she and I were, her kindness struck me in these letters, and I felt loved.

I stuffed all my mail into my pack, shoved the box of food under my arm to sort through at the hostel, and walked down High Street to the Potomac River. Here again, I noticed the dramatic mountain cliffs dangling high above the junction where the Potomac joined the Shenandoah. As I crossed the rustic footbridge, I marveled at this earth, feeling deep gratitude for the mountains and rivers. I walked away from West Virginia's country roads and entered Maryland, my sixth state. *1,000 fucking miles.*

•   •   •

There was one thing I understood about the AT so far: the trail was a constantly shifting corridor of faces. After many days with another hiker, my path could slip away from his, never to overlap again. Or it might take an unexpected turn and intersect after weeks or months of separation. There was no logic to the comings and goings. We were just wild animals, part of a great migration, progressing ever northward. I felt a kinship with most of the hikers I met, and even if we passed only one night together, they earned an indelible place in my heart. I often didn't get to know much about them because conversation revolved around the water options north or how to duct tape your boots together or who had extra Pop-Tarts. In one particularly enlightening discussion, Thor educated me on how to do a proper farmer nose blow so I could get all the snot out while walking. I had no idea what his college major was going to be, but his advice improved my day-to-day life, and my nose, significantly.

Both new and old friends filled my three days and fifty miles through Maryland. Charlie Hustle, an older guy named Satori, and Plato and Angel were nearby most of the time. I also passed a few nights with section hikers Dad and Sam, who made me slightly jealous with their sweet father-son relationship. Despite having some laughs with these folks, and all the love I had received in the previous mail drop, I fell into loneliness. I ached for the people I'd laughed with, sung songs with, philosophized with. My trail family. Bud was one of those people, and we crossed paths regularly. He, however, was incredibly independent and had no interest in adjusting his schedule for anyone. That, on top of the fact that he stopped at every town, store, hostel, road crossing, or bean pole that offered any inkling of civilization, meant our paces didn't line up. I was sometimes amazed he had made it this far with all the stopping he did. I wasn't one to talk, considering the rate with which I'd depleted my funds.

My mom had sent my Walkman to Harpers Ferry, but the tape player was broken, and I couldn't listen to the Dave tape Full Moon had given me. The radio worked, and so I walked alone, listening to classical music, *Car Talk*, and *The Savvy Traveler*. The folks on NPR made the time slide by and gave me something to focus on aside from the heat, the bugs, and my hurting feet.

Entering Pennsylvania, the forest looked scarcely different than the Maryland forest, and yet, crossing the Mason-Dixon line felt significant. Every day the scent of musty dry leaves, the rot of fallen trees, and the smells of the summer forest bombarded me and brought to mind my childhood. I couldn't believe that in two and a half weeks I'd be home. At the Delaware Water Gap, where the trail entered New

Jersey, my parents were going to pick me up for a few days off. Being so close only made me want to move faster.

I did the four miles from Toms Run Shelter to Pine Grove Furnace State Park in an hour, Bud not far behind me. I hadn't eaten all morning, and my stomach roared with hunger. The big day had finally come—The Half-Gallon Challenge.

The park had a typical camp store, which sold everything from ramen to kerosene. Satori was already on the porch, midway through his vanilla half-gallon. I wasn't sure if the smidge of revulsion on his face was nausea from so much dairy or just his normal weary thru-hiker look. I inquired in the shop about the Challenge and was told the official rules: one hour to eat a full half-gallon, any flavor of ice cream, and it did not break the rules if you barfed it all up afterward. The prize was a tiny wooden ice cream spoon that was hardly a prize at all. Still, I wanted to win. Bud purchased Moose Tracks and sat at the table with Satori. Just before noon, I too bought a half-gallon of Moose Tracks and dug in.

It went well. For a while.

We watched the clock, strategizing that the best way to do it was to spread it out over the full hour, even if the ice cream turned to milky soup by the end. I loved the freedom to shovel in spoonful after spoonful of tiny peanut butter cups and swirls of fudge, knowing that my body could handle it. In fact, my body craved it. Satori's time ran out just as he finished his box. We congratulated him on his impressive success.

Thirty minutes. Forty minutes. Then, my fatal mistake dawned on me: the flavor. Moose Tracks was indeed the yummiest, but that was its downfall. The peanut butter and fudge added calories and took up stomach space. Plain vanilla would have been a much wiser choice.

I slowed.

Bud gave up halfway through his carton.

I took a few more desperate bites, but with my stomach groaning, I had to stop. At sixty minutes, I'd succeeded in eating three-quarters of my half-gallon. I'd failed. My only bragging right was that I'd eaten more than Bud had.

In the afternoon, Charlie Hustle arrived, along with two guys named Biohazard and Groove. When my ice cream had digested, we hacky sacked, and I imparted my vanilla wisdom as they prepared to take the Challenge. Take the path of least resistance; go simple.

The day I did the Half-Gallon Challenge was also my parents' thirtieth wedding anniversary. I called them from Pine Grove Furnace and learned they were heading into New York City to dine at Tavern on the Green. The day sounded nice, not what I would want, but typical for them. After all these years, I still wondered what my mom saw in my dad. I'd seen their wedding album, photos of their early days together in the Air Force, images of young parents with Nate and me as babies. They were always smiling. They seemed happy back then. Could they still be happy now? In my mom's letters to me over all these weeks, I didn't hear togetherness in her words, I heard busyness. He went to work and on golf trips. She did things with her girlfriends and attended church events. Now that their kids had flown the nest, what was their relationship about?

Dad marked their thirtieth with a diamond ring, which she said was a gorgeous gem. Though this piece was an heirloom his mother had recently passed to him, my father often bought my mother beautiful jewelry. It was how he showed love, by buying things. A tiny voice inside me questioned whether it was actually love, or guilt, perhaps even control, that prompted these presents.

As I'd gotten older, the fights between my father and me got louder and harder, and I began to get gifts afterward. There was no acknowledgment of the attack, no chance to heal the gaping wounds, but within a few days, a token might turn up on my dresser. A pretty ceramic vase, a rose, a glass trinket. It was never what I would have chosen for myself: a book, writing paper, a movie ticket. He gave items based on how he wanted to see me, not on who I actually was. I wanted my father to love me, wanted him to apologize for his attacks, his rage, his irrationality. The little tokens didn't feel like love. They felt like bribes.

The phone call disheartened me. My mom was a grown woman; she could make her own choices. And yet, the thought niggled that she wasn't happy. Thirty years later, he continued to try to buy her happiness. I wondered if it was still working.

•   •   •

I missed Jurnee. We had spent the majority of the first half of the trail together, and I felt like we should still be together. He made everything more fun. His lighthearted presence would have been welcomed when I arrived at a Pennsylvania shelter for lunch one cloudy afternoon and found it occupied by Wee Willy the Prince of Wales—the surly yellow-blazer I'd met back at Kincorra Hostel—along with two male hikers I didn't know, and a handful of weekenders. The weekenders kept to themselves, but the others called into question my feelings of hiker kinship.

I sat at the picnic table and dug through my food bag for bagels and powdered hummus. As I mixed the powder with water, one of the unknown hikers introduced himself as Sidewinder. He was tall and blond, wiry like a snake. He slipped onto the bench next to me and complained. The rocks, the sun, the clouds, the shelters, the water, and the hills all sucked. Apparently, nothing about the trail was meeting his expectations. I nodded in silence, stuffing food in my mouth, wishing I had not stopped there.

"Are you out here alone, girl?" asked the gray-haired man sitting in the shelter.

Aghast that a complete stranger would call me "girl," I turned and raised my eyebrows at him. "Yeah," I replied. "Are you?"

"Don't you know who I am?" The man was probably in his late fifties, and I didn't remember ever seeing him before.

"No. Sorry." I turned back to my food, slathering more hummus onto the bagel. He walked over to the picnic table. He wore dark, dirty clothes. All hikers' clothes were grungy, but this guy's seemed more so.

"You've heard of me. I'm Junker."

"No. I haven't."

"Sure, you have. I'm Junker."

"I said, no." He paused and scratched his head, then wandered back to the shelter. I choked down my dry food, increasingly uncomfortable and hoping they would shut up and leave me alone.

"She's one o' them hikers that just shoots through the woods," said Wee Willy. He sat at the edge of the shelter too, as corpulent and repulsive as ever. I had to wonder how such a large man had gotten such a small name. Compared to him, who until now I'd never actually seen in the woods, I supposed I did move fast. "Do you even know what's on the other side of a white blaze?" he demanded. "Or all you do is look at your feet?"

I glared at him.

"A tree!" he yelled. "A tree is on the other side of a white blaze, and you should pay attention to the trees!"

I had not met this kind of behavior on the trail, and it made all my warning sensors perk up. "Do you know my name?" I asked Wee Willy. "We've met several times." When a dumb look crossed his face, I went on. "I'm Tamarack. Do you know what a tamarack is? It's a tree." *You fat asshole.*

"Are you *sure* you've never heard of me?" asked Junker, coming over to me again.

I shoved the rest of my bagel in my mouth, stuffed my gear into my pack, and left the shelter. I'd rather slide off the side of Blood Mountain than spend one more second with these jerks. I'd even rather be smothered by Slow Buffalo; at least he wasn't dangerous. There was something ominous about these men, and my interaction with them made me miss Jurnee all the more. Knowing I couldn't catch him, I clung to Bud and Charlie Hustle for a few days, keeping away from Sidewinder, Junker, and Wee Willy.

•   •   •

Everyone said the hiking in Pennsylvania would be easy but rocky. The rumors were true, and the trail morphed into long, flat ridges, punctuated by steep drops into and out of deep gaps. It also became a river of jagged rocks with no even place to set a foot. Though I paused most days for extended lunches and languorous naps basking in the sun, my daily mileage increased.

After a nineteen-mile hike into Boiling Springs, I needed to stop for the night. I took an overpriced room at the old Highland House B&B, hoping that Bud and Charlie Hustle would join me to offset the cost. They arrived and agreed to bunk up, but the owner got annoyed and upped the price to more than they wanted to pay. After they left to stealth camp down by the river, he lowered the price to what he'd originally offered me, but it took both my traveler's checks, leaving me with nothing. Later, Bud bought me a beer at the tavern. As we bitched about the weird Highland House, I wished I'd gone to camp down by the river, too.

I again received a considerable haul of mail at the post office, and thankfully another traveler's check. There were more cookies from Tish, M&M's from Marilyn and Bob, and lots of letters. I shared the cookies with Bud and Charlie Hustle, but as I packed all the remainders into my pack, I noted how odd it was that aside from them, no other hikers were in town. Bud and Charlie Hustle left Boiling Springs as I sorted my food box and sent a package to New Jersey. As soon as I could, I bolted from the unfriendly town. I would catch them along the way, definitely by lunchtime.

From there, the trail entered the Cumberland Valley, a stretch of fifteen miles of low, flat land between ridges. There were no preserves or parklands, and the trail wove through the valley along roads, farmland, and private property easements. It was a muggy morning, and I moved quickly, wanting to get through the unpleasantness of exposed road and farm walking and back into the woods. I walked, looking for my friends, looking for anyone else, but the day passed in eerie solitude. Once out of the valley, I climbed the next ridge up into the trees and pressed on another seven miles to the Thelma Marks Shelter, where I knew I'd find Bud.

Instead, I found Groove, sleeping off to one side of the damp shelter. I dropped my pack on the other side and looked around. It was one of the worst shelters I'd seen. The wooden beams sagged. The floor was moist. A mud puddle covered the ground in front of the opening. The place drooped under an abysmal shadow that felt induced by emotion, rather than the actual dark clouds that rolled in that evening. I filtered water, made dinner, and studied my maps, always listening up the trail, waiting to hear the footsteps of my friends.

When Groove woke up, he groggily told me he'd been sleeping off a drinking binge from the night before in Duncannon. He made a campfire that burnt away some of the darkness of the place. He was a nice, cute guy, and I was glad for the company. Particularly when he reminded me of the shelter's history. I'd heard the story but forgotten that nine years ago a thru-hiker couple was murdered here. It had been tragic and gruesome and had shaken the whole community. The memory of death on the Appalachian Trail was long, and though nothing here showed anything had ever been amiss, the place radiated unrest.

A cold rainstorm blew away the heat of recent days, and my radio informed me that the temperature would drop to fifty-two degrees. I'd sent my medium-weight sleeping bag home after the concerts, and now all I had was a thin fleece blanket. I put on all my clothes, which didn't include my fleece gear anymore, and snuggled down under the lightweight cloth. When night came, I accepted Bud would not be showing up. I spent most of the night shivering and falling in and out of sleep, dreaming that I was a detective trying to solve a murder case that refused to unravel.

I heard Groove leave early, before light had even broken. I didn't want to move my frozen bones, so I stayed put. I was counting on the sun to warm me. But the sun never showed its face, and the rain persisted. I thought about that day outside of Troutville where Jurnee, Biscuits and Gravy, Shaggy and Scooby, and I laid in bed watching the rain and doing nothing. I wished they were with me, laughing and making the dreariness subside. I wanted to tell them I'd figured out how to pee with my pack on. I wanted to hear their jokes and be told I was a badass. I knew I couldn't pick my walking days, and never grasped so strongly the phrase I wrote in the register: "No rain, no pain, no Maine." If I went out in the storm now, I wouldn't have enough clothes to get dry and warm once I got to my destination.

The lure of pizza made me move. I tucked most of my clothes into my pack to keep dry, wearing just shorts and a t-shirt despite the cold. At midday, I set out for five miles into Duncannon. I slipped on the pointy rocks that covered the trail, my boots splashing into the mud. I concentrated on keeping my balance and not breaking an ankle. Moving reheated my body, and as I made the final descent into town, the rain let up.

Wingfoot said that Duncannon was once called the "Jewel of the Susquehanna," but I'd never in my life seen a place sadder and more depressed. The trail weaved right through town where few houses looked inhabited, and most buildings were boarded up and lights shut off. I'd heard a lot about the Doyle Hotel, and some hikers claimed it was an AT icon not to be missed. I'd also heard that a lot of people had died there, and when I walked past the dilapidated old building, not even the promise of a bed, shower, and an escape from the rain could convince me to cross that threshold. Instead, I sought out the Italian restaurant.

I was hoping for a warm slice, but inside, I found an ice-cold pizzeria that had no pizza until dinner time. The man behind the counter growled that he'd make me a sub sandwich, which I agreed to purchase only because he seemed more like a mobster than a restaurateur, and I didn't want to piss him off. The rain had started again, so I couldn't eat outside. I sat in a greasy booth choking down a dry sandwich as my skin froze under the blast of the air-conditioning vents while two young boys sitting in the other booth smacked at each other. Still chewing the last bite, I left the restaurant, planning to push on as far as I could. *Once you're wet, you're wet.*

The AT crossed a wide elbow of the Susquehanna River along the Clark's Ferry Bridge, a four-lane highway with a narrow sidewalk protected behind concrete pylons. Vehicles of all sizes maneuvered around eighteen-wheel trucks. They sped by, assaulting me with continuous waves of water in my face and loud screeches in my ears. I was so wet that I might as well have swum across the river. It was a horrible, terrifying, and utterly brain-numbing half mile. By the time I got to the far side of the bridge and back into the woods, I was ready to quit the AT.

I cursed and thrashed up the next three miles, angry at the weather and the trail. I hadn't seen another thru-hiker all day, and the rain continued to pelt down. At the shelter, I met a dad and daughter who joked about picking a hell of a weekend for a three-day trip. They were friendly and offered me some good cheer and a piece of the steak they were cooking. I appreciated their kindness, declined the steak, and continued to wonder where Bud was.

I didn't warm up again that night and puzzled at what had happened to the hot days of Virginia and Maryland. I lay exhausted, shaking, thinking about how people die in cold temperatures. I'd read that you just drifted off to sleep and never woke up. That didn't sound too bad. At least I would be able to get some rest. I pulled out my silver Mylar emergency blanket and tucked it around myself. I pretended it helped, but I didn't feel any warmer.

On the third day of not seeing any other thru-hikers, I began to feel like I had spun off into some bizarre alternate reality. I knew humanity still existed because I crossed paths with a minister and his youth group, several southbounders, and a couple of weekenders. But my thru-hiking peers had vanished. The impression of a different reality increased with the presence of Warren, the first person I'd met on the trail—including the obnoxious yellow-blazers—who truly terrified me.

He had the sort of nondescript face of an average-looking person who could blend into the background and go unnoticed; the perfect appearance for a serial killer. We leapfrogged a few times, and each time we passed each other, he stood and stared at me. I tried to make conversation, but he answered in short sentences, never revealing much about himself. I knew I shouldn't be alone with him and never stuck around if other hikers weren't nearby.

The rain passed. The sun warmed the air to a near-perfect seventy degrees, but the nights remained frigid. Each day I rose to walk, stiff and aching, hoping just to make it closer to the Delaware Water Gap. Some other thru-hikers did finally reach me. Funk That, Circuit Rider, and Ulysses sped past, doing a thirty-mile day, stopping to chat briefly. I left notes for Bud and Charlie Hustle in the registers, but they were gone. The pattern of the trail had become predictable, some of the ridgelines even beautiful, but the longer I walked alone, the more I struggled with my emotions, with questions of why I was out there. I contemplated calling my parents and asking them to pick me up in Port Clinton, eighty miles early.

I'd passed the halfway mark and felt like I should have some plan for when I finished the trail. I still didn't have a job. I hadn't met the perfect guy to run off with. I certainly didn't want to go live at my parents' house. Day-to-day trail life engrossed me, and I struggled to imagine the end. My eighty-five-year-old Great-Aunt Jeannette had written to me recently. She counseled, "No doubt, you'll always carry some of the mountains with you for the rest of your life." I knew she was right. But what was the rest of my life going to look like?

I had time to figure it out, so I let it slip to the back of my mind. Instead, I tried to cheer myself in the dismal days of Pennsylvania by making lists of positive things I didn't want to forget about the trail: Cool, fresh spring water. No traffic jams! No honking! How to have relationships with people, regardless of all the superficialities. Being able to eat as much of anything you want. It changes your perspective on a lot of things.

Indeed, the trail did change my perspective. I once thought I should pass every single white blaze; now I saw that the trail, and life, were not so black and white. I argued with myself that I should push on, not skip ahead to New Jersey. I should stick to the original plan and arrive in Delaware Water Gap next week. But after days of hiking through cold and rain alone with only weird nutcases nearby, I needed a reroute. My trek was about completing the trail *and* being happy along the way. Finally, at 501 Shelter, twenty-three miles from Port Clinton, I decided to take the path of least resistance. I stopped at the shelter on a small side road off the AT. The couple who lived next door sold snacks and soda to hikers, and I used their phone to call my parents. I asked if the next day, Sunday, Father's Day, one of them could drive to Port Clinton and pick me up.

Doing this, I would skip eighty miles. Instead of returning to this point on the trail, I wanted to slackpack New Jersey. I schemed that if I hiked southbound, I'd run into all my old friends, catching up with people I'd lost along the way. I could hike long days and return home to my own bed every night. I could listen to Dave. I could cuddle my cat. I could go see a movie with my friend Don. I could forget about these unfriendly, solitary, rocky days of pouring rain and tales of murder.

So on Father's Day, while I raced across the ridge into town, my father drove from northern New Jersey to Port Clinton, Pennsylvania. Like my Aunt Jeannette had written, these mountains would always be a part of me. But for now, I was going back to civilization. I was going home.

SLACKER

Entering my avocado-green bedroom in New Jersey was like traveling back in time. Twenty-three years of life piled high against the walls, overflowed out of the closet, crammed onto the bookcase. I could barely see the dark green carpet, barely get to the single bed that my mom had lovingly made up for my return. Everything I owned was in this room or in boxes in the basement.

I dumped my dirty pack on the floor and headed straight for the shower. I had come to love taking showers, watching the dirt run off my legs and swirl down the drain, feeling my fresh, clean skin reemerge. After the last months of the outdoors being my home, having my own bathroom and my own bedroom, upstairs from a full kitchen, with my car parked in the driveway was irresistible luxury. As I looked through my dresser drawers for clothes I hadn't been wearing for the past 110 days straight, I felt like I'd landed on some familiar yet unknown planet. I had thought of this house so many times, considered stopping the insanity of my hike and returning to these avocado walls. But now, surrounded by boxes of memories, I felt upside down.

For most of my youth, my childhood bedroom was a soft lavender color, with a border of curled up yellow cats near the ceiling. When I became a teenager, I wanted to upgrade from the childish design to a more mature space. My mom and I looked through book after book of wallpaper and paint samples, considering myriad options for my small room.

AMANDA K. JAROS   195

I knew I wanted a smooth avocado-green paint, and Mom suggested picking a wallpaper for one wall to balance it. When I came upon a jungle print of greens and pinks, I knew I'd found the one. But on the next page, I discovered a complementary wallpaper, a simple off-white with thin pink and green vertical threads which gave it a fabric-like texture. I loved this unique paper and couldn't decide between the two. I pressed Mom to let me be creative: two walls painted green and one wall of each of the two papers.

When we presented the scheme to my father, his missiles launched.

"What are you thinking!" he yelled.

It was a demand, not a question, and I didn't know how to answer.

"No one makes three walls different!" he bellowed. "We'll never be able to sell the house with a bedroom that looks like that!"

"Are we planning on moving?" I couldn't resist asking, knowing the answer to be no.

"It will bring down the resale value of the house!"

Was I a bad person for wanting three walls of my bedroom to be different? Was it an extravagant request? Would it ruin the house? If the answers were yes, I wished he could have explained it to me. I didn't understand why instead of working together to figure out a solution, everything with my father became a battle.

Mom jumped in to respond, nudging me to leave the room. "Steve, let's just think about it for a few days. It might be fine."

Tense and disappointed, I went upstairs. I could hear his loud voice insist that this was the stupidest thing he'd ever heard of. "Three walls different!"

Her equally calm voice responded. "We can always repaint the room after she goes to college."

It wasn't often that Mom could redirect the attack and de-escalate the situation, but that time, miraculously, she did.

I sometimes thought my mom should take lessons from my grandfather, Ed, who had spent fifty years calming his wife's mood swings. As a child, there was not a stitch of doubt in my mind that my dad had gotten his anger problem from his mother, my grandmother,

Worth. The woman scared me. She made me think of the cackling old witch that Hansel and Gretel stumbled across deep in the forest. It seemed like the children ought to trust her, but really, she was about to burn them alive.

Worth yelled like my father, but more often, she was picky, vindictive, or passive-aggressive. She demanded things be her way, and whether her demands were met or not, she criticized and condemned. Worth's persistent negativity dominated many conversations, from her recurring tirade about Tiger Woods ruining the game of golf to her prattle about a friend or family member's inappropriate clothing, hair, or behavior. She railed about "those Mexicans" taking over her "respectable" white Los Angeles neighborhood. I cringed and shrank in my chair when she said these things as we sat eating chips and salsa at her favorite Mexican restaurant. Of all her grandchildren, she most often focused her wrath on me. A simple statement that I had once won a game of Solitaire brought on a firestorm of insistence that I was lying. No matter the topic, she pressed on the issue, any issue, until I conceded she was right.

Quite the opposite of Grandma Worth, Grandpa Ed was loving and generous with his grandchildren, and he could sometimes soothe her or get her to back down. I wondered what had made my grandmother so rageful at the world. Had her parents abused her? Maybe her own mother had never shown kindness. Maybe she had dreams for a life that hadn't included three daughters, one son, and the monotony of motherhood. There were a million stories that could explain her ire, her hatred of the world and everyone in it. But I could never know.

Worth made choices as a mother that deeply affected her children. In her attempts to control everything, she alienated her goofy and sensitive son, teaching him he was never good enough and never worked hard enough. I grew up hearing stories of fighting and more fighting. My father lived in a household where a broken plate, a forgotten sheet of homework, or a cookie taken without permission could bring on a wealth of out-of-proportion reprisals. More damaging than sending the boy to bed without supper or forcibly extracting an apology or even receiving a belt beating from his father, Worth withheld her love from him. Whether it was a genetic mental illness or behavior passed on from generation to generation, my father left his childhood and went out into the world with indignation and fear hanging over him, ready to impart this legacy onto his own children someday.

I didn't see this volatility in my brother or cousins, but by high school, I saw the inklings of it in myself. I explained away my sad moods and stormy anger as the hormones of growing up and the result of living with an unstable man. But deep down I knew—the mood swings, the temper, the depression—I was like my father and grandmother. I didn't know how to handle my emotions, but I vowed to myself that if I ever had a child, I would remove myself from the family, I would leave forever, I would die rather than raise my voice to him. I refused to destroy my future child's self-esteem over an ice cream box or a wallpaper choice. I would not pass on the anger and explosiveness. The scourge had to end with me.

•   •   •

The day after I arrived home, Mom had plans to go down the shore with her friends for a few days. She regretted she was going to miss my time at home, but I assured her I would be there through the next weekend. Dad left to go golfing, and thus I spent my first day off sorting through my food boxes, washing laundry, and flipping TV channels. It was a welcome respite, but by evening, I felt anxious to get back to the trail.

I'd lived in New Jersey for most of my life, and yet I'd never hiked in the Kittatinny Mountains. I didn't even know their name until the previous winter as I prepared for the AT. These hills weren't like the steep ascents and descents of the Virginia mountains. Instead, they were an extension of the long, flat ridgelines and deep gaps of Pennsylvania. Still, surrounded by rural farming communities, the Kittatinny Mountains were as wild as the Garden State got.

Dad agreed to help me slackpack during the week. I parceled out the seventy-two New Jersey miles into segments of twelve to twenty miles. Each day, we would drive two cars to a road crossing where I would leave my car. Then, he'd drive me north and drop me at another road crossing, and I'd walk back.

On the first morning, we wound our way west from our suburban town, and after a few wrong turns, arrived where the AT crossed Millbrook Road. I parked my car by the trailhead and climbed into his. Dad had a tee time again that day, and though it was still early, I knew he was going to be late. I navigated as best I could north to Route 206, but the windy roads turned us around, and we got lost.

My stomach clenched. I didn't want to mess up his day. I hastened to figure out where we were and which direction to go before he got upset. *Fuck, he's going to explode.*

But, he didn't. He held it together, and when he dropped me at the trailhead, he offered a genuine smile and wished me a good day. I jumped out of the car before the mood changed and strapped on my purple day pack.

After months of receiving trail magic, I decided to use slackpacking as a chance to repay a drop of that kindness. I'd filled my pack with apples and oranges to pass out to my fellow hikers. Along the fifteen miles, I knew I would find welcome recipients. Despite the food, my pack weighed nothing. Hiking became floating. The sun shone hot, but my clean hair and body felt light and fresh. Even if I got sweaty and dirty, I had a warm shower in an air-conditioned house awaiting me that evening. The ridgeline stayed at about 1,500 feet, and I cruised along the flat, often grassy, trail, eager to cross off miles.

Not knowing any of my friends' locations, my anticipation rose with every bend in the trail. I first came upon Hurdler, whom I'd met a few times down south, then All Downhill from Here, whom I hadn't seen since the Smokies. We chatted for a few minutes, and I gave them fruit before we walked on. When I stopped for lunch on Rattlesnake Mountain, I saw a familiar brown dog run up. It was Elwood with Fairweather close behind, whom I had last seen on the tiny strip of grass between Burger King and McDonald's in Front Royal. He stopped walking when he saw me.

"What are you doing here?" he said.

I stood up and smiled. As I explained, Dogman walked up, and I laughed happily as his jaw dropped.

"Shit! Tamarack! How the hell did you get here?" He hugged me. "You're so clean," he said.

When I inquired about Alta, he said he'd sent the dog home to his parents in Connecticut. The heat was too much for the poor pup. I explained about Dave, Pittsburgh, hiking alone in Pennsylvania, and that my parents lived an hour from there. As we talked, No Sub and Disco came up too, and I offered the treats to four grateful friends.

Eventually, they moved north, and I moved south. A deer fly homed in on me as I walked, but I swatted it away, unperturbed. With the ease of a day like this, not even annoying bugs could get me down. My parents had gotten me a new Walkman, and I listened to Dave, singing out loud, feeling joyful, ticking off songs and miles.

And then, out of the trees came Biscuits and Gravy.

"Halooo!" I called, gleeful to have found them.

Like Dogman, they were shocked to see me, and again I explained.

"Do you guys want to come home to my parents' house tonight?" I asked, giving them pieces of fruit. "Hot shower, warm dinner, soft bed."

"Absolutely!" Biscuits said.

I zipped on down the trail to my car, and a few hours later, drove to another road crossing to pick them up. When we arrived home, Dad was returning from his golf game.

"I hurt my back on the course," he said when I asked about his day. "And I didn't play my best."

I tensed, expecting the anger that the golf course so often elicited in him. But he surprised me again with his good cheer and offer to buy us pizza from the local Italian place. While Biscuits and Gravy made use of all the home amenities, Dad went to pick up dinner.

I was so surprised that Dad hadn't reacted in anger that I made note of it in my journal. As a child and teenager, most diary entries that included my dad also included all capital letters spelling out my hatred. But there were good memories that didn't always make it into the diary. Memories of times when he was the dad I wanted. Memories of his strong arms throwing a young me into the rollicking waves as we played in Lake Michigan. Memories of him making me laugh with his silly skits for the family talent show. Memories of loving him. There were times. Times he tried. Times he succeeded.

•   •   •

After dropping off Biscuits and Gravy, I spent the next day on an eighteen-mile slack at the very northwest corner of New Jersey, the highest point in the state. I walked through the crystal-clear, blue-sky morning past High Point Monument, standing tall at 1,804 feet. This time, instead of carrying the food and treats, I'd left a cooler by my car with a sign saying *Thru-hiker food.* I filled it with soda, fruit, carrots, and candy. I passed a few of the same hikers as the previous day, but still no sign of Jurnee. The miles disappeared as DMB serenaded me through my Walkman. My favorite song, "#41," came on, and I belted out the words. It felt as though Dave had tapped right into my heart when he wrote that song, and I sailed, more than walked, along the mountain ridge. Just Dave and me alone together.

When Mom returned from the shore, she and Dad wanted to hike with me. Her friend, Susan, and a friend from my church youth group, Erin, also wanted to come. I had a twelve-mile stretch through the Delaware Water Gap National Recreation Area that I thought they could handle. On another warm day, we did the car shuffle, left the cooler of food with the big sign, and hit the trail headed south.

"Look at me," Dad said, strutting down the trail with a goofy walk and tone of voice. "I'm an AT hiker."

"Funny!" I said, looking back at him. He wore his Michigan Track t-shirt and an orange ball cap and was using a single walking stick. He had on a small day pack and carried water and lunch food. Mom and

Susan trailed him, both wearing fanny packs with water bottles, Erin behind them.

"I'm hiking on the AT," Dad said. "So, I'm an AT hiker!"

"Yes, Dad," I said, playing along with his silliness. "You're awesome."

"Now, Steve, this hiking is serious," said Susan, who was rarely serious. "We old folks need to focus on keeping up with these kids and not break an ankle. I don't want to get left behind out here in the wilderness."

"True," I replied. "Erin and I could ditch you all pretty quick."

We soon started passing northbound hikers, including Towhee, whom I'd last seen in Maryland. She was as bird-like as ever and chirpily introduced her current hiking buddies, Mr. Green Jeans and his sons, eleven-year-old Pigpen and fifteen-year-old Speedy Feet. We met an older couple called Crazy Legs and Teddy Bear and a guy called Long Haired Freaky People, who fit the name perfectly. I'd heard of a guy named Indiana who carried a guitar and hiked with Sunshine West, and I enjoyed finally meeting the unlikely pair: he was a short, speedy fellow, she a bulky, plodding woman. Each time we came across another hiker, we'd stop and talk. Sometimes, I'd introduce my parents and companions, but other times, I could see that my hiker friends wanted to keep walking, so I simply told them about the cooler of food and moved on.

When we met Slow Buffalo, my stomach lurched into my throat. Same old Buffalo—same fast cruising speed, same black bushy beard, same lopsided grin when he saw me.

"Whoa, Tamarack," he said, stopping in the trail. "You're here."

"How're your knees?" I asked awkwardly. My worlds colliding threw me off kilter. I introduced him to my parents and friends, calling him one of my best buddies from down south. It was true. He had been. And I missed the fun we'd once had. But after several uncomfortable minutes, I announced we needed to keep hiking, and we bid Buffalo goodbye.

Not yet out of earshot, Susan whispered loudly, "Was he the one bothering you?" Apparently, Mom had told her friends about my time with Slow Buffalo.

"Shhh!" I responded. "I don't want to be a jerk about it."

"Ooh, what'd he do?" Erin asked, coming up beside me.

I explained how things had soured, silently hoping that more time apart would allow that if I saw Slow Buffalo again, we could simply be friends.

Coming into Sunfish Pond, we met Kaybek, whom I greeted with a hug. We stopped in a sunny clearing to chat, and my funny French-Canadian friend charmed everyone. If I hadn't come up to New Jersey, I may never have seen him again. As he gave me a wink when he left, I remembered how much I adored him.

At Sunfish Pond, my group was ready to take a long break.

"It's beautiful," Mom said, as she and Dad peered over a low rock outcrop into the water.

"Who knew there was a huge lake in the woods up here?" Susan said.

Most people thought of New Jersey as all cities and turnpikes and bumper-to-bumper vehicles, and to a great extent it was. But Sunfish Pond and the Delaware Water Gap Recreation Area defied that appraisal of the state. This large pond was a stunning remnant of New Jersey's glacial past. All shades of green trees and laurels sloped down right to the rocky water edge. Dragonflies zipped to and fro. Toads croaked. The forest extended for miles all around, and the pond mirrored the blue sky and puffy clouds perfectly. Not a single skyscraper or highway in sight.

From there, the trail made a gradual descent for four miles down into the Delaware Water Gap. When our snacks and drinks were finished, we strolled back to the car. The long rocky meander through the afternoon tired everyone out, but my crew was proud of their twelve miles. As much as I enjoyed their company, jokes, and questions, I was also glad it was just one day.

When we got back to my car and the cooler, I discovered a parking ticket. It was a handmade, cartoonish drawing of a hiker with a huge pack. On the other side, Kaybek had listed all the violations I'd racked up for parking there, including: *Not for slackpack zone. French parking only. Do not feed the wildlife. No Mountain Dew in the box.* Leave it to Kaybek to make me laugh even when we weren't together.

•   •   •

I woke in my soft bed to the noises of my parents moving about downstairs. I kept my eyes closed, not wanting to come back into reality from my dreams. There was no pressure to get moving since for no particular reason, I'd decided to take another day off. With each day at home, I could feel myself sink further into indolence. Life there was pure leisure; everything—books, TV, the movie theater—was available at any time. Food filled the fridge and electricity lightened every night. Even the strains on my body disappeared; I wasn't taking ibuprofen daily anymore.

When I opened my eyes, I saw the green and pink jungle print on the wall. I rolled onto my back, looking over at the off-white fabric-like paper on the other wall. Dad had finally given in, and I'd gotten the room I wanted. It was a bright, colorful space that I had loved. And now, I didn't fit in it.

I spent the morning in the bedroom with my cat, listening to music and sorting clothes to give away. All my piles of stuff made me think of Full Moon and Bud. We'd had so many conversations about excess, about how *things* don't make a person happy. I could see that more than ever now. When I was on the trail, aside from a few extravagances, like sandals and a book, I carried only the things that I needed to survive.

The pile of clothes on the floor, on the other hand, stressed me out. For the past four months, I had two t-shirts and one long-sleeved shirt, and I'd done fine. Did I really need a dozen different white t-shirts, along with another dozen colored ones? I didn't even know where they all came from. It was easy to pick out shirts to get rid of, but that was just the beginning; there were pants, dresses, sweaters, shoes. Much too much. I wanted to go back to only having two shirts, to having the simple daily goal of climbing the next mountain, of walking, sleeping, eating.

But the simple life would not last forever; I needed to do something after the AT and thus far, I'd only had one offer. I'd gotten a call from a Ranger named Jim at Hovenweep National Monument in Utah. He'd kept my name from last year's Student Conservation Association application and was offering me an internship starting in October. It was a remote park, an hour's drive to any town. I considered taking the position solely for that reason; perhaps it would be a good place to land while I navigated leaving the trail and entering back into society.

I packed up a box of clothes for the church rummage sale and stashed it in the basement with all the other boxes. I didn't fit in the childhood bedroom I had fought for, not because of all the stuff, not because I was an adult and shouldn't live with my parents anymore, but because in the process of hiking 1,300 miles on the Appalachian Trail, I had grown up.

•   •   •

"Well, God damn, look who it is—the Poor Helpless Female!"

I laughed and ran to Jurnee for a hug.

"Hey, old man," I said.

"I heard about a crazy slackpacker chick in these parts. Didn't realize it was you, kid!"

"Well, why carry a heavy pack, when you can slack!" I said, spinning a quick twirl to show off my light pack. "I think you could use a shower. Want to come to my parent's house tonight?"

It was an unnecessary question, and we arranged where I'd pick him up in a few hours. I cruised as fast as I could go along another stretch of New Jersey trail, eager to spend the evening catching up with my friend. My parents were glad to meet Jurnee after hearing so much about him. And after a big dinner and hours of conversation, he and I agreed, as we so often did when we were together, to take another day off.

In some ways, this stop at home felt like all my college breaks, and it wouldn't have been complete without Don. Don was my first, best, and for many years only male friend. He'd always been there for me, ever since eighth-grade graduation when I was mortified to be the tallest girl in the class. The teachers lined us up by height, having us process into the auditorium two by two, alternating girls, then boys, which put me dead last. Worst of all, because there was an odd number of students, I had to walk down the aisle all by myself, for everyone to stare at. I was sure that the entire auditorium was judging me, so unattractive and abnormally tall, walking alone at the back of the line. The only thing that eased my humiliation was that Don was the tallest boy in our class and in line ahead of me. As we waited for the procession to move along, we stood in the hallway together and he made me laugh. I felt intense relief when the procession was over and I made it to my seat in the bleachers, next to him, where he whispered jokes to me throughout the ceremony. It was the moment when I realized how fun and kind boys could be.

After high school, Don and I became closer. We hung out on summer and holiday breaks, going to dinner or the movies, and once we turned twenty-one, out for drinks. He'd been writing to me along the trail, telling me about his student teaching gig and his travels to Russia. When I got to town, he was eager to show me his new car, and I was eager for him to meet Jurnee.

The two hit it off and had a great time telling stories about me, teasing and joking. I basked in their attention, feeling adored. We pored over my pictures from the trail, and Don showed pictures from his Russia trip. We ate tacos with Mom and went out to a movie in Don's new car. Having Jurnee at my home was strange, and yet, spending a day off felt right. I was submerged in a rare bubble that difficulty and struggle could not penetrate, a bubble that my father could not pop, a bubble I wanted to stay inside forever.

After a week of sleeping in my childhood bed, however, I had completed the New Jersey miles, and when we took Jurnee back to the trail near the border of New York, I would hike on with him.

Before my dad left on a work trip, I thanked him for all the driving he did; I couldn't have slacked without him. As he hugged me goodbye, I silently offered my gratitude for his good mood. Even though they had only walked one day with me, after meeting all those hikers and spending time with Biscuits and Gravy and Jurnee, my parents seemed to have a new appreciation for the AT. I hoped they now saw that I wasn't just an outlier freak doing something radical. There were people, regular people, who were doing the same thing. Perhaps for the first time they understood that the AT was a community, one that their daughter belonged to.

•   •   •

We returned to the trail on the kind of day where merely glancing out the car window at the sunshine made sweat drip down my forehead. I hadn't felt that kind of heat since those brutal days in West Virginia and Maryland. Mom drove us to Route 517 near the New Jersey-New York border. It was about ten miles until the AT officially crossed into New York, and from there, 800 miles remained. The trek had always felt endless, like I was walking on a treadmill, logging miles, but going nowhere. Now, leaving New Jersey, Katahdin was more than a dream, it was a real place that day by day came into clearer focus.

That hot day, however, I didn't want to get back on the treadmill. I felt feeble from so many days of easy hiking, eating, and lazing about. My next food drop wasn't until Kent, Connecticut, about 110 miles north, and my pack weighed as much as a black bear. Jurnee thanked Mom for her hospitality and then took off, leaving me to say goodbye alone.

I felt nauseous from the heat and was almost ready to trade the simple life for the air-conditioned life. I could hop back in the car, calm Mom's fears, and let the cool air soothe me. I could ride home, settle back into my avocado-green room with one wall wallpapered in jungle print, another wallpapered in off-white fabric, and ease back into excess. But I would never be a thru-hiker if I went back. Because I was never going to Springer Mountain again, never walking through snow and heat waves and rainstorms again, never slackpacking New Jersey again. This was it. This was my chance. And I would never forgive myself for stopping now.

I remembered something Cameraman had said to me way back in North Carolina, "You don't have to go fast or go far, you just have to keep going."

Just keep going.

HEAT AND PESTILENCE

Gnats. Mosquitoes. Bees. Ticks. House flies. Black flies. Horse flies. Deer flies. And those tiny flecks of invisible bugs that dive bomb the eyes and zip up the nose. They were a pestilence in cahoots with the devil. Which these days came in the form of the sun. The heat was relentless. The nights offered scarce relief, as the mosquitoes enjoyed that prime feasting time. It hardly even seemed to get dark in July, like the sun was taunting us, a constant reminder that it was only a short spin away before it would again continue its efforts to burn us alive.

New York was rocky, but not in the same way as Pennsylvania. Instead, the mountainsides had giant, bulky rock formations, which forced difficult scrambles. In one place, I physically squeezed through a crevice called the Lemon Squeezer—a narrow passage between two bulldozer-sized rocks. The trail also lost the delightful flatness of the New Jersey ridges and resumed the incessant roller coaster of ups and downs.

Jurnee was on a schedule of rising before the sun to beat some of the heat, while I struggled to wake before nine o'clock, then trudged miserably through the mugginess. A few days into New York, he took off early again, leaving me a note that he was headed fifteen miles into the town of Bear Mountain to get a hotel. I didn't want to push that far and pay for another hotel. Plus, the Graymoor Friary was only another seven miles beyond Bear Mountain, and I planned to stop there the following night, so there was no rush.

I pushed through another hot day, and after about eleven miles, I made it to the trail leading 0.6 miles to West Mountain Shelter. I was starving and rain began to drizzle. I considered pulling out my tarp and throwing it down at the junction, but decided despite the extra mileage off the AT, a roof would be more pleasant.

I approached the shelter to find an unkempt man huddled in the corner, smoking. His shabby gear spread out across most of the space, and his dog, a white but dirty pit bull, guarded the other half. I said hello and dropped my pack on the picnic table. He mumbled a reply. At our voices, the dog perked up, looked at me, and barked.

"Shut up!" the man yelled. He leaped up, grabbed the dog's collar, and hit its head. Hard.

The dog squealed and cowered.

I watched this exchange in disbelief. As far as I knew, no one else was stopping at this shelter tonight. Its occupants would be this man, his scary and scared dog, and me. Dread twinged in my stomach along with the hunger pangs.

I drank some water and pulled out a CLIF Bar and my map. I glanced into the dark shelter to see where I might squeeze in my sleeping bag. The man had left little space. My back ached, and I needed dinner. Not even two hours of daylight remained, and I didn't think I could make it to town, but the stale smell of smoke wafted past, and I knew I couldn't sleep in a smoke-filled shelter.

"Do you think you could smoke outside?" I asked.

"What the hell," he said. "Who do you think you are? I can smoke wherever I like." He scowled at me and blew smoke in my direction.

The dog growled and started barking. He hit it in the chest, yelling again.

"Well, I best be getting on down the trail," I said, gathering the few things I had taken out of my pack. "My friends are expecting me," I added with emphasis.

I heaved the pack, grabbed my trekking poles, and didn't look back as I raced away from the shelter.

I told myself I would stop at the first level patch of ground I came across and set up my tarp, but every step had me pushing for three more. Panic pursued me, along with the certainty that the man was close behind, stalking me for my insolence and vulnerability. I looked over my shoulder many times as evening closed in. The five miles disappeared in a gray blur. I climbed one steep side of Bear Mountain and descended the other in near darkness. I could barely see where I was going, partly for the coming night and black clouds, but also for the haze of fear that stung my eyes.

The town of Bear Mountain wasn't actually a town; it was Bear Mountain State Park headquarters, where there was an inn and post office. When the park lawn and pond came into view, I felt frantic to find someone I knew.

Where the hell is Jurnee?

I approached the bright light spilling out of the inn and saw Sunshine West step out the door, aptly dressed in yellow and orange hiking clothes. I had only met the stocky, round-faced woman a few times in passing, but I was deeply relieved to run into her there. Though they weren't a couple, I knew she hiked with Indiana, the short guy who carried a guitar, and I wondered whether he was in the area too. She informed me that rooms at the inn cost $100, and after a brief discussion, we agreed to find a motel and share a room.

Wingfoot offered scarce information on nearby towns, so I used the inn's pay phone to call a taxi. We asked the driver to take us to a motel and ended up in a shabby, roach-infested room. But three hours and five miles farther than where I thought I'd be, I didn't care. It was cheap and dry, I could finally cook dinner, and no creepy guy was threatening me. As I settled into the motel bed, the adrenaline trickled out of my system, and I slept.

•   •   •

A black bear paced in circles inside the enclosure. I stood watching him, imagining his frustration. I turned my gaze from the bear to the plaque in front of the cage, which noted that this spot, inside the Trailside Museum and Zoo, was the lowest point on the AT: elevation 124 feet above sea level. Nearby cages held a fox, a bald eagle, coyotes, and many other animals which were injured or unable to survive in the wild.

It was a small, well-intentioned zoo that allowed city people the chance to see wild creatures. Even though I knew the animals were being rehabilitated, the cages seemed so unfair. I'd seen many wild animals the past four months; the peregrines rocketing through the sky in Tennessee, the coyote dashing through the field in Virginia, the black bears stomping away from Aunt Tortoise and me in Shenandoah. Those animals knew freedom. Those animals could choose where to wander, what to eat, when to sleep. The bear in the cage continued his laps around the pen. This wasn't where he was meant to be.

I'd never liked zoos; I didn't like the despair in the animals' eyes as they butted up against hard and fast walls that could never be surmounted. As a child, I could relate to that despair, and I didn't have an outlet to cope with my own. My father's irrational behavior bore into me, excavating a gaping hole in my core that grew bigger each month and year. Writing in my journal was the only thing I had to help me process my experiences, to record a reality that otherwise went unseen by the rest of the world. None of our church friends, Nate's and my schoolmates, or my parents' coworkers knew about my father's unhinged rage. He worked hard to present himself as a goofy jokester, a hard-working family man, an athletic marathoner. The discrepancy between how he acted with his family and whom he showed off to the world confused me.

I thought surely my aunts and uncles knew. Yet, I was uncertain. At a family gathering with Mom's siblings one Christmas, Dad snapped at me for taking his spot on the couch as we all watched a movie in the living room. I stormed away in a huff of eight-year-old frustration, the moment just one more bubble of lava in the volcano known as life with Dad. My reaction was out of proportion to the incident, and Uncle Rick followed me to my room where I was crying in the dark.

"You know," he said, putting his hand on my shoulder. "You can tell me anything."

I sniffled and wiped my face on the pillow.

"And I have to keep it a secret because I'm a lawyer," he went on. "I won't even tell Aunt Barbara if you want."

I said nothing, but as he turned to leave me in the darkness, I wondered what he knew. And what he didn't.

By eight years old, I knew my dad would be sorry that he treated me this way if I was gone. Perhaps having similar thoughts, Nate tried to run away once. The attempted escape resulted in Mom's worry and panic until he returned several hours later, but Nate's action resulted in no change in the household dynamic.

I wasn't brave enough to run away. I didn't know the word suicide as a child, but I understood that if I was dead, my father would regret his behavior. Perhaps he would even see the pain his actions caused and apologize. Of course, I'd be dead, but that would serve him right. I made my will, something characters in books always did, allotting cherished trinkets and stuffed animals to friends and cousins.

By high school, I thought about the different ways one might extinguish oneself. I didn't know how to do that if you didn't have a gun, which I hated anyway and would have been too scared to touch. I could slit my wrists, but that would be awfully messy. The most pain-free option would be drug overdose like several of my movie star crushes. I didn't know what any of the pill bottles in my parents' cabinets were, and I hated the idea of ending up in the hospital with people trying to save me. I didn't really want to die, I just wanted out. But I remained an animal trapped in the cage of my father's aggression, walking in circles until I might one day be sent back into the wild.

On the trail, I had found freedom. I woke up every day in the woods, packed my gear, strapped it to my back, and walked. Some days I didn't want to. Some days the heat and bugs were awful. Some days there were creepy guys who freaked me out. But I was no longer in a cage; being there was my choice.

From the zoo, the trail went up and down and up and repeated the crests and falls for seven miles to the Graymoor Friary. Wingfoot noted that the Franciscan Friars of the Atonement had opened their doors to hikers for twenty years. That year, they offered their large baseball field for camping and welcomed hikers into their dining hall for dinner and breakfast.

A smattering of colorful tents spotted the grassy area near a wooden pavilion. As I walked up, I could see several dirty hikers lounging about, clothes hanging from the ceiling, stoves and food bags atop the picnic tables. Sunshine West was setting up her tent, and Crazy Legs and Teddy Bear sat at the edge of the pavilion complaining, moaning about this and that discomfort, smoking. Towhee was nearby talking with a weedy old man named Greenfoot, who had a white, bushy beard. I met a young guy named Seeker who made me laugh, and another guy named Canada who impressed me with his shelter. He had an A-frame tarp like mine, except he'd brilliantly sewn mosquito netting on the sides, fully protecting him from the pestilence. Knowing that we had both planned to stop at the Friary, it was strange, however, that Jurnee was not there yet.

Holly and Dooley were also at the pavilion awaiting dinner. The two were an attractive, calm pair. They'd started together in Georgia and somewhere along the trail had decided to get married. They'd been making plans as they hiked, and in two weeks, they would arrive at their wedding atop Mount Greylock in northern Massachusetts. It would be a simple event, and their families could get there via the road to the top of the mountain. Holly made sure we knew that all thru-hikers were also invited, and I hoped my timing worked out to attend.

After weeks apart, I'd caught up to Slow Buffalo. We hadn't spent the night in the same place since Troutville. He remained aloof all evening, not encroaching on my space. I hoped it was a sign that he had let go of his infatuation. Despite his coolness toward me, he still managed to make sure we talked. He implied he was hiking with Towhee now, and I couldn't help but wonder if he was trying to make me jealous.

The ragtag hiker crew traipsed up the hill behind a monk in a brown robe who had invited us to dinner. He ushered us into the high-ceilinged dining room and showed us to a long rectangular table reserved for thru-hikers. The meal was a plain, non-vegetarian affair—hot dogs, sauerkraut, baked beans, and reconstituted lemonade—and I was grateful for the generosity.

As the monks said a prayer ahead of the meal, I glanced over at the tables of men with balding heads and bulky physiques. Despite their brown robes and my stained blue t-shirt and shorts, we weren't that dissimilar, the monks and me. We had all arrived there seeking something. I presumed they sought a greater connection to their God. I was on a journey to find a connection with myself. Had they found what they were looking for in monkhood? What would I find when I made it to Katahdin?

•   •   •

I didn't expect to see fireworks on the Fourth of July, partly because I was in the woods, and partly because of the rain. I sat in the muggy RPH Shelter watching it pour down, wondering whether I should move or not. It was ten o'clock in the morning, and I didn't want to stay there, but going on would be misery.

I'd spent the previous night at a tent site a few miles back. Seeker and I had hiked most of the hot day together, enjoying each other's company and discussing philosophy. After a long detour to a state park snack bar for ice cream and French fries, we were both ready to stop before getting to RPH Shelter and camped in a tiny site enclosed by laurel. At RPH, I pulled out the register to see if Jurnee had signed in. He hadn't.

In fact, Jurnee had stopped signing the registers altogether, which irritated me, and I intended to tell him off when I caught up. According to the book, everyone else in the nearby cohort had been there, and I sat in the shelter reading their entries as the rain came down.

I looked at my map again, realizing that, as always, there were no options but to keep putting one foot in front of the other. I saddled up my pack and headed out. RPH followed a one-lane road for a short distance before heading back into the woods. I walked aside the road avoiding puddles, raindrops bouncing off the pavement up onto my boots and water running down my pack and raincoat onto my legs. A gray van pulled up next to me and a middle-aged man with a white t-shirt covering a round belly rolled down the window. He introduced himself as the Merry Hiker, a thru-hiker from a few years back.

"You interested in a home-cooked meal?" he asked. "My wife Mary's putting on quite a spread for the holiday, and we're hoping to bring along a few hikers."

"Uh, yeah!" I couldn't believe his timing. If he had come by five minutes later, I would have turned off the road back into the woods and missed him.

"I've got Greenfoot's pack, here. He's slacking the next ten miles, and I'm picking him up at Depot Road. Happy to pick you up there too in a few hours. Our air conditioner's on the fritz, but we have a breezy porch you all can sleep on."

As I dumped my pack into the back of the Merry Hiker's van, a thought flashed past about the soundness of this idea. I was giving my entire life, my pack, to a complete stranger who had come out of nowhere and offered to take me home, to Poughkeepsie of all places. Four months ago, I would have bolted from this offer. But I wasn't that girl anymore. I wanted a Fourth of July meal and a breezy porch, and the Merry Hiker was pretty much Santa, so I grabbed a water bottle, confirmed our meeting point, and set off into the rain.

That evening, I knew that going with Santa was the right choice when I saw corn on the cob, potato salad, macaroni salad, green salad, cheesy garlic bread, and burgers with all the toppings spread out like a king's feast on the table, with ice cream, watermelon, and cantaloupe waiting in the wings. I filled my plate.

I heart Poughkeepsie.

The Merry Hiker, aka Bill, and his wife, Mary, were some of the kindest people I'd ever met. Bill had loved his time on the trail years ago and continued to miss it. Since he lived thirty minutes from RPH Shelter and its easy trail access, Bill went there every weekend during the summer to offer trail magic. Mary had gotten used to his wanderings and always made extra food in case he brought home more mouths to feed. This time, they'd opened their doors to four of us: Greenfoot, Holly, Dooley, and me.

The rain stopped, but moisture hung in the air like steam from a shower. Bill and Mary's adult son came for dinner, along with a couple of their friends, all accustomed to having smelly strangers in their midst. The assorted group sat next to several overworked box fans, eating and discussing both trail life and Poughkeepsie life. We planned to watch Boston's Fourth of July fireworks show on TV until the power went out all over the neighborhood. Even the electricity couldn't handle the heat.

The front porch would have been breezy if there had been wind, but the oppressive heat stagnated in the small room as Greenfoot, Holly, Dooley, and I tried to sleep. Thoughts of my future arose again. Whatever came next, I knew I'd spend time on a trail crew or as a ridgerunner or just stopping by the trail and leaving snacks. I'd been given so much; I had to somehow return it.

•   •   •

New York seemed to replicate the interior of the sun. The pestilence and the 100-degree heat made me feel like I was being worn down to little shreds of skin that would peel right off. When I arrived at the last road crossing in New York, I granted myself a half-mile side trip for a pint of Ben & Jerry's at Tony's Deli. The ice cream heartened me, as did meeting Porter, a tall, thirty-something, wiry guy with glasses who had a reputation for being super nice. I liked him right away, which might have been because we eagerly commiserated about the heat and bugs, or because he actually was super nice.

The next day, I crossed into Connecticut. A trail angel had left a *Welcome to Connecticut* sign and some Gatorade at the border. *My tenth state!* I tried to rejoice as I guzzled a bottle of the warm liquid, but the drink did nothing to cool my sun-beaten skin. I slogged on, hoping to make it to Kent, my next mail drop, and a place to cool off.

After hiking twelve and a half miles, I found Porter and Kentucky at the Mt. Algo Lean-to, sitting in the shade, sweating. I'd never met Kentucky before, but it didn't take long for me to see that he was a near-replica of the creepy guy back at Bear Mountain. He was smoking in the shelter, a stack of beer cans next to him, only lacking the scary dog. I wasn't sure if he was a thru-hiker, but he didn't look like he'd be walking anywhere anytime soon.

"I think some more ice cream is in order," Porter said, looking at me. "Whaddya say, Tamarack? Stop down to Kent?"

It was 0.3 miles down the hill, then 0.5 along the road into Kent. I got the sense that Porter didn't want me to stay at Mt. Algo alone with Kentucky any more than I did.

"Air-conditioning," I croaked. "I need air-conditioning. And pizza."

"It's a larch day, eh?" Porter said as we strolled out of the clearing.

"Huh?"

"This heat seems to be wearing you down," he went on. "You're more of a larch today than a tamarack."

"More like a triple-larch day. I feel like crap."

Half an hour later, on a mission to Pizza Garden, we walked by the elite Kent Boarding School and crossed the Housatonic River into the swanky village of Kent. The town had classic New England charm, with old stone churches, a covered bridge, and big white houses with wide front porches. Pizza Garden, on the other hand, was in a flat-roofed building from the 1970s. I didn't care what kind of architecture it had, as long as it had pizza and air-conditioning.

The manufactured icy air pierced my damp skin, and goosebumps materialized immediately. Slow Buffalo sat in a booth finishing his meal, and when he saw us, he motioned us to join him. Porter went right over, but I hesitated. I wondered how this would play out. I tensed when Porter invited him to hang out while we ate, but the meal unfolded with little awkwardness.

After a stop at the post office for my mail drop, I met up with Porter and Buffalo again at the outfitter. They were talking with a southbounder named Tim who was headed to the next town over, New Milford, to stay in a hotel. He invited Porter, Buffalo, and me to join him, which would cut the room rate considerably. I was wary of sharing a room with Buffalo; it had been a long time since we'd spent time together. Still, it was a good offer, and I figured I could survive a night with Buffalo if it meant a night with air-conditioning.

·   ·   ·

The trail out of Kent followed the Housatonic River for several days, winding next to the river, then through patches of state forest and parkland. The same cohort surrounded me through Connecticut's fifty-one miles: Porter, Slow Buffalo, Indiana, Sunshine West, Towhee, Ironhorse, Icehouse, Kaybek, Holly and Dooley, and Yogi and Boo-Boo.

I'd taken so many detours and ice cream breaks I'd lost track of how far ahead or behind Jurnee might be. Then, I met a hiker named Falcon, who had seen Jurnee back at Bear Mountain. Falcon told me that Jurnee had sprained his knee that day and was probably off the trail. I felt punched in the stomach.

How could that be? He wouldn't, he *couldn't* leave altogether. That was not acceptable.

I realized that I'd expected to hike Katahdin with Jurnee. We had started this journey together, we had to finish it together. But even if he healed and returned to the trail quickly, I was so far ahead that I might not see him again. This information crushed me, and I wanted to leave the trail. This far north and people were still dropping out. Maybe one of them would be me.

Even as I contemplated leaving, I kept marching on. I walked by giant rock slabs, sparkly rivers, deep ponds, and wildflowers in bloom, but it became a blur. If there was beauty in these hills, and I knew there was, I didn't see it. My moods fluctuated. I might start a day peppy and ready to cruise, but a long uphill or an awkward stumble or the thought that Jurnee really was gone could sink me. I pushed myself up and down the hills, swatting the bugs away from my eyes and nose, a salty layer of sweat always caked to my skin. A part of me wanted to slow down and meditate by the riverside, seek out inspiring views, and stop and smell the flowers. But I couldn't. There was a constant pressure to tick off miles, both for the fact that this whole affair was getting tiresome, but also because I wanted to keep up with the cohort.

Slow Buffalo seemed content with friendship, and he and Porter lightened my days. We hacky sacked at every snack, lunch, and camp break. My skills had improved somewhat, but I still had poor control.

"Dang, Tamarack, watch where you kick that thing," Buffalo joked after I flicked the hack with my foot and it zipped right past his ear and into the bushes.

"Better behave, or I'll aim next time."

"That could be your superpower," Porter said. He switched to a deep voice-over voice. "Fighting evil-doers with a single flick of her toe. It's *Hacky Girl!*"

"I'd better practice more then," I said, laughing. "Actually, the other name for a tamarack, besides larch, is hackmatack. That would be a really good superhero name."

"What would Porter's be?" Buffalo said, kicking the hack back to me. "He's got garlic breath from all the calzones and pizzas he coats in garlic."

"Oh yeah, totally," I agreed, completely missing the hack. "Meet *Garlic Boy!* One breath and his nemesis falls dead away."

Porter chuckled, hitting the hack back and forth from one foot to the other with ease. "Buffalo's?" he asked.

"Jolly Ranchers," I said, after thinking for a few minutes. "He sucks on those all day. He could spit them out in an endless stream like bullets."

"Beware, enemies, it's *Jolly Rancher Man*," Porter said, again in the voice-over voice.

Kicking the hack, I felt the old ease Buffalo and I once had. Still, I made sure that Buffalo and I weren't ever alone. The cohort was around, and for a while, the dynamic worked.

The lowlands of Connecticut morphed into the rising foothills of Massachusetts. Over each hill, we came to another road, that led to another general store or coffee shop or grocery, which enticed Porter, Buffalo, and me to stop again. Schlepping through the hot forest beat me down, but the town stops lifted my mood. We hopped over the hills together to Falls Village, then Great Barrington, then Upper Goose Pond Cabin.

The afternoon we arrived at Upper Goose Pond Cabin was another muggy one. The large, red building was maintained by the Appalachian Mountain Club, about a half-mile from the nearest road. It had lots of bunks, a kitchen, and a caretaker who kept the place tidy and made brownies for thru-hikers. There was a pond available for swimming or canoeing, and flat spots in the woods for tenting or hacky sacking.

I'd been trying to get Ironhorse to hack with me all week, but he always claimed exhaustion. He finally conceded when I started a game with Icehouse, Porter, and Kaybek.

"Oh, Tamarack, I'm too old for this," he complained, lurching awkwardly after the hack.

"No way!" I replied. "You're hiking the frickin' Appalachian Trail. You can handle this."

"My legs already hurt enough. I don't need to make them work more."

"But you're so fun to play with," I said. His slow foot-eye coordination caused him to consistently miss each hit, which he comically exaggerated, making me laugh. "Keep trying."

That evening, I sat in the warm living room of the cabin with several other hikers as Indiana played his guitar. Indiana and I had been spending more time together, and I'd learned that he was a guitar maker and hadn't wanted to go six months without his instrument. When he played music, he turned serious and reflective, a vast difference from his usual sarcasm and wit. He had strong opinions about everything and rarely held them back. The more familiar we got, the more he teased, and I did my best to keep up. He'd teased me about my height, calling me a giant Amazonian jungle woman to which I countered that his very short stature and scruffy brown hair reminded me of an Ewok. But when Indiana played music, the poetic, quiet side that he often hid, came out. I was glad he showed it in his art.

In the cabin, Towhee hummed along with Indiana's original songs and sang the familiar tunes, her sweet bird-like voice soothing. The rest of us sat in a circle tapping our feet or nodding our heads. *Jurnee should be here.* At that thought, a wave of emotion that wasn't exactly sorrow or happiness overtook me.

This is nostalgia.

I didn't know you could feel nostalgia for something that was happening in the moment, but that's what it was. Hard and soft, dark and light, that moment contained everything. There was so much suffering on this trail: blisters and snow, injuries and fears, heat and pestilence. And yet, one hour out there with these people was a thousand times better than a week anywhere else I'd ever been. Anywhere else I could imagine. The Merry Hiker was right to miss this life. I understood, wondering how I would ever be able to move on.

•   •   •

The Cookie Lady's house sat right next to the trail, where she offered a large field for hikers to camp. I set up my tent near Indiana, Buffalo, Towhee, Sunshine West, and Ironhorse. We lounged in the late afternoon heat, hiding in the shade like lions. Sunshine and Towhee went to a nearby town for food and brought me back a pint of Ben and

Jerry's Bovinity Divinity. I slathered the ice cream on the homemade cookies that the Cookie Lady bestowed upon us that evening. As the heat of the day faded, we watched the fireflies' sparkly show light up the lawn.

Not all insects are a part of the pestilence.

Indiana and I walked together much of the next day's ten miles to Dalton, Massachusetts. The gathering spot in town was Tom Levardi's house, which lay directly on the AT route. Tom offered his yard for camping, and we knew we'd find friends there. Indeed, when we walked up, Porter, Icehouse, and Kaybek sat at the picnic table in the yard, dealing with various camp chores.

A few minutes after I dropped my pack and joined them at the table, Tom himself came out to greet us. He brought out a pitcher of ice water, then asked if Indiana and I wanted a bowl of ice cream. After our eager nods, Tom disappeared into the house and returned with two large silver bowls, each with several scoops of chocolate and vanilla ice cream, hot fudge, nuts, and whipped cream. It wasn't just a bowl of ice cream; it was a massive sundae. Awestruck, we thanked Tom before he left us to our business.

Porter was lacing up his boots. "I've gotta get moving," he said. "I talked to my wife, and she's ready for me to come home. All this stopping is fun, but I need to start doing more miles."

I stepped away from my ice cream to hug him, knowing I wouldn't see him again.

"Take care of yourself on those larch days," he said and smiled. "Use your superpowers if you have to."

"Okay, Garlic Boy," I said, nodding. "Don't you go too long without another ice cream stop." *Or without a hack circle, or evening of music, or a laugh with your friends.* "Or you might not make it."

THE LONG GREEN TUNNEL

Mount Greylock rose regally at the western edge of Massachusetts. At 3,491 feet, Greylock was the highest point in the state and the highest point on the trail since Virginia. For many weeks, I'd been hiking through river valleys, across rock piles, and along low ridges. Greylock was a reintroduction to the world where mountains dominated. From there, the AT left the town-to-town hopscotching and entered the rugged ranges of New England.

My pack tugged at my shoulders as Towhee and I set out together from Cheshire, our last town stop for a while. Seventy-five mountainous miles lay between me and Manchester Center, Vermont, where I'd get my next mail drop. We spent the climb chatting about our hiker friends and what we thought the Green Mountains of Vermont and the White Mountains of New Hampshire would be like. Over the previous few weeks, I'd appreciated Towhee's kindness and friendship. And despite her gentle demeanor and light-hearted attitude, she was one of the strongest people on the trail.

My feet throbbed, as always, but the eight miles passed with an ease I hadn't expected. The trail builders there, as opposed to on every other inch of this trail, had a slight understanding of switchbacks and had mercifully incorporated that knowledge into their work. I breathed hard, but the steep sections were more exhilarating than difficult. When the trail leveled out near the peak, I remembered the deep sense of accomplishment I felt summiting a mountain.

The top of Greylock, however, was not the forest oasis I preferred to find after hauling my aching body up the side of a mountain. Instead, I encountered a mess of tan service buildings and a red and white radio tower. Past that, the trail emerged onto a paved road and a wide, meticulously manicured grassy field. A circle of sidewalks wound toward the impressive, 100-foot-tall Veterans War Memorial Tower. The smooth stone spire protruded from the center of the field like the turret of a castle, atop which perched a giant glass ball that shined like a beacon in the hazy afternoon sun.

Across the field from the tower stood Bascom Lodge. The cobbly stone building reminded me of Bilbo Baggins' hobbit house in *The Hobbit*. The lodge was much larger than Bilbo's house, of course, with a central two-story building and a one-story wing angling out on either side. The latticed windows and stone chimneys poking above the brown roof made the whole thing appear cozy and inviting.

Though I could have done several more miles that afternoon, the next day was Holly and Dooley's wedding, and Towhee and I planned to attend. We dropped our packs outside and went through the stone archway front door to ask about space in the bunkhouse. The entire lodge was booked, but the manager offered us a room used for storage. We could crash in there for ten dollars or a few hours cleaning floors and windows in the reception hall. We accepted, willing to work in exchange for a roof over our heads.

Hikers poured onto the summit of Greylock all afternoon. There were day hikers with mini packs and weekenders with bursting packs. There were a couple of southbounders headed to Georgia, one of whom was the first Black thru-hiker I'd met. And then came the usual crowd. When Sunshine West arrived, Towhee and I invited her to join us in our storeroom, pleased to have a girls' room to ourselves for a change.

In the fading evening, Slow Buffalo, Kaybek, and I got a hacky game going in front of the lodge. Soon, a boy named Tony, maybe fifteen years old, wandered toward us. I'd met him the day before in the lowlands hiking with his boy scout group. He sidled up to me and stepped into the circle asking if he could join us.

"Of course," I said, and tossed him my hack.

He missed it on the first try, then tossed it back to me, and I sent it around the circle.

"So, you come here often?" he asked, looking at me with a raised eyebrow.

"Huh?" It was the strangest question. Then I heard Buffalo stifle a chuckle and realized what this kid was up to.

"I hike a lot. I'm going to hike the AT in a few years," Tony said in a forced deep voice. When the hack came his way, he missed it again.

"That's great," I replied. "It's an amazing experience."

"Maybe you and I should go somewhere private and talk more about it."

At this, Kaybek and Buffalo both snorted with laughter.

"Oui, Tamarack," Kaybek said, chuckling. "You teach the boy some things."

I glared at him. Kaybek hit the hack toward Tony, and it arced through the air. This time Tony made contact. He kicked it so hard that it moved across the wide sky and sailed high above Bascom Lodge, finally coming to rest atop the stone chimney.

"My hack!" I screamed.

Buffalo let out a guffaw. Kaybek grinned. Tony shrank and looked at the ground.

"Gee, sorry," the kid said.

"Sorry, my ass," I replied. "You'd best get my hacky sack down off that roof before you get off this mountain, or you'll regret it, young man."

He spluttered an uncertain response, unsure what to do. I stomped away to ask the front desk manager for a ladder. Luckily, the hack had only gone up a single story, and the chimney could be reached from the peak of the roof. I hauled a ladder from the back side of the building, and with Tony, Kaybek, and the lodge manager standing by, Buffalo climbed up and retrieved my hack.

"My lady." He bowed as he handed it back to me.

I thanked him and turned to Tony, who muttered another apology before scampering away.

"Well, you scared him off girls for a while," Buffalo said.

"Little punk."

·   ·   ·

Saturday dawned humid and hot. All morning, shiny cars arrived at the top of Greylock, and Holly and Dooley's smiling friends and family emerged in flowery dresses and pale suits. The other half of the growing crowd was sweaty and stinky, wearing stained shorts and t-shirts. A lot of hikers had pushed long and hard to get here for the big day, having hiked with Holly and Dooley farther south. Some had yellow-blazed to not miss it. There were both new and old friends: Falcon, Creeper, Biohazard, Poopajack, Greenfoot, and Golfer. Though one group of wedding-goers belonged in *The Great Gatsby* and the other in *Lord of the Flies*, everyone mingled and chatted as we awaited the appearance of the bride and groom.

The ceremony would be held on an overlook to the east, and when the Gatsby folks meandered away from the Veterans War Memorial Tower, the hikers followed. Dooley appeared in khakis and a white shirt, his thick red hair combed back, his bushy beard trimmed and clean. Then Holly came walking from the lodge on the arm of her father, wearing a simple white sundress and a straw hat. The couple radiated happiness as they took each other's hands. I slipped my arm through Kaybek's as we watched Holly and Dooley stand atop one of the many mountains they had climbed together and promise to climb many more.

Afterward, the party moved to the rustic dining room inside the lodge. The families had organized a huge buffet, and while the family members stayed inside to eat, we hikers took our plates and sat on the grass outside. Maybe it was the abundance of food, the kindness of strangers, the vows of love, but though I didn't have one sip of alcohol, I felt drunk. I flirted unabashedly with Kaybek and Biohazard. Both of them were sweet, funny, and flirting back. I told myself I hadn't come out here to find a man or get into a relationship, but I'd been entrenched in a world of men for months, and I wanted a physical connection. But was there even one guy out here, besides Slow Buffalo and fifteen-year-old Tony, who found me remotely attractive?

Things with Slow Buffalo were deteriorating again. Tony had been more direct with me in the first few minutes we spoke than this man I'd known for four and a half months who couldn't voice his affection—an affection I did not reciprocate. Buffalo had returned to acting as if I were a cheating girlfriend and had taken to hovering around me. As I flirted with the guys at the wedding, I noticed the scowl on his face and the sullenness of his attitude. I'd thought we could move on and be friends, but after the wedding I doubted it.

The reception passed as all receptions do, with cake and laughter and photographs. Holly asked Indiana to play his guitar, and as he strummed out some gentle songs, people danced. The music wafted over the crowd as Dooley danced with his mother, and Holly with her father. I watched their closeness and their sweetness with their parents and wondered if I would ever get married, if I would ever have a ceremony on top of a mountain and a big buffet lunch and a dance with my father.

A hot flash washed over me, and the space felt suddenly stifling despite the big fans blowing air through the room. My stomach roiled, and I went outside, trying to suck air deep into my lungs. I made my way to the short stone wall and sat alone, looking up at the giant glass ball atop the memorial. There was something wrong with me. I would never get married. If my time in college and on the AT was any indication, maybe I'd never even have a real relationship.

I took deliberate deep breaths, using my paper napkin as a fan to cool my face. I noticed a group of four guys walk up from one of the trailheads. They wore daypacks, and when they came by me headed for the lodge, the blond one paused.

"G'day. What's with all the cars?" he asked, pronouncing the word cars more like cahs.

"Some hikers got married," I said. "We hikers hiked up, but their families all drove up."

"You hikers?" the dark-haired one asked. "What do you mean?"

I explained about the Appalachian Trail and thru-hiking. They were impressed and sat down to talk more.

"I have to ask," I said, "your accents, you're Australian?"

"Righto," one replied. "We're from Queensland."

"Hey, I've been there!" I exclaimed.

I told them about my study abroad program and asked them about Australia. I wanted to know where they came from and what they did there. They, however, were more interested in my AT stories and wouldn't let up with the usual million questions: How much do you eat? What about bears? Let's see your blisters.

I felt heartsick listening to their voices. Their accents jolted me back to the beachside bar and the dry, fruit-scented air I'd been so keen on a mere two years ago. At the time, I didn't know why I wanted to go to Australia. I knew little about the country and knew no one from there. I'd seen the flyers hanging up around my Michigan campus and after talking to someone in the study abroad office, my wanderlust got the best of me. It wasn't until I'd been in Sydney for a few months that I realized why I'd gone. It was geographically just about as far from home, as far from my father, as I could possibly get. I was on the other side of the world.

I'd lived near the university in a house with other American students. Though I wanted to get to know some Australians, I was shy, barely even speaking to my professors, and staying with my American peers. I talked to my parents weekly; simultaneously missing them and relishing the vast ocean between us.

A few months into my semester, they surprised me by telling me they were coming to visit. They figured they would never have the opportunity or reason to make the trip again, and my dad's free flights made it an easy decision. They made a reservation at the Holiday Inn on the beach of my suburb, a ten-minute walk from my house, and we planned out an itinerary. I enjoyed playing tour guide. I introduced them to my friends, made them ride the buses, and took them to museums and the Opera House. But their appearance unsettled my life; I was just touching upon my independence, and my father's presence made me feel like a child again.

They wanted to see the Great Barrier Reef, so we booked a few days at a hotel in Mackay, Queensland, a popular resort town with many options for getting out on the water. Though I was anxious about a long weekend in close quarters with my parents, the timing was ideal. My study abroad program was hosting a dance, and since, naturally, I didn't have a date for the event, it was just as well I was in Mackay.

My parents and I made our way north as winter advanced in the southern hemisphere. Though Queensland winters were nothing like New Jersey winters, cool, damp weather hung over Mackay. After two chilly days snorkeling on the reef, we all agreed that staying on dry land was preferable to another day on the water, and we got a tip for an easy rainforest walk. Dad drove our rental car out of the city, commenting repeatedly about being on the "wrong side of the road." I navigated, following both the map and the directions from the front desk clerk at our hotel. We almost missed the trailhead, which had only one other car in the scrubby parking lot and a minuscule sign by the road.

The forest was unlike anything I could have imagined. The trees scraped the sky, their wide trunks a deep, chocolate brown, their leaves a shiny, olive green. Many had multiple branches rooted in the ground making them look leggy and labyrinthine. I ran my hand over the variety of leaves and barks, touching the smooth and rough and grooved textures, filing away the feel of each to write in my journal later. We seemed to be the only humans ever to pass here, and as we meandered through the leafy tunnel, I felt the pressure of constant interaction with my parents lessen.

Everything was soppy and wet, and none of us had proper shoes for the soggy trail. I wore white Keds, Dad his running shoes, and Mom her aerobics sneakers. We avoided the mud puddles, alternately looking into the canopy while trying not to trip on the many roots that crossed the path.

After about a mile, we came to a marshy pond where we discovered that someone had indeed been there before us: a bench. We stopped for a snack. As I ate, I reveled in the nature all around me, the ripples on the water, the unfamiliar grasses growing out of the marsh, the teensy black spots and what appeared to be blood on my white shoes. I bent down to look more closely; the black flecks were writhing and moving all over my now mud-splattered Keds.

"Oh, my gosh!" I yelled, causing both my parents to turn their heads. "My feet, oh, my gosh! I'm covered in leeches."

They looked at my feet, then their own, and immediately started swatting at their shoes.

"My feet are bloody!" Removing one of my shoes I found that the leeches had crawled inside and attached all over my sockless feet. I didn't do well with blood, particularly my own; the one time I'd donated blood, I passed out. My breath quickened; I felt woozy.

"Oh, dear," Mom said. Both my parents were wearing socks and had managed to acquire only a few leeches around their ankles. But my flimsy fabric shoes were no match for the determined masses of bloodsuckers. Mom bent down in front of me and used a stick to push off the unattached leeches, but the attached ones were more of a problem. I started to cry.

"Calm down," Dad said. "They're just leeches."

Calm down? Did he see what was on my body? I gasped for breath.

Mom and I scraped the leeches from my feet, taking some skin along with them, knowing we'd have to do it again when we got back to the car. We stuffed our snacks back into our pockets and returned the way we came.

The forest was gross and ugly. I hated it, hated the rain, the mud, the creatures. I kept my eyes on the trail, tip-toeing while moving as fast as I could. Back at the car, I sat with the door open, bent over my bloody feet, pushing the leeches off with a stick, still in tears.

"Stop crying," Dad insisted loudly. "You're fine."

"I'm not fine!" I yelled at him, anger overtaking my fear. "These things are awful!"

"They're tiny little bugs. You're being ridiculous!"

"I'm not!"

"Steve…"

"And they ruined my shoes." I sucked in my breath.

"We're not bringing those shoes back to the hotel."

"What do you mean? They're my shoes."

"They're bloody and disgusting, you're not putting them in this car!"

"Well, we can't leave them here. There's no trash can or anything." A haze came over my eyes. My body flashed hot, and I started to shake.

His voice rose. "They're garbage, and we are not bringing them with us. Go put them off in the woods."

"That's littering!" I screamed at him. My hands quivered with rage, my breaths shuddered as they went in and out of my lungs. The hatred of so many years, so many incidents threatened to erupt from beneath the very surface of my skin. "I am NOT leaving my shoes here for someone else to clean up. That's a terrible thing to do!"

He screamed that we were leaving them. Then he bent down, picked them up, and thrust them into my hands, jolting my body with the impact. "GO!"

I flinched. My eyes blurred; my body shivered. This was my father. *My father.* The man who was supposed to protect me, support me, and listen to me. I'd gotten so little of that. So little of the understanding I thought I deserved. I realized I never would. A piercing scream rose up from deep within. It needed release. Someday, somehow, it would escape.

I took the bloody shoes and walked to the edge of the parking lot by the faded sign. I set them down neatly next to each other, as I would have if I were placing them in my closet. With tears still running down my face, my body still quaking, I walked barefoot to the car and got in.

He drove us back to the city. We did not discuss the incident further but returned to our hotel and ordered dinner. I took a hot shower, trying to wash away the anger and regret along with the mud and caked blood. I was powerless. I hated how he dominated and disregarded me, but even more, I hated myself for letting him. Even in Australia, a million miles from home, he could waltz into my life and ruin my day, my week. He could turn me into something I didn't want to be—a person who left their disgusting trash in the rainforest. Before my hair was dry from the shower, I was counting the hours until they would leave for the airport to fly home.

•   •   •

Entering Vermont corresponded with the beginning of the Long Trail, a 273-mile trail that wound north through the Green Mountains. For the next 105 miles, the AT and the LT would follow the same route until Killington, where the AT turned east to New Hampshire, and the Long Trail continued north to Canada.

The day after the wedding, I entered Vermont and stopped to avoid the oncoming rain at the Seth Warner Shelter. There I met Molly and Ben, a couple of hikers starting the LT. I sat in the shelter, my camp chores long since completed, listening to my radio and writing in my journal. The couple rushed around camp, testing their gear for the first time, trying to keep everything dry, and groaning about the weight of their packs. I couldn't help but laugh when Molly offered me a candy bar to lighten her load. On my first night on the trail at Springer Mountain Shelter, I had been like them, so unsure, unsettled, unaware of what lay ahead.

Did I know any better now what the future held? Not really, but I had whittled my pack down to a decent size. My body had become accustomed to taking a beating every day. And after four and a half months, this had become a simple, stable life. Comparing myself to these hikers, I was impressed that I had changed so much.

As I moved into Vermont, my hiking cohort spread out again along the trail, some making up time and pushing twenty-mile days, others, like me, dropping mileage to readjust to the mountains. Vermont felt very different than everything before. In the previous four states, I had crossed a road every hour. In Vermont, I might cross one road a day.

The trail was not only deeper in the wilderness, but more rugged. Any resemblance to the mildness of the middle states was gone. There was no messing around.

The forest reminded me of the northern, Canadian, evergreen forests. Spruces and pines and hemlocks and cedars dominated the rocky terrain. Russet-colored pine needles carpeted the ground and crunched beneath my feet. I'd heard the AT called the long green tunnel. Traversing the Green Mountains, lush evergreen branches capped every bend in the trail, and the AT fully embodied that name.

I got good radio reception and listened most days. With the mountains increasing in size and the trail increasing in steepness, the music and news programs distracted me from the miles. I heard that John F. Kennedy Jr., his wife Caroline Bessette, and her sister died in a plane crash. I knew little about them except what I learned in history class about President John F. Kennedy. I wasn't a follower of these beautiful, so-called American Royals, but I knew they were too young to die and in such a disastrous way. My throat choked up as I walked. I was immersed in a simple life, but news like that plunged me back into the real world. Very soon, I would be returning to that world, a world of heartbreaking news stories, a world of tragedy, a world in which I often felt like I was drowning. Perhaps I ought to get serious about deciding what would happen next.

What physically came next was Manchester Center. I hitched the five miles into town and made my way to the Episcopal Church, which offered its congregation hall for hikers to sleep in. The usual crew was in town, but I also met up with Pizza Guy after many months apart. As we hacked in the churchyard, he told me he'd left Blisters and was searching for Batgirl. He'd fallen in love, but had also fallen behind, and was on a mission to catch her before the end.

I spent the afternoon doing laundry, visiting the post office, and eating ice cream at the Ben and Jerry's shop. My boots, the lightweight pair I had bought in Waynesboro, were scraped and tattered, and the treads were worn completely flat. I visited both the local outfitter and the Eastern Mountain Sports store.

I knew it was a bad idea to buy new, unbroken boots and walk off into the wilderness, but I had to do it. The old pair would not see me through the upcoming ranges. I settled on a dark brown, ankle-high EMS pair and adjusted them the best I could. I left the store with moleskin and a hope that blisters wouldn't decimate my feet.

Kaybek, Slow Buffalo, and I dined together that evening at the Quality Restaurant. I hesitated to eat somewhere that proclaimed its greatness in its name, especially since the ancient building with faded teal awnings screamed mediocrity. But it turned out to be a quality place, the price was right, and they served beer.

We piled our wonky table with fries, burgers, and beer. After a while, we stepped up to the bar, switching to margaritas and cigarettes. As the alcohol and nicotine flooded my bloodstream, I noticed Kaybek took every opportunity to touch my hand, my arm, my shoulder. He flirted with me. I flirted back. Despite this, Buffalo continued to hang out with us, suggesting we do shots. I did one lemon drop, then drew the line. I watched the two of them throw a few more back. The more Kaybek drank, the funnier he became, his English slurring back to French. Buffalo shifted as well, sliding into a more sullen demeanor than I'd ever seen. I got the distinct drunken impression that he was trying to outdrink Kaybek.

I proposed ice cream and put my arm through Kaybek's to walk over to Ben and Jerry's. I hoped Buffalo would take his leave of us at that point, but he persisted, and the three of us stumbled down the street for a late-night bite to dilute the alcohol. I managed a giant bowl of Chocolate Chip Cookie Dough, amazed that I could pack more calories into my already stuffed stomach. When I returned from a trip to the bathroom, I noticed that the two of them had stopped talking to each other and both were frowning.

I tried to continue the fun, attempting to get them to sing some Dave with me as we walked back to the church, but the lightness of our evening escapade had suddenly darkened. There was a playground in the churchyard, and I sat on a swing, dangling my feet and humming

Dave. Our conversation had stopped; there wasn't much else for the three of us to say in the middle of the night.

I jumped off the swing to head inside to bed. Kaybek grabbed my hand and tugged me back. I could barely see his eyes from the nearby streetlight, but I knew he wanted more than a wander around town with Slow Buffalo. I did too.

I recalled that the only way to deal with Buffalo was directly. If I wanted him to leave, I would have to say it out loud.

"Buffalo," I said, looking at Kaybek, "why don't you go inside? We'll be there in a minute." I stepped even closer to Kaybek.

Buffalo froze on the spot, and I could sense his eyes on me. I heard him exhale a quiet sigh before he turned and disappeared into the darkness.

"I want to kiss you," Kaybek whispered.

I leaned toward him and kissed him first. He was slightly taller than me and wrapped his arms around my back and pulled me to him. I felt my knees melting and was glad his arms were there to hold me up. After a few minutes, he pulled away, taking both of my hands in his.

"Before, earlier, Slow Buffalo tells me he likes you," Kaybek said. "You know this?"

"Yes, yes, I know. Please kiss me again."

"I do not want to hurt his feelings."

"Oh, geez," I said, dropping his hands and stepping back. "Seriously? If he actually liked me, shouldn't he say it to me? Why's he telling you? He's not my boyfriend."

"You no are interested in him?"

"No! Not at all. And I'm so sick of him trying to claim me."

I let out a loud sigh and headed toward the church.

So much for that.

The congregation hall was dark. Several AT, LT, and southbound hikers were already asleep. I stumbled over to my gear on the linoleum floor as Kaybek went to his spot on the other side of the large room. I pulled out my sleeping bag and rustled around, trying to get comfortable on the thin Ridge Rest pad. It would be hours before I could sleep; the alcohol was thick in my system as was the anger. I couldn't even make out with someone without Buffalo getting in the way. *Who the hell does he think he is?*

A tap came on my shoulder, and Kaybek whispered, "Tamarack."

I opened my eyes, and my head spun as I sat up. He took my hand and led me across the dark hall. There had to be something sacrilegious about having sex in a church, but I went with him anyway.

We passed into the hallway leading toward the kitchen, where Kaybek opened a door to an adjoining room. A storage room of some sort. He clicked the door behind us. Then he pushed me up against the wall and kissed me hard.

"Okay, oui?"

"Oui."

He kissed me again. I wrapped my arms around his neck and kissed him back.

•   •   •

The church people needed the congregation hall for their weekly bridge club, so hikers had to vacate for the morning. I could barely crawl out of bed from the hangover, but I dragged myself to the shower before I got kicked out. Most people had already hiked on, and I didn't know where Kaybek was. In my hungover state, I knew there would be no hiking for me that day. Once I was clean and my gear was tucked away in a corner of the hall, I took my throbbing head and my journal to the lawn by the swings and leaned against a broad maple tree. I was thinking about spending my day recovering, drinking coffee in the bookshop, and eating more ice cream when Kaybek walked up. He wore a bandana tied around his head and his boots were laced up. He was prepared to hike. He dropped his pack and sat next to me.

"Tamarack, that was fun." He gave me a sly smile.

I grinned. *Man, he's sexy.*

The smile faded, and he looked suddenly serious. He reached over and put his hand on mine. "This does not mean we hike together now. We no are a couple. You understand this?"

"Yes, I understand." We'd been dancing around this attraction for the entire time we'd known each other. Now we'd acted on it. And now life would move on.

Kaybek leaned over and kissed me again. His blond stubble scratched my chin, reminding me of the other places on my body his beard had scratched the night before. Then he stood up, put on his pack, and we said goodbye. I was surprised that I accepted this, that I didn't want more from him. But I adored him no matter what, and it felt right. I was mostly pleased to know there was one guy on the trail who found me attractive and was willing to do something about it.

•   •   •

Blisters formed on my heels within hours of leaving Manchester Center. I limped in my new boots through a sixteen-mile day, not looking forward to arriving at my destination, Big Branch Shelter, where I knew Buffalo was planning to stop as well. He'd taken the day off when I did but had been brooding since I'd made him leave Kaybek and me alone at the swings. I couldn't remember how harshly I'd spoken to him that night, but apparently, it didn't matter because he still hung around, waiting, expectant. His moping increased; he seemed to have lost his friendly Buddhist sensibilities back in Massachusetts.

Sunshine West also had taken a dislike to me. The best I could surmise was that she was jealous that Indiana and I were spending more time together. They'd generally been a team as long as I'd known them, but Indiana had a wife back home in Terre Haute. Regardless of the details of their relationship, I didn't see how my friendship with Indiana negated hers. I wasn't attracted to Indiana, he was very short after all, but I liked him a lot. He'd begun teaching me a few chords on his guitar, and I looked forward to spending time with him at the shelter each evening. We had developed a kind of bickering, sibling-like relationship. Our banter made me think of Jurnee, except Indiana was more pointed and political in his comments. He was a smart ass, but I never took him seriously.

The cohort trekked through the Greens of Vermont, closing in on Killington. I didn't have a mail drop there, but I planned to meet up with the couple who had lived across the street from me during my entire childhood. I was looking forward to a night off in a soft bed. As I trod by every shade of green in existence, I passed time flipping through radio stations. One afternoon, I stumbled upon an unintelligible rock song. When it ended, an announcer stated it was the Woodstock Festival. The thirtieth anniversary event was happening over in upstate New York that very weekend. I listened to another horrid song from Kid Rock, then turned the dial.

I plowed through the hot day, blisters popping inside my sweaty boots. Even in the shady forest, the heat pressed down, and I was glad I wasn't at a sweltering concert. I flipped back to the festival channel, and to my astonishment, Dave was playing. I stopped on the trail and laughed and raised my hiking poles in the air.

Dave was everywhere on this hike, and I was falling more in love. As I made my way north, Wingfoot's guidebook assisted me in navigating trail mileage and towns. Dave's music helped me navigate my emotions; from the philosophical to the angry to the rapturous, there was a song to match each one. I'd written lyrics in the registers and my journal, sang the songs a thousand times as I walked, been enchanted in Virginia when the music floated through a campground like ether, and made a pilgrimage to Pittsburgh. Now I discovered the band live on the radio as I made my way through these green mountains; sometimes I felt as if Dave was right beside me on this trek. The words filled my head as the notes filled my heart. The band played several songs at Woodstock, increasing their intensity to match what I imagined was a very hot and bothered crowd. I jammed down the trail, floating, singing, and by the time they played an encore of "Ants Marching," I had forgotten about the intense pain in my feet.

I sped into the shelter, excited to tell Indiana and Sunshine about hearing Dave.

"Sounds like a fucking mainstream nightmare," Indiana said in his usual tone. "Probably a muddy field full of drunk frat boys taking advantage of topless sorority girls."

"It's good that I like you," I said. "Otherwise, I'd take you down for that kind of trash talk." We'd bickered many times over Dave, and I knew he said these things to razz me. Indiana was an excellent musician, but I liked to tease him back. "You just wish you were as awesome as Dave."

"He's a rich, pretentious poser," Indiana said, scoffing. "Can't even play the guitar."

"Jealous!" I hollered.

Sunshine rolled her eyes and turned back to digging through her food bag.

•   •   •

At Sherburne Pass and the road to Killington, I called my old neighbor, Roberta, who picked me up within the hour. She and her husband Peter had moved to Vermont from New Jersey a few years before and still kept in touch with my parents. They were a wealthy couple who had cats instead of kids and had offered to take me in for a night. When I walked into the spotless bedroom with an attached bathroom, I felt like a wild boar being let loose in a palace. My filthy gear was going to stain their white carpets and sheets, but I tried to leave the dirtiest stuff outside and took a shower immediately upon arriving.

I would have been happy to spend the next morning soaking my feet in their hot tub and eating a big meal, but while Peter golfed, Roberta whisked me all over the state of Vermont, wanting me to see the state's ski areas. My interest in ski resorts rivaled my interest in golf courses, but I acquiesced as she drove me north to see Smuggler's Notch and Stowe. I focused on the impressive mountains she pointed out, Mt. Mansfield and Camel's Hump, rather than the slopes decimated for human entertainment and sport. We stopped at the Von Trapp Family Lodge for authentic Austrian fare and photos. Finally, the day bore real fruit when we arrived at Mecca, also known as the Ben and Jerry's Factory in Waterbury.

Roberta and I toured the colorful factory and learned the history and philosophy of the company. We received samples of Bovinity Divinity, Smores, and Chai Latte, and she won a Phish Stick. I bought a waffle cone loaded with Chocolate Fudge Brownie, Vanilla Caramel Chunk, and Peanut Butter Cup. I wanted to tell someone at the factory how important Ben and Jerry's had been to me on the AT, *in basic terms, very;* how many pints I'd devoured, *at least twenty-five so far;* and that I loved their motto, *If it's not fun, why do it?* But I wasn't sure whom to tell except Roberta. So, I bought a bumper sticker, and we headed back to Killington.

My whirlwind driving detour all over Vermont was more a day out of author Bill Bryson's playbook than my own. And after another night in Roberta and Peter's pristine home, I was eager to get back on the grimy trail where I belonged. It was time to move past Killington and the Greens and cut east, toward the river of jagged mountains ahead— the Whites. That range stood huge and imposing, and within its depths, the AT cut through. Beyond that, farther north, at the end of the long green tunnel, was Katahdin. I could not yet see her from any mountaintop, but with each step I took, she grew larger, mightier, and more brilliant than ever before.

KRUMMHOLZ

I'd slept in a wide variety of strange places over the past months, but the dank basement of a frat house was by far the worst. Wingfoot called Hanover, New Hampshire, "the most sophisticated town on the AT," and while the home of Dartmouth College might be sophisticated, the fraternities which offered space for thru-hikers were far from cultured.

When I got to town, I found Buffalo, Sunshine West, Indiana, Glider, Ironhorse, and Doc all at Panarchy. In its glory days of the early 1800s, the white, imposing, column-fronted house must have been a beautiful sight. But today, it was a frat house like all the ones I'd partied at in Ann Arbor: beer-stained pool table, peeling wallpaper, apocalypse-ready furniture, and a healthy population of cockroaches that some people adopted as pets. A few students were in residence over the summer, but they acted oblivious to the hiker crowd occupying their house. I was grateful for a free roof over my weary head, but as I staked a corner of the basement near Glider and Sunshine West, an uneasy, dark feeling I recognized too well set in.

Throughout my first years at college, I had been imprisoned in the depths of a major depression. I functioned, but barely, hiding the extent of the black hole from my friends and family. The depression diminished when I went to Australia. For a while, sunshine and beaches dictated my days and broke me out of that dark place. It lurked, though, under the surface, waiting. In the two years since then, I had held it at bay, my senior year by drinking and partying, and after that by immersing myself in life at Baxter State Park. But I teetered at the edge, aware that any disappointment or momentary sadness could cause me to fall into the black hole again.

Over five months on the trail, I had seen my moods go up and down dramatically and regularly, but I hadn't become depressed. Until Hanover.

A weight much heavier than my full pack settled onto my chest. I woke in the mornings, unable to pull myself out of my sleeping bag. Once I did, the days seemed to stretch into a hazy infinity with no clear purpose or direction. Regardless of the weather, I saw everything in gray.

I tried to drown the feeling at a frat house party but ended up drinking and smoking too much and spending a nauseous night on the hard basement floor. I guzzled caffeine for long hours in the local coffee shop, staring out the window, composing gloomy poems. I even tried to scare myself out of being sad and saw *The Blair Witch Project*, which I learned had been filmed near the AT in Maryland. I hated movies about bad things happening in the woods, but I saw it anyway. It did nothing to change my mood.

The weight pressed on me as I lolled in Hanover. Wanting attention, knowing he would give it, I didn't even push Buffalo away. We watched movies on the maroon, mildewed sofa in the frat house living room. He waited on me, making popcorn and getting drinks as we sat close to each other. He wasn't a bad guy. Why couldn't I scoot over closer, as I would have if I was sitting with Kaybek or Full Moon? It would have been so much easier. I searched, but I could dredge up no romantic affection for him. Instead, I let him hover like a mosquito, no energy to raise my hand and swat him away.

I called my parents, forcing happiness into my voice, refraining from any talk of sorrow. Their happiness for me was evident and gave me a brief lift. They offered to come up to Maine and get me when I finished. The idea surprised me; I hadn't once considered how I would leave Baxter State Park or the state of Maine once I had completed my hike. I figured I'd deal with that when the time came. However, their plan made sense; they'd drive up, spend a few days, then bring me home.

But home to what? To New Jersey? To my childhood bedroom full of clothes and stuffed animals and piles of knickknacks? Nine months ago, I didn't have a career, a boyfriend, a long-term plan. With about six weeks left to hike, not one of those things had changed. I was as lost and aimless as ever.

My mail in Hanover reinforced this notion. One of my sorority sisters wrote to me with the news that she got engaged. My friend who had spent a semester in Australia was back in the States and fleshing out her future grad school plans. And another friend landed her dream job at Morgan Stanley in New York City. They were all busy moving forward, starting important things. What was I doing? Sitting in coffee shops, watching movies, learning to play a few chords on my friend's guitar. Hiking the AT was incredibly self-indulgent and not helpful to society in any way. I finally saw what my father had seen all those months ago: a lazy, privileged young woman who needed to pull herself up by her bootstraps and find a damn job.

It was Buffalo who got me to escape the Hanover abyss. He was having such a novel experience partying with the fraternity that he repeatedly declared his intention to stay all week. I didn't want to reject him again outright, but I knew if I left during his fun, I could get ahead and be on my own. My motivation was nil on a day thick with humidity, but I promised myself one more afternoon in the air-conditioned coffee shop and a pint of Ben and Jerry's Chocolate Fudge Brownie in exchange for leaving when cooler evening air blew in. Town departures had never been easy, and this one required Hacky Girl superhero strength. I heaved my full pack and dragged myself a mile and a half out of town to Velvet Rocks Shelter.

The sole inhabitant of the shabby shelter was the eccentric Long Haired Freaky People. I set up my tarp nearby and watched the glowing yellow sky dwindle. I climbed into my sleeping bag in the blackening forest, waiting for the caffeine to work its way out of my system before I could sleep. The woods were dark, but nothing like that creepy

Panarchy basement that I was relieved to be leaving behind. As I dozed off, I scanned my body, searching for the heavy weight, hoping I had left that behind too. A noise crackled nearby. I sat up like a shot. *The Blair Witch*!

That shit was scary. *But not real.*

I forced my eyes closed and lay back. I relaxed my muscles, trying to let go of the tension. The noise crunched again. I breathed. *There is no creature in these woods that means me harm. I will not carry this fear with me.* And anyway, there were a thousand things a hell of a lot scarier than the Blair Witch.

.   .   .

For a few days, I leapfrogged with Indiana and Sunshine West. Indiana taught me more guitar chords, informing me I could now play any Bob Dylan song. That seemed about as likely as me becoming Bob Dylan, but I enjoyed his attention and insisted on practicing when we were together. We continued to joke and bicker while Sunshine continued to send me pointed looks. She finally confided her true irritation: she was due back home to start work. She might have to skip up to the 100-Mile Wilderness, the final 100 miles before Katahdin, so she could finish. I tried to reassure her with the old *hike your own hike* phrase, saying that each of us had a different path to take, but I wasn't sure it helped. I felt guilty enough about my Pennsylvania skip, if I had to miss all of New Hampshire and most of Maine, I would have felt crummy too.

Towhee was also in the area, along with her husband Dave, who had left their beagle, Ben, at home and driven their ancient gray van from North Carolina to slackpack a few sections with her. I'd also caught up to Living Water, Plato, and Angel, none of whom I'd crossed paths with in months. I was glad friends were nearby, and I met new hikers every day, but I plowed forward at my own pace, step by step, hoping to get there eventually. The depression didn't exactly lift, but with the stunning daily views, the camaraderie with Indiana, and my unceasing hunger, the depression slipped to the side.

The trail wound increasingly higher and more vertical. I hadn't been above treeline since the previous summer on Katahdin, and looking at the elevation profile on my map made me a bit queasy. The first major hike in the Whites was a 4,000-foot climb to Mt. Moosilauke at 4,802 feet, the highest mountain on the trail in many months. The day before Moosilauke, I swung by the Glencliff post office to pick up another mail drop, which included the fleece clothing I knew I would need from there on out. The massive load of food and gear would have to sustain me through the rest of New Hampshire, 100 miles to Gorham.

The Whites required taking it easy, so I granted myself a full day to do the six-mile climb over Moosilauke and the subsequent 1,000-foot descent to the Beaver Brook Shelter on the other side. I searched for my rhythm across the first flattish mile, adjusting to the increased weight of the pack. I left my radio off, wanting to hear the wind and birds, the crunch of leaves and dirt. When the incline began, my feet felt like they were stuck to flypaper. I stopped to pee and look at the map, then kept on steadily uphill.

There were no views or overlooks to indicate how high I'd climbed, but at some point, the root-covered path gave way to rock underfoot. The forest shifted; everything became stone and sharp angles and conifer trees. My legs ached. I'd been climbing forever; I could feel the top. The air nipped. The forest thinned. The trees shrank as I arrived at the Krummholz, where I paused to give myself a silent cheer.

I'd experienced the Krummholz—a German word that meant twisted tree—the previous year at Baxter State Park. This thin zone of land buffered the lush lowlands from the alpine peak, and for miles in each direction, the spruces and pines were indeed twisted and misshapen. It was as if an invisible horizontal ceiling prevented these trees from growing one inch above their allotted elevation, which in New Hampshire topped out at 4,400 feet. The extreme sun exposure, high winds, and months of snow and ice battered the plants down, creating a unique and beautiful stretch of land.

Reaching the Krummholz meant that I'd made it through most of the climb. Almost there. I collected my breath as the puffy clouds thickened in the sky above. I hiked on, leaving the twisted trees behind, gasping as the cold wind blasted my face.

All my climbs to Katahdin's alpine zone came rushing back in a surge of emotion. The lichen-covered rocks, the spiky clumps of grasses, the utter lack of anything to block the view across the earth. This stark world of apparent emptiness secretly held a whole universe of life between the rocks that most people never even knew existed. I was hot from the exertion but felt chills as I looked down over the mountain, amazed that my legs had brought me this far. I pressed into the wind and followed the stone cairns that marked the path rising to the top.

A weathered, brown wooden sign held up by a large pile of rocks marked the peak. I slowed as I approached the sign, partly from exhaustion, partly because I was looking at the view and not wanting to stumble. The whipping wind cooled me through my sweat-soaked shorts and t-shirt. I dropped my pack and dug out my fleece sweater, which didn't offer enough warmth. I wanted to stay up there all afternoon, but I knew I had a short time before I froze. I needed to celebrate my success quickly.

A white-haired woman and her little dog arrived after I did. As I stuffed M&M's in my mouth, I watched the woman walk up to the sign and touch it. She turned to me.

"How far you going?"

"Maine," I said, pausing from the M&M's.

"You're just getting to the good part," she said. "I'm Grammy GoAT. Did the trail in '88." She held out her hand.

"Wow, that's so awesome!" As I shook her hand, I thought she appeared awfully old. If she'd been a Grammy eleven years ago, how old was she now? "It's great that you're still out here, hiking these big mountains."

"Bah." She waved her hand at me. "They'll never get me to stop coming up here. Once you do this thing, you'll always keep coming back. This trail gets you. You'll see."

•   •   •

White Mountain National Forest was a distinct ecosystem from the rest of the trail, both in the natural features of the steep and rugged wilderness and in how humans could move within it. The AT route was highly regulated by the Appalachian Mountain Club. The frequent and free lean-tos were gone, replaced by a tent site and hut system. The small number of tent sites were five to ten dollars a night, while the huts were full-service lodges maintained by a dedicated crew and placed strategically a one-day walk apart. The fifty-five-dollar price tag included prepared meals, a cot, and restrooms. People wanting to hike across the Whites reserved their spots in each hut months or years in advance. They carried minimal gear as they hiked, eating and sleeping in the huts along the way. This option was out of reach and impractical for most thru-hikers, but the huts also offered work-for-stay for two thru-hikers each night. We could spend a few hours cleaning tables, bathrooms, or dishes in exchange for a spot on the floor and possibly dinner.

If the huts were full, there was primitive camping. It was legal to go off the trail and throw down under some shrubbery. But the regulations spelled out the significant distance a camp had to be from trails, water, huts, or roads. Thru-hikers rarely used this option, due to the difficulty of wandering a quarter of a mile off the trail and finding a flat, open scrap of ground.

When all these options failed, there was stealth camping, which I found to be my only choice the afternoon I arrived at Franconia Notch.

A storm was brewing. I'd already walked nine miles over the Kinsman Mountains, and I refused to climb to 5,000 feet to cross Mt. Lincoln and Mt. Lafayette in a cold rainstorm. I also didn't want to hitch to the town of Woodstock to pay for a hotel. I'd been hearing about stealth camping for as long as I'd been on the trail, but I'd never done it; the good, obedient girl in me didn't want to break the rules or get in trouble. Finally, it was time.

Despite the interstate running through the Notch and the nearby Flume Gorge Visitor Center, I saw no other people. I backtracked a short distance from the highway, then scoped out several areas less than fifty feet from the trail. I found a flat spot where my tarp could tuck in behind a large boulder, somewhat hidden from view, and completely illegal.

I put on my fleece, cooked my dinner, and filtered water from the nearby stream, but I waited until sundown to pitch my tarp. As darkness came, I kept my flashlight off, settling into my sleeping bag debating which would be worse, a midnight visit from the Blair Witch who would scare me to death or a ranger who would kick me out of the woods when I had nowhere else to go. Neither would be enjoyable, and I slept lightly for much of the night.

I startled awake at first light when rain pounded the roof. As I came into consciousness, I felt relieved that neither the Blair Witch nor the rangers had shown up, but I noticed the water running underneath my sleeping pad and decided I'd better get moving fast. I shoved everything into my pack and dashed to the interstate overpass. Water came down in torrents so loud that the cars speeding by overhead were barely audible.

I sat under cover on the gravel, leaning against a gray cement wall and watching the rain. In the dismal scene, my sadness welled again. My friends were dispersed across the range. I had no energy and no options. Tears rose, and I cried along with the water streaming from the sky. Grammy GoAT had said that this experience would stick with me. True, I would never forget it, but not because I wanted to repeat it, but because the loneliness was crushing me.

•   •   •

I paid scarce attention to the village of Woodstock or the chatter of the middle-aged man next to me as we drove. I'd waited all morning under the highway for the rain to stop, but by lunchtime, the weather reigned victorious. I stood in the downpour for thirty minutes before a car came headed in the right direction. The friendly man didn't seem concerned about my drenched clothes and pack soaking the interior of his car, and he puttered along, pointing out landmarks along the route. Tired and cold from the rain, I silently urged him to drive faster and leaped from the car when we arrived at the Cascade Lodge hostel.

There were few hikers in town, and that evening I came across only Teddy Bear and Crazy Legs. Teddy Bear actually looked like a teddy bear, with fluffy brown hair, a round face, and ears that stuck out a little. Crazy Legs was the skinniest hiker I'd met and looked like her bones could easily snap with any stumble on the rocks. Her short, black hair was streaked with gray, and every time I'd seen her, she had a cigarette in hand. This time was no different as they lounged on a wide, worn couch in the common room, next to an open window. The rain continued outside.

"Join us, Tamarack," said Teddy Bear, as he moved their maps off the recliner next to the couch.

The few interactions I'd had with the couple had mostly included me watching them nitpick and criticize each other. But I thought my mood might fit theirs, especially after the heavy sadness under the overpass.

"How're the Whites treating you?" Crazy Legs asked, taking a drag on her cigarette. Her deep, raspy voice labeled her as a person who had partaken in more than her share of cigarettes over the years.

"I'm exhausted actually," I said. "And hungry. These mountains are whipping my butt."

"Yeah, it's different here. It's rough." Teddy Bear said.

"My feet throb all the time," Crazy Legs added.

I nodded vehemently as they told me about their various foot ailments. Though they were complaining, for once, they didn't seem pissed off at each other or the world.

"Besides warping my feet, this trail has changed me," Crazy Legs said, stubbing out her cigarette. "I've learned a lot out here."

"Oh yeah?" Teddy Bear said, turning to her with a raised eyebrow. "Like what?"

"I judge people harshly when I first meet them."

Teddy Bear chuckled. I guessed that this was a significant understatement.

"What I should do is get to know people, talk to them first," she went on, "before I decide who they are."

It was a deeply honest admission and even as I saw this quality in her, I realized I did the same thing.

"I guess it's just a habit from the real world," I said.

"The real world, ha!" Crazy Legs laughed, then took out another cigarette and lit it. "What the hell is the real world?"

"Hey, can I bum one of those off you?" I asked.

She looked at me with disbelief. "See, now, I never would have pegged you as a smoker." She pushed the package toward me.

"I'm not, but it's good every once in a while." I lit one and handed her back the lighter, sucking in the sweet taste of tobacco. The nicotine shot straight to my head and my eyes blurred. "What did you think of me when we first met?"

They exchanged a glance.

"You're a loner," Teddy Bear said. "Don't worry, we both are too. That's how we could tell. But we all need people. As much as she and I get sick of each other out here," he gave Crazy Legs a light jab with his elbow, "we're glad to have each other." She jabbed back.

"It's impressive, though," Crazy Legs said. "You, being out here alone. I'm not sure I could have done this by myself."

"Thanks, I guess," I replied. I breathed in the smoke and looked out the window at the clouds emptying themselves onto the earth.

I'd never thought of myself as a loner, but rather, as someone who always ended up alone. As I talked with Crazy Legs and Teddy Bear, I wondered if I had chosen solitude. Or had it been thrust upon me?

I had no control over what happened to Jurnee, Hercules, Bud, Full Moon, Kaybek, Biscuits and Gravy, Grubby, Porter, or any of the other people I had enjoyed so much. Our paths had simply diverged. Other people I considered friends—Indiana, Towhee, Ironhorse—were in the Whites somewhere. Perhaps I could find them and stick with them. But the reality was, whether by choice or by chance, I was trekking along this trail, through this world, alone. All I really had was myself.

•   •   •

The 4,000-foot climb out of Franconia Notch was a battle. I moved slowly, my body straining and struggling as if I'd never hiked before. I gave myself a long break at the Krummholz before moving up into the alpine zone. The wind thrashed at the mountain, but the rain had passed, leaving a smattering of clouds. The scene reminded me of that day I had hiked across Big Bald, being blown all over the grassy peak. When the wind had shoved me then, I stumbled onto soft grass. Here, however, nothing soft existed. Everything was rock, granite, and more rock.

I spent the morning crossing the sparse, lunar-like landscape up and down Little Haystack at 4,760 feet, then Mt. Lincoln at 5,089 feet. When I came to the final stretch up 5,260-foot Mt. Lafayette, the rain resumed, and I started to shiver. The wind sucked the last of the warmth from my now-wet limbs, and I began thinking about hypothermia. The raindrops were ice shards stabbing my skin. I pushed myself faster, trying to warm up, but there was no evading the cold. I raced down the backside of Lafayette, maneuvering around the rocks, yelling into the wind. The adrenaline drove me over 4,500-foot Mt. Garfield, and by the time I pulled into the Garfield Ridge Campsite, the rain had stopped again. I used my last droplets of energy to set up my tarp, put a few bucks in the self-serve pay box, and cook a dinner of lentils and veggies. The food didn't touch my hunger, but I was desperate for warmth. I stuffed my food bag into the metal bear box nearby and climbed into my bag for the night.

I'd been waking at sunrise, and with clear skies the next morning, I set off early for Galehead Hut, three miles away. If I arrived by breakfast, I might be able to yogi some leftovers. I walked in before nine o'clock, and though I'd missed the food, I was delighted to find Indiana and Satori washing dishes.

"How are you doing?" Indiana asked in that sincere way he did when we hadn't seen each other for a few days.

I told him about my inexhaustible hunger and my detour to Woodstock. He told me that Sunshine West was gone. She'd run out of time and these mountains were too difficult; she skipped up to the 100-Mile Wilderness. I had liked Sunshine well enough, but I didn't miss her negative attitude toward me.

There were only a few other thru-hikers around, and now that I had caught up with a friend, I intended to stay with him. Over the next couple of days, Indiana and I walked and camped together, both glad for the company. He kept on with my guitar lessons and tried to make me laugh as we pieced together the lyrics from strange songs like "I'm My Own Grandpa." Our friendship strengthened, and with it, my sorrow of recent days receded.

The trail rose dramatically up and down from treeline across the magnificent range of 5,000-foot mountains. The landscape of this wild wonderland inspired me, but also hammered me down. The void in my belly continued to increase. Every day I ate as much of my food as I had rationed, but I always finished still hungry. At Zealand Hut, I needed calories more than I needed to be a vegetarian, and gratefully accepted a large bowl of chicken noodle soup from the crew. I was so ravenous that if they'd offered me a slab of beef, I would have asked them to pass the steak sauce. I doubted if even that would ease the feeling of starvation overcoming me.

Wingfoot noted the ruggedness of the Whites and suggested decreasing mileage. Indiana and I complied. When we arrived at Crawford Notch, we decided that instead of heading up the next massive ridge into the Presidential Range, we'd hitch a few miles north to the Crawford Notch Hostel. That evening we sat in the common room chatting with weekend hikers James and his son Mark. They'd been hut hiking, but the weather and mountains had gotten the best of them. They'd decided to cut their trip short and skip the Presidentials.

"Are you two interested in our bunks at Lakes of the Clouds Hut?" James asked. "They're already paid for."

My eyes widened. It was too good to be true. Working in exchange for a night sleeping on the floor was a fine way to get through. But an actual bunk, with two actual meals, at no actual cost, was pure luxury.

"Definitely," said Indiana, "I'm happy to pretend I'm James for a night."

"I guess that makes me Mark, your teenage son," I said.

"Well, yes," James went on, grinning at us, "You'll have to creatively skirt the truth, but I doubt the crew will care."

"Thank you so much," I said to James. "This is really awesome."

The evening grew even better with the two packages of Lipton noodles I found in the free box and added to my regular mac and cheese. Further generosity came from the biker group also staying in the hostel who shared their leftover mashed potatoes and tortellini. Later, a hut worker returned from town with a pint of Ben and Jerry's for Indiana and me. I tucked into bed grateful for the trail magic but with an achy emptiness overtaking my body.

•   •   •

I strained uphill thousands of feet, one step at a time fighting gravity across the southern Presidential Range. I rose once more past the Krummholz and into the dreamy world of lichen and stone. The sun was high, and the mountains stood angular and jagged with peaks of gray and blue. When I rounded the trail from behind Mt. Monroe and saw Mt. Washington, I had to stop and right myself. On the east coast, our mountains didn't rise to elevations where oxygen levels were noticeably lower, but I felt light-headed and weak. I was exhausted from the long climb, sunburned from a day of walking fully in the sunshine, and starved from my ongoing hunger. But none of that compared with the overwhelming massiveness of the mountain. At 6,288 feet, Washington was the highest peak in New England. It could snow on any day of the year up there and it held the highest wind speed recorded on earth. I was nothing next to this giant. I followed the AT as it weaved between Monroe and Washington, feeling puny in every sense of the word.

The gray shingled walls and roof of the Lakes of the Clouds Hut blended in perfectly with the landscape. Washington loomed above the building as I walked up to the dirt clearing surrounding the hut. Wingfoot called it "Lakes of the Crowds," and I had to agree. Trail crews, hut crews, researchers, and day and weekend hikers wandered in every direction. I dropped my pack next to the building and leaned against it to have a snack. I had to wait for Indiana to show up before checking in since he would be the one posing as James. I didn't know how far back he was, but I didn't like being amongst the crowd, so I decided to take a jaunt up Mt. Monroe.

The peak was about 300 feet above the hut, and it was a short, easy climb without my pack. I had the top to myself to contemplate the range. Washington still stood a thousand feet above, and in the other direction, a wave of mountains spread out like an ocean. *So many mountains!* And Georgia so very far away. It was hard to imagine I had once been there.

My head ached; I guessed I was dehydrated. When I saw the tiny form of Indiana trekking around Mt. Monroe over to the hut, I headed back down. After we checked in, I lay on the bunk that had been gifted to me and waited for dinner. I thought my stomach might be digesting itself, and when food was placed in front of me in the dining hall, I gobbled it down. Mashed potatoes, cooked veggies, chicken soup, salad, and bread. I asked my tablemates for their discards and the kitchen for any extras they would give. That night, I ate more snacks from my food bag, but nothing filled my stomach. I went to bed hungry and scared that my body was finally giving out.

In the morning, I felt no better. Despite my nausea, I ate pancakes in the dining hall and topped them off with granola from my bag. I packed and left the hut early, wanting to get up to Washington before the crowds.

On the trail from the hut, a giant yellow sign warned hikers of the extreme weather atop the peak. A storm could blow in at any moment and knock people off the mountain. It had happened. Folks in the dining hall had told stories last evening. The 1,000-foot elevation gain in 1.3 miles was akin to climbing a staircase. Weak and ill, I stumbled often on the rocky terrain and struggled to keep myself upright.

When I reached the peak, clouds rolled in. As did the people. Cars and buses full of tourists were already wandering around the weather station, snack bar, and overlook areas. More and more materialized from the world below. I elbowed my way through the crowd to the peak sign and asked a stranger to take my photo. It took several minutes to get people to move aside so I could get a photo alone. Then I wandered to the snack bar, feeling discouraged and ready to quit. I found an uninhabited corner to keep away from the swarm. I felt I might vomit, and yet I knew I needed to eat. I bought a veggie sub and potato salad then had more of my granola. It helped, but only slightly.

When Indiana showed up, he offered me some of his mini bagels. He sat with me for a while, waiting to see if I perked up. We had planned to do fifteen miles across the northern Presidentials today. But walking one more step on rocky terrain, where I could be blown off the ridge at any moment, starving and achy, not sure if I could stand straight, was simply not possible. Madison Hut was only about six miles away, but even that seemed unmanageable.

"I can't do it," I croaked.

"Sure, you can," Indiana said. "You're an Amazon woman."

"Yeah, no. I'm done." I hated myself for saying it, but I knew I couldn't walk any farther. "I'm going to take the shuttle down."

"Are you sure?" Indiana said. When I nodded, he added, "Then I'll see you at Pinkham Notch this evening, right?"

"Right."

After he left, I sank further. I was bailing on one of the most scenic and stunning sections of the trail. But my body would not cooperate, and I could not hoist my pack. I purchased a ticket for the shuttle to Pinkham Notch, then lay on a hard bench clutching my belly for three hours until the shuttle company had enough riders to make the trip. I watched the happy, clean, well-fed tourists come and go. I couldn't judge them anymore. They had taken the easy way to the top, and I would take the easy way down. I hid at the back of the snack bar and avoided everyone, not wanting to run into any other thru-hikers and explain why I wasn't hiking.

I cried on the shuttle ride. The dark sky threatened rain again, but I should be out there in it. The weather was as fickle as my moods, and when I exited the van at the Pinkham Notch Visitor Center, the sun had returned. I sat on a bench in front of the building and regretted what I had done. Washington glared down at me from on high. *Is the mountain judging me?*

A blond woman with a golden retriever walked by.

"You're a thru-hiker!" She exclaimed.

I said nothing, expecting the usual barrage of questions and comments I wasn't interested in answering. She introduced herself as Deborah and reminded me we had met on Mt. Pierce a few days prior. She was waiting to pick up her friend, Amazing Grace, a southbound thru-hiker.

"You look kinda hungry," she said. "I've got a car full of food if you want some."

My emphatic nodding was all the answer she needed, and Deborah led me to her car. She made two huge veggie sandwiches, then offered a bonanza of fruit from grapes to cantaloupe to nectarines. I sat in the front seat of her car and between bites, explained my ailments and why

I wasn't hiking down off Washington. As I spoke, I knew I was justifying it to myself, not her, and was grateful when she didn't ask questions but instead handed me more food. I thanked Deborah and headed back to the visitor center to clean up in the bathroom.

There was no sign of Indiana all afternoon, and after a few hours, I left him a note pinned to the community board. A quarter-mile from the visitor center, the AMC offered a free camp, and there I set up my tarp and ate dinner. I kept looking up the trail, willing Indiana to show up.

I didn't want to be alone again. It was so much more fun with Indiana. We teased and joked, but then that sweet side of him came out. Underneath his Oscar the Grouch exterior, he was a cuddly, caring Elmo, and now and then he let it show. Like a few days before, when we'd stopped at Ethan Pond.

"Wingfoot says that tamarack trees line the shore," I said to Indiana as we had walked out of camp that morning. "We have to go there."

"I've seen enough Tamaracks on this hike," he replied.

I rolled my eyes at him. "Har, har."

"Yes, of course, let's stop," he agreed.

In the bright sunshine, Ethan Pond was more of a sparkling gem than a pond. The water rippled placidly, reflecting the deep blue of the sky above. All along the shoreline, the scraggly, soft green tamaracks took up most of the real estate. Other kinds of conifers mingled in places, but my namesake prevailed. I'd never seen so many in one place.

"Remember, they're the only pine that loses their needles," I said. "They're unique and perfect. Like me." I batted my eyes at him in an exaggerated way, expecting him to retort with a comment about my mediocrity, my ordinariness, my flailing abilities.

Indiana looked out over the pond, contemplating. "What am I gonna do after the trail when you're not around?" he said.

His sentimentality caught me off guard. Indiana had become one of my best friends, and I didn't know what I was going to do without him either. But I hadn't expected him to *say* it.

In Pinkham Notch, I wasn't worried for Indiana's safety coming down off the Presidentials; he had probably stopped early. I worried about what I would do over the next days if I wasn't with him. Alone, I might sink into depression again. But as I got ready for bed, I told myself to relax. The windiest mountain in the world rose high above, where at any moment, a storm could sweep up and blow you off course. I had avoided that fate, and there, far below, for the moment, I was safe.

•   •   •

I returned to the visitor center in the morning for the six-dollar all-you-can-eat breakfast. I ran into Greenfoot, who'd slept in the bunkhouse and hadn't seen Indiana either. We talked briefly before he set off for the climb out of Pinkham.

From there, the trail moved northeast to traverse the Wildcat Range, the final twenty miles of New Hampshire which ended at Gorham, near the Maine border. Indiana and I had planned to do that stretch in two short days. My trek through the Whites had left me weak and defeated, and I didn't want to struggle anymore. I debated for an hour or so, while I took down my tarp and packed up my gear. But the ache in my stomach and the pain in my head decided for me. I replaced the note on the community board, then walked out to the road and stuck out my thumb for a hitch.

I was immediately picked up by Maggie, the woman who ran The Barn, a well-known and loved hiker hostel in Gorham. On the drive, I told Maggie of my starvation and said I was looking forward to a lot of sleep at her place.

"Well, you know we also run a real bed-and-breakfast," she said. "That might suit you better in your condition."

When she told me the price was forty dollars, I shook my head. "It sounds lovely, but I can't afford that."

"How about you do some work for us, and we'll lower the price?" Maggie replied. "You can wash windows or vacuum the rooms. Even better, I could use your help watching my toddler while I get some work done."

By the time we pulled into the Libby House B&B, we'd made a deal. And instead of turning left to The Barn where the hikers stayed, Maggie showed me into the purple Victorian house with the sprawling wraparound front porch. She didn't ask me for anything but showed me right to a gorgeous cream and pink-colored room with a four-poster bed topped with a puffy white comforter.

I peeled off my stinky hiking clothes and dropped them in a pile, then took a hot shower. I thought about James and Mark, Deborah, Maggie, and all the complete strangers who had gone out of their way to be kind to me. Maybe I looked exceptionally ragged, maybe they could feel the guilt of skipping thirty-five miles exuding from my skin, or maybe they were just good people trying to do good things. Whatever their reasons, I felt cared for as I climbed into the soft bed and cuddled down under the comforter. This was a thousand times better than where I'd slept at the beginning of the state: the dark, dirty basement floor of Panarchy. And while I relished sleeping on the hard earth, atop a cold ridge, under a thin tarp, with the wind and rain raging outside, I was deeply grateful to be in this divine bed. I fell asleep within minutes and didn't wake for thirteen hours.

•   •   •

My days in Gorham focused on sleeping, eating whole pizzas, hacky sacking, napping, and helping out around the B&B. I had fallen into a crew of old friends that included Ironhorse, Biohazard, and Dogman, who remained one of the top two cutest guys on the trail. Pizza Guy and Batgirl were also in residence. My initial delight in catching up with my old dummy taco stuffer friend faded after Batgirl and I spent an afternoon lounging on the couches. Her self-importance had skyrocketed from its already considerably high point after Pizza Guy had declared his undying affection. I enjoyed reminiscing about Virginia with her but remembered why we had parted ways all those months ago. Towhee and her husband, Dave, arrived with a dozen funny stories about van life. Indiana also turned up, beaten down by the Whites and ready for his hike to be over.

I hadn't played hacky sack in weeks thanks to both Indiana's indifference to it and the adverse rocky terrain, so at The Barn, I pulled in Biohazard, Pizza Guy, and a reluctant Ironhorse for a game. The four of us stood in the driveway, the hack flying back and forth along with the jokes and stories. I kicked the hack to Ironhorse, who tipped it, sending it flying into the road behind him. Before any of us could move, an eighteen-wheel logging truck roared by, flattening the hack to the road.

"Mr. Hacky!" Ironhorse cried out.

I screamed and rushed to the road to scoop up my hack before another vehicle came by. Its beans were dropping out of a minor hole on one side and a gaping wound on another. It was dirty before, but now the red, yellow, and green stripes were almost black.

"I'm so sorry," Ironhorse said.

"I can fix it," I replied. With a needle and thread from Maggie, I spent a half hour doctoring my little hack.

"You've pulled it back from the brink of death, Dr. Tamarack," Ironhorse said when I showed him the patched beanbag. He grimaced. "Does that mean we have to play again?"

"You kicked it into the road on purpose!" I accused him jokingly. "Just so you wouldn't have to play anymore."

"I wish I had that much control over my kicks." He gave me a sheepish look. "Ah, I mean, yes, let's play again."

Ironhorse was like a favorite uncle. Like Teddy Bear and Crazy Legs had said: I needed him; I needed all these other people. One of the best medicines I could take for my aching body and beaten spirit was to laugh with my friends. In Gorham, I felt myself healing.

Until then, most of the things in my life had just happened to me. I had made choices to go to the right college, to attend the church and join the sorority, to wear the fancy dresses and pantyhose because those were the norms I had been given. That was whom my family, my peers, my society expected me to be. For many years I accepted that reality. And each time I attempted to step away from that prescribed version of myself, from what my father thought was right, be it with a colorful bedroom, a philosophy-based diet, or a longing to see the world, I was met with a violent effort to snap me back into place.

But I had made it to *this place, this moment* out of my own profound volition. Going to Australia had been the first step out of the box they had put me in. That taste of freedom had led me to Baxter State Park, which led me to Georgia, which led me to walk 1,830 miles to Mt. Washington, New Hampshire, which led me to skip the Wildcat Range and come to Gorham, which led me to sew up a hacky sack that a fifty-year-old man I adored named Ironhorse had kicked into the street. These choices were mine.

I wasn't sure what choice I would make after the AT. Maybe I'd get the dog I wanted. Maybe I'd go west and work at that National Monument, Hovenweep. I was a loner, in the sense that I needed to do my own thing, go my own way, and hike my own hike. But if I skipped a few mountains or my parents didn't like the direction I went or on any given day I walked zero miles or twenty, good or bad, dark or light, up or down, they were my steps to take, and it was up to me how I walked them.

THE WAY LIFE SHOULD BE

A rectangular blue sign nailed to a lichen-covered spruce tree welcomed me to my fourteenth state. The hand-painted, yellow words clumsily printed in all capital letters said:

WELCOME TO MAINE. THE WAY LIFE SHOULD BE.

1,880 miles from Springer Mountain, soaked with sweat and rain from the morning, I dropped my pack and stood by the sign so Indiana could snap a picture. It felt like both a momentous occasion and just another day in the long green tunnel. There was nothing remarkable about the sign or the spot or the moment, but I was back in the state I had fallen in love with the previous summer. The end was very near. In 280 miles, two more mail drops, and about three weeks, I would climb Katahdin and complete this journey.

But Maine wasn't going to make the last miles easy. The day after entering the state, Indiana and I left camp early to tackle Mahoosuc Notch, the hardest mile on the trail. It wasn't actually a trail, but rather a mile of giant boulders to scramble over and under and around and between. The boulders covered in damp moss caused me to slip, while the dry, gritty ones scraped my hands and knees as I crawled across. In a few places, we took off our packs. Indiana would creep through a narrow, jagged gap, then I'd pass our packs over and crawl through after him. Evergreen trees covered both sides of the notch, and several had fallen over this mess of rocks, offering us further obstacles. I moved so slowly—pausing to assess each step, looking up to avoid hitting my head on a rock, feeling my muscles shake under stress—I wondered if I was even moving at all. We inched through, alternately laughing and swearing at the madness of the trail, with the sun never breaching the ridge to shine on us.

After about two hours, we emerged from the cool shadows to the base of Old Speck Mountain. Indiana strode on, undaunted by the past mile and the climb ahead. I stopped for lunch, my limbs aching from the strain of bouldering. After four days of sleeping and eating in Gorham, I had felt powerful enough to keep hiking. But Mahoosuc Notch and the prospect of Old Speck had me rethinking my strength. On the first steps of the steep climb, I began to cry, wondering if I would make it to Katahdin at all.

When I hauled myself into the lean-to at Speck Pond, I found Indiana, Towhee, Yogi and Boo-Boo, Flash and Merit, and a section hiker with an English accent. After the difficult few miles, most of them were doing various camp chores and soaking in the warm end-of-summer afternoon. Indiana, however, was resting next to his full pack. Ready to leave.

Like so many hikers, Indiana had run low on funds, food, and patience. The end was calling us all, and he needed to make miles. As Indiana bade everyone goodbye, I didn't know what to say. I knew I wouldn't see him again. I held back my tears until he left, then retreated to my tarp. Like so many relationships I'd built on the AT, this one's time was up.

That evening, the sun and clouds put on a show. I lay on my back, looking up, as layer within layer of clouds changed shape, bleeding color into each other and morphing into iridescent pinks and oranges. The mountains around me turned purple, melting into the deepening indigo sky. It was a singularly spectacular and ephemeral event.

I wanted the color to linger. To keep filling my soul with light and hope. I'd wanted Indiana to stay. Like I'd wanted Jurnee and Full Moon and Bud to stay. I'd wanted to hold on to so many of my friends, and yet, I never could. Like the sunsets, they slipped away. I kept my attention on the changing sky, glad to be resting. I knew I would sleep well that night, after such a draining day. A few stars popped out, white specks of glitter a billion miles away. The darker it got, the more stars lit up, until the full Milky Way was a dazzling wreath of sparkles.

When Indiana had said goodbye earlier, he'd taken on that tone of kindness that he often hid. "Take care of yourself, Amanda," he'd said. He'd used my real name, which was odd since he usually called me by some random nickname. This felt personal; this felt like he knew me. I realized he did. These months, walking with these people, I had been more fully myself, more fully open and alive than I'd been in my entire life.

Without them, without this trail, who would I be?

•   •   •

I trucked through the dreary morning. A misty rain had blown in, but I needed to keep going; I couldn't wait for better weather. Head down, I kept my eyes on my feet, my thoughts alternating between what to eat for lunch and what to do after Katahdin. One question was much easier to answer than the other. I heard a snarfle ahead and jerked my head up to see a giant mass of brown. Actually, two giant masses of brown.

Ahead of me stood a car-sized male moose with a velvety antler rack at least five feet across. Next to him was an equally large female moose. Both ignored me, a mere ant to their goliaths, and continued chomping on leaves. I'd seen moose the previous summer at Baxter, but always from a distance, across a pond, through a forest. These two were close. And spectacular.

I gingerly unbuckled my pack and crouched down, hoping I wouldn't scare them, hoping no one else would come along and disturb this moment. I watched them, rapt. They appeared to be the most awkward creatures, with wide bulky bodies, knobby knees, small heads at the ends of their thick necks. Yet, they sauntered through the forest, turning left and right to grab their favorite leaves, perfectly adept at their work. Their skinny legs and big hooves allowed them to maneuver the terrain without any hint of clumsiness. I watched until the last rustle of leaves had stilled.

When I got to the shelter that afternoon, I told Flash and Merit about the moose. I couldn't quite put my awe into words, but they were impressed, wishing they had seen them too.

Moving at a similar pace, I spent a few days with Flash and Merit. Flash was about my age, dark-haired and handsome. Merit was his gray-haired father and just plain sweet. As kind as they were to each other, their interactions also held a slight edginess. I imagined after five months together patience might be a tad thin.

"Should I put up the tent or get the water?" Merit asked.

"Well," Flash said, struggling to keep from patronizing his dad, "as you see me here with the water bag pumping water, why don't you put up the tent."

"Oh, okay."

Merit's strength was waning. He'd run out of ibuprofen, so I shared mine every day. In exchange, he'd been giving me Snickers bars and servings of the pudding he and Flash made for dessert every evening. It was a good trade since I was running out of food.

Since the Whites, my hunger hadn't dissipated. When I'd sorted through my last mail drop, I estimated I wouldn't make it to my next drop in Stratton. Luckily, the upcoming town of Rangeley had resupply options. In the meantime, I accepted anything extra anyone offered, whether a garlic clove, a few ginger snaps, or a crumbling Pop Tart.

Along with Flash and Merit, I crossed paths with other thru-hikers—Towhee, Batgirl, Pizza Guy, Greenfoot, Yogi and Boo-Boo, Diamond, Sly Fox—but once I wasn't hiking with Indiana anymore, I turned inward. I was on my own again, not tied to anyone. I had the freedom to stop and spend a whole afternoon lying on a pebble beach at a secluded pond, watching dragonflies, and writing in my journal. I looked at the maps and decided how far to hike based on my food bag and my belly. I walked each day alone, forcing myself to consider what came next, never getting much further in my thoughts than each small segment of trail that remained. To Rangeley, to Stratton, to Monson, to Katahdin.

How many summer mornings had I awoken, packed up, and strode into a town I only knew as a dot on a map? Each time, the food, the locals, and the scenery was an array of possibility. It was like docking at a port for the first time after a long stretch at sea, wondering what culture I would find. Walking into Rangeley was no different. I went to Our Place Cafe where I ate two huge pancakes, a veggie omelet, and toast. I also stopped at the IGA to stock up on dry trail food, plus fresh hummus, tomatoes, and chips for lunch.

I needed a new book to read, so I stopped at a trinket shop. The two elderly women behind the counter identified me as a hiker and began chattering.

"We don't get too many hikers in here," one said. "They typically don't buy bead necklaces and paperweights." She giggled at herself.

They asked several questions, and I told them I'd been hiking since early March. They both gasped.

"Oh, my dear, congratulations!" the other one said, clapping her hands together. "I wish you were my granddaughter. I'd be so proud."

They advocated for my purchase of *Woodswoman*, by Anne LaBastille, and after several more kind words, I left their store and wandered over to Rangeley Lake. I sat by the water, listening to the motors of a dozen Ski-Doos and speedboats. A white float plane landed and took off. I didn't want to be in town; it was too noisy and busy. I wanted to be in the forest where the loudest sounds were birds calling or wind blustering the trees, where I might stumble upon a moose, where I felt most at home.

Anne LaBastille became my companion for many miles. I dove into her book about moving to an island deep in the Adirondacks with her dogs and making a life for herself from the land. She was alone, and yet she managed to survive. Hell, she thrived. As I turned each page, Anne became my hero. I wanted to be her.

I camped near the shelters so I could share a story or a laugh with others. But I spent the days pounding up and down the mountains alone, thinking about Anne and solitude and why that appealed to me. When I was a child, if I was shut in my bedroom with a book, playing in the woods, or hiding in my closet, I was content. More importantly, I felt safe.

On the last miles of my journey, solitude felt appropriate. I needed the space to try to understand what I had been through for the past months. I didn't know if I would ever be able to find closure from this experience, I didn't know if I'd ever be the same again. But I needed time to tie up the loose ends that flailed around wildly in my heart.

•   •   •

In Stratton, I took a zero-mile day. My body was emaciated and sore, and I needed to lie on a bed and watch TV. I went to the White Wolf Inn where I found Angel, the German girl, whom I hadn't seen in a few weeks. She had ditched Plato and yellow-blazed to get away from him. I told her about my experience with Slow Buffalo. She confided that she was happier alone, and I congratulated her for taking control of her situation. Flash and Merit were there too, along with a handful of other hikers, but I hunkered down in my room for the day. When I went out to the diner, I didn't see any other thru-hikers. The town was quiet and empty.

I talked to Nate for the first time since I'd been in New Jersey. He and a buddy had rented a house near the Air Force base where he was newly stationed in Phoenix. He offered for me to come and stay with him while I figured out what to do next. We hadn't lived together since I was thirteen and he left for college, and I didn't know whether we could get along well enough to live together. Still, I was touched that he offered and told him I'd think about it.

I called and talked to Mom. She said that I'd gotten another call from the ranger Jim at Hovenweep. I needed to let him know if I wanted the job. *Why can't I decide?*

Then she told me that Great-Aunt Jeannette wanted to take my cousin Emily and me to Kyoto, Japan next spring to see the cherry blossoms bloom. At eighty-five years old, Aunt Jeannette had considerable savings that she and Uncle Dick had amassed over the past sixty years. She was a traveler but didn't feel safe traveling alone since Uncle Dick died. Her solution was to take her extended family on trips all over the world. I was thrilled that Emily and I were next on her list. *Maybe I could climb Mt. Fuji!*

I remembered but didn't remind my mother about the missiles my father had launched a few years ago when I had broached the idea of my visiting Emily when she lived in Japan. Back then, despite my dad's attempt to quash my desire, I'd begun making plans, studying basic Japanese, and collecting maps. My father never gave his approval, but he did give me an airline standby pass, and I promised to repay the fifty dollars. Then I flew across the ocean to Tokyo and wove my way through a foreign language and an unfamiliar culture to reach Emily in Kochi. For a week, I slept on her bedroom floor in her host family's house as she showed me around her Japanese life.

Now, Aunt Jeannette was proposing to take us back there. My father couldn't protest this. He couldn't protest any decision I made ever again. That era was over.

•   •   •

The terrain through Maine was like riding an undulating wave. I sailed along smooth stretches near 1,000 feet. Then I'd ascend a 3,000-foot river of rocks. Some of the bare peaks touched treeline, but the mountains weren't as expansive as the Presidential Range. I stayed enclosed in conifer green, rolling along until I came to an overlook or bald peak. Each time the trees broke open, I looked north, straining to see if I could see the Greatest Mountain.

As much as I wasn't sure what came next, I also wanted this trail to end. I was done with the pain, the blisters, the starvation. I walked each day beaten and worn and suffering. Like the trail itself, all at once flat and steep and lush and rocky and up and down, I also was hot then cold then strong then weak then begging for the finish line then never wanting to leave. Regardless of how I felt, I got up and walked again.

Ten, eleven, fourteen miles, to another pond, another peak, another night of sleeping outside under the stars.

Two days past Stratton I came to a single-lane road. At the AT crossing someone had painted in big yellow letters *2,000 MILES*. Here, in the middle of the woods on a tiny back road, I stood 2,000 miles from Springer Mountain, Georgia. My throat tightened, and I bit my lip. I thought back to the 100-mile party that I'd had with Slow Buffalo, Jurnee, Paranoid, Algae, and Hercules. The beginning. *My beginning.* A lifetime ago. We'd all been so amazed and proud of accomplishing 100 miles. I'd had a dream that I would someday get to 2,000 miles, but standing there, I couldn't believe it was real.

I dropped my pack, pulled out a Balance Bar, and scarfed it down in three bites. *"Water for everyone!"* Jurnee had quipped. I raised my bottle to him, to them all, to myself. Then I hefted my pack and kept walking. 160 miles to go. Time was flying away from me.

·   ·   ·

When I came upon a tiny sand beach at East Carry Pond, I had to stop. The sun blared down, and I needed a swim. I stripped off my shirt and shorts and waded out into the clear water. I floated on my back, closing my eyes and letting the sun warm my cold skin.

When I'd lived at Baxter the previous summer, sometimes I would swim out as far as I could into Togue Pond, which lay under the gaze of Katahdin. I'd flip onto my back and puff up my chest with air as my skin would numb in the cold. With my ears submerged, the water muffled all sound. I'd float, looking up at the reflection of pond melting into mountain melting into sky, letting the wilderness consume me until only a blurry blue remained.

Now, the Greatest Mountain wasn't within view, but over the past six months, wilderness had definitely consumed me. This trail had taken me in, spun me around, and was about to spit me out back into the so-called real world. My time living at Baxter had ended. *All things do.* It was time to go on to whatever whirling, twirling experience life offered up next.

I heard a familiar warbling call and rose up, treading water. A pair of loons glided across the far end of the pond. Behind them trailed three balls of fuzz, following their parents, trying to keep up. They were headed toward me; I watched them approach. They seemed curious about this strange bobbing head in their lake. I edged back toward the shore. When they saw me emerge from the water, they sped off in the other direction.

I was lounging on the tiny beach when Biohazard caught up. He joined me in the sunshine and filled me in on his latest scene. A rotund yellow-blazer named Lone Wolf had taken to operating a slackpack van for Old Blue, the retired cop I had met down south. Others were welcome to join in, and Diamond, Sly Fox, and Fleischman were all partaking. Lone Wolf would stock up on food, and drive the van ahead to a designated spot, then Old Blue and the others would hike with a day pack to the arranged location. Biohazard was still carrying his own gear, but he stayed with them in campgrounds or towns, eating and drinking well.

I understood the desire to not carry the backpack anymore, but I also thought they were cheating. Then I stopped myself. Didn't I slackpack New Jersey? Had I learned nothing? It was their hike to hike. Not mine. As long as they were respecting others, respecting the planet, I could respect them.

I pulled out my hacky sack, insisting on a lunchtime hack break. As we played, Fleischman walked up and jumped into the circle. In all those months, my hack skills had not improved much, but it was still one of my favorite ways to pass an afternoon with friends.

•   •   •

I'd crossed many rivers on the AT, some large ones on busy highway bridges, some narrow ones which required careful fording, balancing with my hiking poles, and getting my feet wet. The Kennebec River, however, posed one more unique challenge on the AT. The wide span of water in the backwoods of Maine had no bridge and was nearly chest deep. For years, hikers had forded the river, but it had an intense and variable current that had pulled more than one person under. After a death a decade back, the Maine Appalachian Trail Club set up a shuttle. Wingfoot gave a long list of warnings for hikers still wanting to ford, but the ATC officially sanctioned route had become the canoe. For a few hours each morning a guy named Steve, known as The Ferryman, transported hikers and their gear to the other side. I didn't need any more major challenges in my life, so on the first day of September, I arrived at the riverbank promptly at nine o'clock to hop in the canoe.

The hills on both sides sloped gently down to the dark river, which had a vastness that felt more like a lake than a flowing water body. The water swelled by, lapping the shoreline. Fleischman and Biohazard were there, but they decided to wander downstream to look for a place to ford. I wished them luck, and when The Ferryman docked in the sandy reeds, I climbed into the front seat of his red canoe. He was wicked nice and chatted as we paddled. It took several minutes to cross, and I was glad I chose the boat; the current out there was strong.

I spent the day stuck in my head, singing Dave, pondering the next forty miles to Monson. Did I want to push hard and get this thing over with? Or should I take my time and wring out every last drop of this experience? When I arrived at the road crossing near Pleasant Pond, I found Lone Wolf sitting in a camp chair next to the van. I said hello and was preparing to press on another half a mile to a lean-to when he offered me a beer.

"Well, sure," I said. "I guess I could use a beer today. Thanks."

I wasn't completely comfortable sitting alone with Lone Wolf. I didn't know him well and had little to say, so I let him ramble on about himself. Halfway through my beer, Biohazard and Fleischman showed up. We got to hacking, and by the time Old Blue and a cute southbounder with a Maine accent named Dogeye arrived, I was on my third beer.

"Okay, team," Old Blue announced, "let's get to camp and get some dinner. I'm starved."

They gathered up their things. I made to do the same and hike on to the shelter.

"Tamarack," Biohazard said, "come with us."

I hesitated. Their buoyant energy was a stark contrast to my mood and my recent days of solitude. I wasn't sure it was my scene.

"I'll buy you vegetarian food when we stop for steak," Lone Wolf grumbled.

"Come on, girl," Old Blue chimed in. "You need a break."

"Okay." I gave in. "But ya'll are paying my tent site fee."

"Done," said Bio. And I climbed into the old van with the motley crew of men.

•   •   •

The New England Outdoor Center was a car campground like all the others I'd ever seen. Lone Wolf pulled the van into a parking spot near a few picnic tables and flat, dirt tent pads. Tall pines dotted the campground, not offering each campsite much privacy from its neighbors. Fortunately, the place wasn't packed with partying vacationers who would keep us awake. As it turned out, we were the campers reveling into the wee hours of the night. The beer flowed as Lone Wolf barbequed lots of meat. I cooked a regular camp dinner, but he had indeed bought me apples, bananas, and a loaf of bread when we stopped at the store.

I hadn't sat at a campfire in weeks; fires weren't allowed in the Whites, and before that, it was too hot. I looked into the leaping flames, mesmerized by the sparks flying up and the tinges of blue in the hottest nooks of burning wood. Months ago, back before the Smokies, Melissa had asked whether I was going to hook up with a group. Since then, I'd been a part of many groups, some consisted of several people, some were uncomfortable, and some lasted only a day. The fire jumped and danced, and as I looked across it at the faces of these gruff, meat-eating, slackpacking men I did not know well, I felt at ease. They weren't just one of my many groups, they were my tribe. And I was thriving amongst them.

I went to bed drunk and warm. Before I sloshed off to sleep, I wrote a few notes in my journal. If I could thrive here, over 2,000 miles of uphills and strangers and unknowns beyond every twist in the trail, I could thrive anywhere.

Today was a day when all was right with the world.

THE GREATEST MOUNTAIN

My apparent solitude through Maine was an illusion. I was actually surrounded by a large cohort of hikers, a day or two ahead and behind. I overlapped with them in Monson, many of us staying at Keith and Pat Shaw's boarding house. The white bunkroom was sparse and clean, several bunks lined up in rows. The dinners and breakfasts were all-you-can-eat and very cheap. Hikers packed around the small dining table passing bowls of broccoli and mashed potatoes and meatloaf. Some folks called Shaw's one of those vortexes that sucked people in for days or weeks. The town itself had the basic amenities, like a laundromat and general store, but there was little else to do. However, I could understand the appeal. We were about to enter the 100-Mile Wilderness; no towns or roads, no camp stores or ice cream stands. This was it, the last stop before Baxter State Park, before Katahdin, before the end of the journey.

Studying the final page of Wingfoot's mileage chart, I realized I had a mere nine days of hiking left. Nine days of getting up in the morning, packing my gear, and stepping onto the trail. Nine days of pushing myself to the limit of my strength, of walking in peace and silence. Nine days of singing aloud with no one around to hear. Of leaving or receiving notes in the registers, of cooking oatmeal for breakfast and macaroni and cheese for dinner on my one burner stove, of a layer of grime coating my skin.

Nine days is nothing.

There were quite a few hikers in Monson that I didn't know, but Flash and Merit were also there enjoying a day off. As were Diamond, Angel, and Charlie Hustle. The Lone Wolf and Old Blue slackpack gang now included Fleischman, Biohazard, and a very tall Israeli man named Simba with wild curly brown hair. I was amazed to meet up with Hillbilly again, whom I hadn't seen since way back at Wapiti shelter in central Virginia. I finally met Magellan, an older woman with short, gray hair whom I'd been hearing about for weeks. Magellan had joined up with Batgirl, Pizza Guy, and Towhee. I privately called them the Batgirl Tour, due to Batgirl's domineering direction of the group. I wanted to hang out with women for a change, but because I didn't follow Batgirl's lead, she didn't include me in their activities. Instead, I hacky sacked with Hillbilly, Biohazard, and Charlie Hustle on Shaw's lawn.

Unsure whether to stay or go, I dawdled in Monson for a day and a half. I lounged against a huge pine in the yard, enjoying the summer scent of evergreens floating on the air. I contemplated the end, realizing that I'd see my parents in less than two weeks. I'd hoped to talk to my mom before the 100-Mile Wilderness, but I wasn't able to reach her. She had sent a thoughtful, congratulatory letter, and I read it over several times, savoring her pride.

I collected one last, large pile of packages and mail from the post office. A dozen friends and family sent letters of congratulations, including Slow Buffalo. He'd stayed in Hanover for two weeks and, knowing he wouldn't see me again, wanted to wish me well as I entered the wilderness. Our paths had diverged for the last time, and I told myself to remember the fun we'd had and let go of the rest. He was a part of the tribe, after all.

Alongside a final box of cookies from Tish was another package of M&M's from Marilyn and Bob, and snacks from both Tucker J and my friend Don. It was a bonanza of sweets and love that I would share with the other thru-hikers. I sliced open my final brown cardboard box and dumped the contents onto my cot in the hostel bunkroom.

Back in my parents' New Jersey dining room, I had packed up twenty-three boxes with no real idea what I was getting into. And yet, it had worked; I'd made it to number twenty-three. The usual Ziploc baggies of pasta, rice, dried veggies, and fruit tumbled out. CLIF Bars and Balance Bars, a roll of film, more writing paper and toilet paper, and a big bag of GORP. And there at the bottom were the final three trail maps. Fresh and dry and clean, never been used. The maps that would take me to Katahdin.

One of my favorite parts of backpacking was looking at the maps. I loved the compass directional in the corner, the oddly shaped, blue bodies of water, the black lines of differing thicknesses with road names, the minuscule terrain lines indicating elevation, and most importantly, the bright red line weaving back and forth across all these landmarks labeled *Appalachian Trail*.

When I was in high school, before I'd ever been on a hike on a trail in the wilderness, before I even knew what backpacking was, I bought a book called *50 Hikes in New Jersey*. I wasn't athletic, and it would be a physical challenge, but I wanted to go hiking. I looked up the numbered hikes within driving distance; the blurry black and white maps were difficult to read, and the topographical lines were hard to differentiate, but I pored over the options. I studied each corresponding description and imagined what it would be like to walk on those trails. A breeze would rustle the tall trees above me, birds would sing, and flowers would spring from the dark earth next to the path. I would adventure to ponds and overlooks and rocks the size of houses where I would stop and take deep breaths and fall more in love with my planet. Out there, somewhere, I would find peace.

Hiking boots were essential to this plan. I went with my parents to the Eastern Mountain Sports at the mall where I would one day work. We wandered in, Mom stopping at the fleece jackets, Dad heading for the cases of sports watches. I went directly to the wall of boots. It was tall and imposing, covered by dozens of boots and sneakers and sandals each on their own mini shelf. The variety astounded me, but my eye was drawn toward one. I asked a sales associate to bring me the pair with light brown suede and teal green canvas. Size 10. They were ankle high and sturdy, yet soft. They had thick, black treads to prevent slippage or toe-stubbing.

The boots fit. The color was right. My heel didn't rub. They were beautiful and tough, protecting my feet from all the harms of the world. They would take me all the places I knew I needed to go.

Then something happened. Something always happened. A tone of voice. A grumpy mood. A perceived infraction. My father got angry. Hiking was stupid; the price was outrageous; I was ridiculous. He didn't launch a full attack in the store, but the rage simmered under the surface, growling, seething, waiting for a moment in private to strike. I cried and wiped my eyes with my sleeve. The sales associate stepped away.

Sitting on my cot in Monson, surrounded by my pile of hiking food and gear, I couldn't remember why Dad had gotten angry that day. But I remembered I didn't leave EMS with the boots I'd so desperately wanted. I didn't own a pair of boots until the summer I worked at Baxter when the Student Conservation Association program gave me the pair of blue Montrails as a part of my compensation. I also remembered that I did not go on even one of those fifty hikes in New Jersey. Without boots, I couldn't step into that world.

Now, I'd worn through four pairs of boots. My feet had pounded approximately 2,060 miles. I'd walked 184 days across the east coast of America. I didn't have to imagine the adventure or peace or pain of hiking anymore. Now, I knew it.

•　　•　　•

Keith Shaw wove wildly across the center line, looking everywhere except at the road. As he drove, I clung to the armrest. I hoped I hadn't made it this far only to die in a car crash and breathed in relief when he pulled into the trailhead parking lot. I hauled my pack out of his vehicle into the warm afternoon air and waved goodbye. Loaded with all the extra treats, my pack felt as heavy as the day I started up the Approach

Trail. But I took my time on the gentle and friendly terrain, headed ten miles to Wilson Valley Lean-to.

After about four miles, I came to a clear pond and stopped for a swim. The cool water reinvigorated me, but I nicked my bare toe on a rock and started bleeding profusely. As I sat holding a bandana to the injury, I took deep breaths, not looking at the cut so I wouldn't get woozy. It was a small price to pay for the benefit of such a glorious watering hole. Many ponds dotted the 100-Mile Wilderness, and I decided I'd stop and swim at as many as I could, avoiding the sharp rocks, of course.

Later, I came to the scenic Little Wilson Falls and Big Wilson Stream which I had to ford. As I had many times in Maine, I debated with myself whether it was better to wear my boots through the water to protect my feet from the rocks and have soggy feet the rest of the day or to cross the river barefoot, protecting my boots but potentially hurting my feet. With an already cut toe, I opted to protect my feet. I picked my way across, icy water pouring over the tops of my boots, turning them into leather buckets. On the opposite shore, I stopped to check my toe and wring out my socks.

No one else showed up at the lean-to that evening. I spent the night alone with the giant spruce trees and the chipmunk family in residence. I tossed the rodents a few tiny macaroni noodles and watched them skitter around chasing each other for the bounty. I enjoyed their antics, much more so than the mouse who woke me up in the darkness chewing through my food bag.

The next day, I took it easy again, trekking the rolling path nine miles to Cloud Pond. The day was clear and warm, but as I cooked dinner, the sky warned of a storm brewing. When I'd arrived, the lean-to had been silent, but by evening Charlie Hustle, Hillbilly, Patches, Gruff, Skydog, and Redstripe all showed up. They said hello as they went by to make camp down by the pond, but I didn't join their loud banter and slept alone in the shelter.

The rain came down intermittently all night, and I woke to a loud pattering on the roof. Tucked in my sleeping bag, I felt the air thick with moisture on my face and knew the trail would already be soaked through. *I could stay here today. And never leave.*

I pulled myself up to sitting, glancing at Charlie Hustle and the others down by the pond. They were all packing up, undoubtedly drenched. I scooched back against the lean-to wall and watched as they streamed out past the shelter, one by one heading farther into the wilderness. All except Hillbilly, who relocated to the shelter and spread out his wet gear on the other side.

"Those folks were sure motivated this morning," I said, pulling on my fleece pants inside my sleeping bag. I stood up to get my food bag down from where it was hanging and assess any mouse damage.

"Yeah, man," Hillbilly responded, "They're always in such a rush. What's the hurry? Katahdin ain't going anywhere."

"I'm gonna stay here this morning. What's the point of hiking in the rain?"

"I might stay, too," he said. "I've got more food than a 600-pound hoarder with a McDonald's addiction."

I laughed, wondering where he came up with these things. "It'll probably clear up later," I said. "Then we can hike."

"Yeah, probably."

But it didn't clear up. And Hillbilly and I didn't leave the lean-to. I learned that his real name was William, he was from North Carolina, and he smoked a lot. For a while, we stood where the ceiling was the highest and tried to hacky sack. The main goal was to prevent the little ball from flying out into the rain and mud.

"You know, we started on the same day back at Springer," Hillbilly said.

"Did we?"

"Yeah, I remember you at Hawk Mountain Shelter," he said, kicking the hack to me. "You had that massive pack that towered over you." He raised his hands above his head to show my pack height, a fleck of ash falling off the cigarette he held.

I didn't want to admit I didn't remember him from then. "I remember you in the Smokies."

He chuckled. "You hated me back then."

"Uh, no, I…"

"Come on, admit it."

"Well, I didn't know you. You made obnoxious jokes. You're more fun now."

"Riiight," he said with a sarcastic drawl.

We kicked the hack back and forth until we bored of it. Then retreated to our respective sleeping bags to prepare for more chatting, reading, and doing nothing.

Around lunchtime, the Batgirl Tour arrived, dripping wet and glad to be under cover. They busied themselves in the center of the shelter, pulling out food and warm clothes. They were loud and rowdy but offered an entertaining distraction in the muted day.

"Perhaps we should stay here tonight, Batgirl," Magellan said, sounding hopeful. The rain had lessened, but the trees still dripped steadily.

"Maybe," Batgirl replied.

"What do you want to do, Batgirl?" Towhee asked her.

Eventually, Batgirl declared that she would be hiking on to the next shelter, seven more miles away.

"Yeah, I think we should go on," Pizza Guy said emphatically. Magellan and Towhee both looked exhausted, but they nodded. Batgirl packed up her things, and they all did the same. They bade us a quick goodbye and left, following her back into the shadowy mist.

"Jesus, can he even make up his own mind anymore?" Hillbilly said before they were barely out of earshot. "Or he's just following with his dick."

"You're hilarious," I said through my chortling laughter.

"Thank you," he said.

I looked at him as he lit another cigarette. "Can I have one?"

"Yeah, man. Thought you'd never ask."

I took a drag of the cigarette, feeling my brain go fuzzy. "So," I began, then blew the smoke out of my lungs, "we should really hike today."

"We should."

"We should."

We sat on our opposite sides of the lean-to, smoking, looking out the shelter opening at the intensifying rain.

"Wanna play hangman?" Hillbilly asked.

I nodded. Then scooted over next to him.

•   •   •

I leapfrogged with the Batgirl Tour, Old Blue's gang, and Hillbilly through the 100-Mile Wilderness. We stopped for breaks and nights together, each following our usual camp routines of cooking, gathering water, washing dishes. We packed into shelters to laugh and whine about the rain, but we avoided talk of what came next. It was hard to believe that the trail would actually end, that anything else outside of this wilderness even existed. We were there in the moment, and the real world, looming at the edge of awareness, would have to wait a few more days.

The days, however, passed at lightning speed, despite being just as long and hard as all the previous trail days. The path morphed into one final roller coaster. I'd climb up one steep mountain, descend all the way down the other side, and be faced immediately with another. My body didn't hurt anymore. I felt strong but numb; the only things of consequence were eating, walking, and attempting to stay dry. I hadn't been forced to hike in too much rain over the past six months, but Maine was making up for that. The dark clouds didn't take their leave after Cloud Pond and rain came and went at random intervals. I wore my raincoat every day, but its waterproofing had long since disintegrated. Water slid down my shorts onto my bare legs pooling at the top of my gaiters, then seeping down into my socks.

One afternoon, I made good time while it wasn't raining, pleased to be drying out. I arrived at a gorgeous, spacious pine clearing next to a pond, ready to camp for the night. As soon as I dropped my pack, a deluge came down. I hustled to pull out my tarp, but all my gear was soaked by the time I climbed inside. Water began to pool under me, and I looked out at the pond, now rippling with millions of raindrops. So close to the end, and still, one more challenge, one more cold and wet night to get through.

I was as hungry as a bear after winter hibernation and was eating through my food bag far too quickly. When I discovered that my bag of mini bagels had molded from the moist air, I thought I might not make it. But I traded Magellan some iodine tablets for a package of Ramen and got one meal closer. I just wanted to finish, to complete this impossible task, to climb Katahdin again. Each time I arrived at another peak, I looked north to see if I could catch a glimpse of Katahdin. She had to be there somewhere. At the peak of 3,650-foot Whitecap Mountain, the clouds again prohibited any views. I stopped for a snack, despite the cool air. Hillbilly walked up, followed by Magellan and Towhee.

"Hey, this is the last real mountain before the end," Hillbilly said, lighting a cigarette, as he did at every break. "We should practice our finishing photos."

"Sure," I said. "We gotta look good on top of Katahdin."

Towhee and Magellan agreed that this would be a fun activity, and we all got out our cameras. We took turns posing by the Whitecap peak sign. I stood with Magellan and Towhee, each of us flexing our biceps like weightlifters.

"We're tough thru-hikers!" Magellan shouted. Towhee whooped.

Then Hillbilly switched places with Magellan and Towhee, and he and I raised our arms in victory, cheering for ourselves.

"We made it!" I yelled, laughing at the camera.

•   •   •

When I finally saw Katahdin, I was thirty-six miles away. It was a rare clear day, the cloudless sky the color of a robin's egg. I came out of the trees atop Nesuntabunt Mountain, and there she was, standing as I had left her a year ago. She towered over all the range, green spreading out like a royal carpet all around her. As ever, she was the Greatest Mountain.

Tears welled in my eyes. My heart felt like a squirrel jumping around in my chest, and I dropped my pack and doubled over, hands on my knees. Joy and sorrow and adulation surged up. It was almost as if every emotion I'd ever experienced exploded within me. It had been such a long road. *But I'm here.*

I felt so light, I thought I could have flown across the lowlands and leaped up onto the tableland. I didn't fly, but my thoughts remained lofty as I hiked one last day through the wilderness. I stopped at Rainbow Ledges, twenty-one miles away, for another view of Katahdin. The ridges and crevices and curves of her squarish form were just as I remembered. I could see that the greenery she wore stopped about three-quarters of the way up her side. Above the Krummholz was the mottled white and gray of pure rock.

Abol Bridge was the official end of the 100-Mile Wilderness. Many hikers stopped there for campground amenities or to hitch on the dirt road to Millinocket, about twenty miles away. It was a stunning spot at the edge of Baxter State Park, along a branch of the Penobscot River. To the north, Katahdin dominated. She ruled the world. I pushed on six more miles to Daicey Pond Campground, leaving just over seven miles for the next day's climb.

The sun shined warmly to welcome me across the Baxter Park boundary. I walked uphill along Nesowadnehunk Stream, passing rollicking waterfalls, trying to comprehend that I had made it back. Who from the previous summer would be there? I knew my former boss, Jean, and my old roommate, Sara, would be, but the rest was unknown.

At Daicey there was a lean-to reserved for thru-hikers, and I made my way to it in the late afternoon. I checked in with the campground ranger, whom I hadn't worked with the previous summer, and waited to see if any other thru-hikers showed up. I took a long swim in the pond, once more under the gaze of my mountain. I soaked my tired body in the cold water, scrubbing my hair and skin to remove the salty sweat. Six and a half months. It had been such a slow progression of walking 2,160 miles, and yet, my mind couldn't keep up. It felt sudden, abrupt, to be there.

One day left to travel.

The anticipation of seeing old park friends, the wondering whom I would summit with the next day, and the bewildering completion of this trek kept me tossing and turning on the hard shelter floor, aching to move, energy coursing through me most of the night.

•   •   •

I left Daicey Pond by seven the next morning and raced the two miles to Katahdin Stream Campground. I dropped my full pack and trekking poles at the door of the ranger cabin and let loose my adrenaline.

I'd climbed each of the four trails to the peak the previous summer, but I'd only done the AT route once. I usually took the more gradual Chimney Pond Trail on the other side of the mountain. The AT was one of the harder trails, requiring the largest elevation gain on the AT, more than 4,000 feet. It was a steep and rocky path, rising approximately 1,000 feet per mile, which entailed climbing hand over foot much of the way.

I didn't notice the rocks, the cool air, my heaving lungs. I didn't think. I trusted my body to do the work, feeling strong and alert, completely able. I paused on the two-hour climb only for short water breaks. I pushed through the twisted trees of the Krummholz, not interrupting my rhythm, needing to get there. Arriving at Katahdin's tableland, I paused to look down over the expansive view and was surprised to see that I'd entered the foggy sky. I looked up to glimpse Baxter Peak, but it was covered in thick gray clouds and hidden from view.

I skipped across the rocks over Thoreau Spring, barely noticing the colorful lichens and tiny, delicate worlds I had been enthralled with last summer. I put on another burst of speed as the last mile of the flat tableland slid away. As I followed the final white blazes painted on the stone stairway, the clouds thickened, and I couldn't see beyond my next step. I didn't slow down. Up and up and up, and the trail dwindled to nothing as I emerged to the top of a large pile of rocks and a big, brown, rectangular sign.

Baxter Peak. Katahdin. The northern terminus of the Appalachian Trail.

I did it. The thought shot through my brain. The only thought I'd had all day. *I did it.*

I went to the sign and touched it. It was brand new, a replacement for the decrepit sign that I had gazed at all the previous summer. The brown wood was smooth, the white paint on the little letters fresh and unmarred. The wind whipped hard as the clouds swirled all about, and I could see nothing but a few feet of rock in any direction. I was in the same place I'd been so many times before and yet everything was different.

The only other hiker there was Dogbone, a guy I'd met once in the wilderness. We congratulated each other, then took turns taking photos by the sign, trying not to get lost in the clouds. I sat for a snack, my body heat fading as the cold air sank through my thin jacket to my sweaty skin underneath. Dogbone bade me goodbye, and I was left alone at the end of the trail.

I'd never been alone at Baxter Peak. The mountain was always crawling with people, coming and going and enjoying and admiring. I yelled, "Thank you!" into the clouds, testing how loud my voice was. Nothing responded. Another hiker could pop through the fog at any moment, but they didn't. I was truly alone. So, I screamed. A piercing, primal scream that had been stuck inside me for years. I let go, and the scream ripped free from deep within. The sound dispersed away into the wild wind, into nothingness, into everythingness, gone as quickly as it came.

After fifteen minutes or so, thoroughly chilled, I touched the sign one last time, then stepped away from the peak. The clouds had risen a bit, and when I dropped to the tableland, I could see other hikers in the distance headed my way. Diamond scurried by, nodding at me. Batgirl,

Pizza Guy, Towhee, and Magellan gave me hugs and high-fives as they passed. When I came across Old Blue, he stopped in the middle of the trail and took hold of my shoulders.

"I'm proud of you," he said, holding my gaze. I smiled and nodded in response, touched that he cared.

I headed down the mountain one step at a time, a litany of Dave songs pouring out of me. I took care on the sharp and steep rocks and paid attention to the trees and flowers and scenery I hadn't noticed on the way up. By the time I made it back to Katahdin Stream Campground, I was starving. I collected my pack and settled at a picnic table to cook a box of mac and cheese I found in the hiker free bin.

That night, Old Blue hosted a party at his campsite. Biohazard, Fleischman, Creeper, Holly and Dooley, Hillbilly, Towhee, Simba, and I all gathered together to revel. Some of us were done, some would summit the next morning. The beer and laughter and friendship filled me up, but there was also an ache. I wished Jurnee was there. I missed him and Full Moon, Bud, Biscuits and Gravy, Indiana, Grubby, Ironhorse, and Kaybek. But on my last night on the Appalachian Trail, I knew it didn't matter whether or not I walked through any given day with these people I adored; we were connected forever by this voyage.

Faint and exhausted, I set up my sleeping bag in a lean-to reserved for thru-hikers. As I lay in bed, an astonishing thought crossed my mind. I did not have to get up in the morning and haul a heavy backpack up an impossibly steep mountain. I did not have to pop any more blisters, ford any streams, or feel the ravages of starvation. I did not have to get up tomorrow and walk. In fact, I did not have to walk anywhere ever again. As I dozed off, I thought that was perhaps the best idea I'd had in 194 days.

•   •   •

Several days later, my parents arrived in Millinocket. My friend Don and his mom, Sally, had surprised me and driven up to celebrate, too.

Their arrivals were full of congratulations and hugs, and I was honored that everyone had come all the way from New Jersey to applaud me.

They all wanted to experience Katahdin. Dad and Don both wanted to climb to the peak, so the five of us set out one morning on the Chimney Pond Trail. The day unfolded with possibly the most perfect hiking weather I'd ever experienced: white gold shining sun, the wispiest breeze, and air clear as a perfect diamond.

By the time we reached Chimney Pond Campground several miles in, Mom and Sally were ready to stop. We left them to enjoy the backcountry campground as Dad, Don, and I hiked on. The Chimney Pond Trail was scrambly in places, and we had to traverse a scree slide.

I led the way, moving slowly, watching them both to be sure they found their footing. We pushed our legs and lungs hard; one last battle against gravity. They were both amazed when we emerged onto the tableland and saw the rocky alpine expanse rising to the peak. We could see for miles in every direction, and I knew they were feeling the spark of inspiration I had found atop this mountain. The whole world was so very small and blue and green and magical from up there.

We joined the groups of colorfully dressed hikers at the rock pile at the peak. We relaxed and snacked and enjoyed the view. When the area thinned out, we asked another hiker to take photos of us. We stood behind the new sign, Don on one side of me, Dad on the other. We smiled big for one shot. Then Dad said, "Say cheesy, stinky feet!" and all our mouths opened, laughing. I asked for one more shot and threw my torso forward over the sign, face flat onto it, hugging it from the top, happiness washing over me.

We had a long way to go to get back down, but I was reluctant to leave, not knowing when I would ever return. The only way I could get myself to pack up was to promise I would come back and hike this mountain again every year. No matter what.

As we tucked away snack bags and water bottles, Dad turned to me. He said, "I'm proud of you," and hugged me tightly. He was deeply proud; I could see it on his tanned, freckled face. I had always wanted his pride. I had always wanted to be good enough, smart enough, pretty enough for him to stop attacking me, to stop the inferno of his rage that scorched my life. But everything I was, was not enough. And as a child, each time I thought I had grabbed hold of something solid, I'd find that it dissolved into a stream of charred sand that slipped through my fingers. Always out of reach.

Now, I had found my footing on this stable and unwavering rock beneath my boots. A powerful wind whipped across my body, and I stood atop the Greatest Mountain and realized that I didn't need my father's pride anymore.

I am proud of myself.

•   •   •

On the day before my parents had arrived, I'd gone to Millinocket to get lunch and groceries. Hikers were trickling in and out of town, and I wanted to see who was around. The main street of Millinocket was run down and unimpressive, but I knew hikers would congregate there because there were restaurants and a couple of bed-and-breakfasts.

I stepped outside the diner onto the sidewalk and heard a loud whistle. I looked up the street into the sun. There, tall and lean, wearing a bright pink t-shirt from a thrift shop, was Bud. I screamed and ran toward him. I smashed into him, wrapping my arms around him, never wanting to let go.

We both laughed until I peeled myself away.

"You look good, girl," he said. Then he put his arm around my shoulders, pulling me to him again.

"You," I paused, "have hair!" He had stopped shaving his bald head and now had a thin layer of dark brown hair sprouting on top. "What are you doing here? I thought you were way behind."

"No, I was right behind you for a long time," Bud replied. "I hurt my hip coming into Abol Bridge and hitched over here to see if a few days of rest would help."

"Oh no! So, you haven't done Katahdin?"

"Not yet. I've hiked it before, so technically I'm done," he said. "But it'll be a bummer not to get to do it again this trip."

Despite this, Bud was positively glowing.

"We did it," he said, grinning. "We made it all the fucking way."

"We did it." I grinned back. I grabbed his arms and jumped up and down and yelled, "We did it!"

For a brief moment, I rose and hovered outside of myself, looking down on these two worn-out hikers standing in the street carrying on like wild monkeys over a pile of bananas. We were those hikers I had seen last summer, depleted and raw, emaciated and dirty, clothing in tatters. I was exhausted. I was empty. I had sweated and cried and laughed and clawed my way to this place, and along the way, I had been completely cleared out of everything I used to be. And now, I could see myself for what I was: full, alive, beautiful.

My whole life suddenly opened up before me and everything, anything was possible. Bud's eyes gleamed with triumph and strength, and I knew mine mirrored the same. Triumph and strength. And I would never, ever let those things go.

EPILOGUE

I heaved my pack one more time and stuffed it into the back of my parents' car. Then I climbed into the back seat and settled in for the long drive back to New Jersey. I looked out the window across the forest tinged with the yellow of autumn, hoping to catch one last glimpse of Katahdin.

I'd promised myself I would come back next summer and hike again, but as we left Millinocket, I understood that life held no guarantees. There was so much I did not know.

I didn't yet know that before the year was out, my mother would file for divorce, that she was done with my father, that she would finally break the silence of our damaged family. I didn't yet know that her decision would wash over me like a river of soothing warm water, tumbling the grains of sand back together, offering relief that the world could start to solidify into something real.

I didn't yet know that she would tell me this late one night, privately, when she and my father came to visit me at Hovenweep National Monument in Utah. That I would spend five months serving in the silence of a desert winter, looking more deeply into solitude and nature and meditation.

I didn't yet know that I would become a ridgerunner at Mount Rogers National Recreation Area and spend a summer giving back to the trail that had given me so much.

I didn't yet know that I would, a few years later, get that dog I wanted so badly. That I would name her Gaia, and she would become my best friend for thirteen years.

I didn't yet know that I had further to go in my journey with mental illness. That I would come to truly understand the words depression, bipolar, therapy, and medication before I could heal.

I didn't yet know that I would settle my life in Ithaca. That I would stop moving, find work, and fall in love with a man who adored me and would do everything in his power to lift me up. That I would gain a stepdaughter and give birth to a son.

I couldn't possibly know what awaited me as I drove away from Katahdin on that September day. But leaving the Greatest Mountain behind one more time, I did know that the mountains and rivers and balds and forests and wild animals would forever be linked to my heart. The rain and snow and wind and heat would not fade from my skin, but forge the very core of who I am. The gifts offered and challenges faced day after day after day would give me a place to begin.

And even twenty-five years later, the love I feel for the people I journeyed with and the joy of each moment I spent sharing the Appalachian Trail with them has not diminished but instead glows brighter and more vivid with each passing year. The Trail has given me the beautiful voyage. And all that's left to say is thank you.

AUTHOR'S NOTE

I took great care to describe all of my experiences in this book accurately and honestly. I hiked the Appalachian Trail in 1999, before digital technology was widely available, and when the Trail measured 2,160 miles. Since then, the Trail's length has been adjusted yearly, based on added and relocated sections. In 2024 it measures 2,197 miles. Names I used for places or organizations also may have changed. Particularly, what I called the Appalachian Trail Conference is now the Appalachian Trail Conservancy. My use of mileage, trail routes, elevation, and names is based on the data from the 1999 guidebooks and my journals, as well as online research that is available now.

Additionally, these stories involving family and friends are told from my perspective, based on my memories and journals. I reached out to friends and family for their memories on certain things, which helped as I looked back over many years. I acknowledge that we all remember things based on our own view of the world and there is more than one side to every tale. The side shared here is solely mine.

ACKNOWLEDGMENTS

This story has been twenty-five years in the making and I am grateful to many people.

Thank you to Aimee Hardy, for her patience with me and my eagerness during the editing process. Her ideas and suggestions made this book so much brighter. Thank you to Black Rose Writing for working with me on this book. Their efforts are making my dream become real.

There aren't enough words of gratitude for my writing tribe. Maria Luiza Brisbane, Lainey Carslaw, Kim Hambright, and Laura Jackson got me through the many ups and downs of writing and submitting this book with their wisdom, laughter, friendship, and support. Their honest feedback on early drafts helped direct my path. Thank you also to Andrea Lani, who is one of the best writers and editors I know. I always trust her insight into my writing.

Thank you to Saltonstall Foundation for the Arts for offering quiet retreat space for NY artists. Each time I retreat to Saltonstall, I walk away a stronger writer.

Like the community support needed to write a book, hiking the Appalachian Trail is not something one can do alone. Thank you to my parents. I would not have been able to complete my hike without their assistance and help. They supported me with food, finances, rides to trailheads, and a place to call home, even as I was finding my own way. Many thanks to all the friends and family who wrote to me, sent cookies and treats, and cheered me from afar; their encouragement got me through many hard days.

I am grateful for all the trail angels I encountered on my hike. Some I wrote about, some I never knew or had a chance to thank. Trail angels are the best of the AT, they make the trail the magical place that it is. I appreciate the Appalachian Trail Conservancy for all the work they do to protect, plan for, and maintain the trail and the hiking experience for everyone.

I could not have hiked those many mountains without Mike Jurnovoy, Paul Gadola, and Mitch Renville. Their love and friendship have extended far beyond that last hike up Katahdin. I am lucky to have met them all those years ago and lucky to still be able to call them my friends. Their excitement for this book means the world to me.

Thank you to my kids, Tahlya and Cedar, for your love, support, and cooking your own dinners some nights as I have walked this path of being a writer. You both inspire me to be better.

My greatest debt is to my husband, Rob. You have patiently and unfailingly supported me in the good days and bad, as I wrote and revised and submitted and faced rejection and succeeded. Rob has always believed in me and always sees the good in my work. This book would not be coming into existence without you.

ABOUT THE AUTHOR

Amanda K. Jaros is the editor of *Labor of Love: A Literary Mama Staff Anthology* and author of *100 Things to Do in Ithaca Before You Die*. Her essays on nature and family have appeared in *Flyway, Appalachia, Terrain.org, Stone Canoe*, and elsewhere. When not writing, she can be found on a trail somewhere, and has hiked the Inca Trail in Peru, several trails in Australia, and is currently working toward completing hikes of the 46 High Peaks in the Adirondacks. She lives in Ithaca, New York, with her husband and son, where she recently took up kayaking and serves her community as a county legislator. Learn more at amandakjaros.com and Instagram @amandajaroschampion.

NOTE FROM AMANDA K. JAROS

Word-of-mouth is crucial for any author to succeed. If you enjoyed *In My Boots*, please leave a review online—anywhere you are able. Even if it's just a sentence or two. It would make all the difference and would be very much appreciated.

Thanks!
Amanda K. Jaros

We hope you enjoyed reading this title from:

www.blackrosewriting.com

Subscribe to our mailing list – *The Rosevine* – and receive **FREE** books, daily deals, and stay current with news about upcoming releases and our hottest authors.
Scan the QR code below to sign up.

Already a subscriber? Please accept a sincere thank you for being a fan of Black Rose Writing authors.

View other Black Rose Writing titles at www.blackrosewriting.com/books and use promo code **PRINT** to receive a **20% discount** when purchasing.

Made in United States
North Haven, CT
04 April 2025

67552020R00166